Selections from the Poetry of t[...]
George Rave[...]

TO THE READER.

DURING my lengthened researches in, and long study of the Pus'hto language, for so many years past, and particularly when making selections for my work entitled "GULSHAN-I-ROH," * I could not fail being much struck with the beauty of some of the poetry of the Afghāns; so much so, indeed, that I long since determined, and, at length, now venture to submit to the European reader, a literal translation of several poems of the most celebrated of the Afghān poets—together with a brief notice of each author—in an English dress.

It must be remembered, that these poems are the effusions of men who never enjoyed any of what we call the luxuries of life; yet how refined are the generality of their sentiments! Of men who lived in a state, such as our own Borderers lived in, five hundred years ago, in violence and in strife, and whose descendants live so still; yet how exquisitely pathetic are many of their poems, and how high-souled and benevolent their sentiments and ideas! Inhabiting a fine country, with grand and lofty mountains, and green and fertile valleys, but with nought more than the bare necessaries of life attainable, how simple and how perfect are their similes, and how true to nature! What a patriotic ardour; what a true spirit of freedom, and a love of country, much of their poetry displays!

It must also be borne in mind, that the greater number of the writers of the following poems, except Aḥmad Shāh, and Khushḥāl Khān, and his sons, were either men, who during their life-time had scarcely left the precincts of their native village, or who had devoted their lives to poverty and religious abstraction. Men, who never wrote for fame; and who never contemplated that the inmost thoughts which had occupied their hearts, would ever meet the eyes of more than a few dear and admiring friends, after they had, themselves, passed from the scene for ever. Never did they imagine that they would appear before any Public, much less a European one, in the Saxon tongue, and translated by a FARANGĪ!

"Far from the maddening world's ignoble strife,

Their sober wishes never learn'd to stray;

Along the cool sequester'd vale of life,

They kept the noiseless tenour of their way."

I have been very careful to render the poems as literal as possible; and have, it will be perceived, endeavoured to preserve the rhyming words, as they occur, in the English as well, more particularly when each couplet ends in the same word throughout.

It will also, no doubt, be observed, that two nominatives sometimes occur, one in each line of a couplet; which is occasioned by the first hemistich of the couplets being put first, where we should, if we considered the English idiom only, put it last. This may cause a seeming quaintness in the translation; but I considered it necessary to follow the original as near as possible, in order to preserve the literal style I had, from the outset, adopted.

The reader should also understand, that Afg͟hān books exist only in manuscript, as was the case in Europe before the invention of printing; and the following poems have been translated from such. Copies of the works of some of the authors herein contained are rare, and seldom to be met with, even in Afg͟hānistān, such as the poems of Aḥmad S͟hāh,K͟hwājah Muḥammad, and (except in the Pes'hāwar district)K͟hushḥāl K͟hān, and his sons; whilst the original manuscript of S͟haidā's poems, as they were first collected and arranged into a volume, and richly illuminated, is in my possession; and no copy of them, that I am aware of, exists, save that which I permitted the descendants on his brother's side to make from my manuscript, which I sent some hundreds of miles for them to examine. Although he was celebrated as a poet, they had never seen his poems before, he having died in India.

Greater variety will be noticed in the poems of K͟hushḥāl K͟hān, than in those of the other Afg͟hān poets contained in this volume; for, like the poets of the West, no subject seems to have been foreign to him; and, amongst other things, he does not spare the failings of his own countrymen, as he found them two centuries since; and probably he will on this account be the favourite with the general reader.

All I can say in conclusion is, that what is good in the following pages must be credited to the authors; and all the failings and imperfections, which are very many, I fear, to their English translator, who, therefore, prays for the indulgence and forbearance of his readers.

H. G. R.

Footnotes

v:* See List at the end of this volume.

REMARKS ON THE MYSTIC DOCTRINE AND POETRY OF THE ṢŪFĪS.

THE poetry of the East, particularly that of the Muḥammadan nations, differs materially from that of the West; and when taken up by the uninitiated, would often appear to be the mere effusions of wild and voluptuous bacchanals, or worthy of Anacreon himself. These remarks, however, pertain more to Persian than to Afg͟hān poetry, which contains less of the, often, bombastic style of the former, and approaches nearer to the simplicity of the poetry of the ancient Arabs. A general subject with the Afg͟hān, as well as other Asiatic poets, is that of love, not *human*, but divine, and a contempt for the people and vanities of the world; whilst other Afg͟hān poets, such as K͟hus͟hḥāl K͟hān, write on any subject that may have been uppermost in their minds at the time, after the manner of Western poets.

The general reader, who would understand many of the poems contained in the following pages, must know that most of the Asiatic poets profess the mystical doctrine of the Ṣūfis, the tenets of which, it will be necessary to explain to him; although Oriental scholars may be supposed to be sufficiently familiar with the subject.

The Muḥammadan writers state, that these enthusiasts are co-existent with their religion; and, probably, their rapturous zeal may have greatly contributed to the first establishment of Islāmism; but they have since been considered its greatest enemies, and it is avouched that their doctrines have, for a long time, been even undermining Muḥammadanism itself. Hence the most rigorous proceedings have, from time to time, been put in practice to repress their increase, but these, as usual in such cases, have had a contrary effect; and Ṣūfi-ism is said to be still on the increase. There is no doubt, but that the free opinions of the sect on the dogmas of the Muḥammadan religion, their contempt for its forms, and their claim to communion with, or rather absorption into the Creator, are all more or less calculated to subvert that faith, of whose outward forms the Ṣūfis profess their veneration.

The tenets of the Ṣūfi doctrines appear to have been most widely diffused over Persia; and, indeed, the great reputation acquired by one of the priests of the sect, enabled his descendants, for above two centuries, under the name of the Ṣafawīan dynasty, to occupy the throne of that country. *

The general name by which this sect of enthusiasts is known, is Ṣūfi, implying *pure*, a term probably derived from the Arabic word صفه (*ṣafah*), signifying purity; and by this name all are known, from the venerated teacher, or spiritual guide, followed by crowds of disciples, to the humble *kalandar*, *darwesh*, or *fakir*, who wanders about almost naked, or only clothed in his *khirkah* or cloak of rags, subsisting upon scanty alms, to support this, voluntarily adopted, life of prayer and religious abstraction.

In India, more than in any other country of Asia, from remote ages, these visionary doctrines appear to have flourished, much after the same manner as in Egypt and Syria, in the early days of Christianity, as testified to by the early ecclesiastical writers, who trace to those countries the mystic, the hermit, and the monk; for there the propensity to a life of austerity was quite a disease. In the Hindū religion also, as well as in the people themselves, there is much that tends to foster a spirit of religious abstraction; and we may thus, with some justice, suppose that from India other nations have derived this mystic worship of the Deity, but without adopting the dreadful austerities and macerations, common among the Hindūs, and deemed necessary for attaining unto this state of beatitude.

To give a full account of the doctrines of the Ṣūfis, would be almost a useless attempt; for traces of it may be found, in some shape or other, in all countries; alike, in the sublime theories of the philosophers of ancient Greece, and in those of modern Europe.

The Ṣūfis affirm, that their creed is adverse to superstition, scepticism, and error; but "it exists by the active propagation of all three." * The doctrines of their teachers are given to their disciples in place of the outward forms and observances of the faith they profess. They are invited to embark upon the ocean of doubt, piloted by a sacred teacher, or spiritual guide, whom they must consider superior to all other mortals, and deem worthy of the most pious and spiritual confidence—in fact, of almost adoration itself. They are devoted to the search after TRUTH, and are constantly occupied in adoration of the Deity. He, according to their belief, is diffused throughout all created things; † and they consider, that the soul of man, and the principle of existence, is *of* God (part of Him), not *from* Him. Hence their doctrine teaches that the soul of man is an exile from its Creator, who is its home and source; that the body is its cage, or prison-house; and the term of life, in this world, is its period of banishment from Him ere the soul fell it had seen the face of TRUTH, but, in this world, it merely obtains a partial and shadowy glimpse, "which serves to awaken the slumbering memory of the past, but can only vaguely recall it; and Sūfi-ism undertakes, by a long course of education, and moral discipline, to lead the soul onward, from stage to stage, until, at length, it reaches the goal of perfect knowledge, truth, and peace." *

According to this mysterious doctrine, there are four stages through which it is necessary man should pass, prior to attaining unto the highest state, or that of divine beatitude; where, to use their own words, "his corporeal veil, which had previously obscured his sight, will be drawn aside, and his soul, emancipated from all material things, will again unite with the divine and transcendent essence, from which it had been divided, for a time, but not separated for ever."

The first of these stages is termed *nāsut*, or humanity, in which the disciple is supposed to be living in obedience to the *sharœ*, or orthodox law, and paying due observance to the rites and ceremonies of religion; for these things are allowed to be necessary and useful in regulating the lives of the vulgar and weak-minded, and in restraining within proper bounds, and guiding such as are unable to reach the acme of divine contemplation and abstraction, who might be led astray by that very latitude in matters of faith, which instructs and enraptures those of more powerful intellect, and more ardent piety.

The second stage is termed *ṭarīḳat*, or the way, in which the disciple attains what is called *jabrūt*, or potentiality and capacity; and he who reaches this stage, quits, altogether, that state in which he is merely permitted to follow and revere a teacher or spiritual guide, and thus he becomes admitted within the pale of Sūfi-ism. All observance of the rites and forms of religion may be laid aside; for he now, it is supposed, exchanges what is called *œamal-i jismānī*, or corporeal worship, for *œamal-i-rūḥānī*, or spiritual adoration; but this stage cannot be attained, save by great piety, virtue, endurance, and resignation; for it is necessary to restrain the intellect when weak, until, from habits of mental devotion, grounded upon a proper knowledge of its own greatness and immortality, and of the Divine nature, it shall have acquired sufficient energy; since the mind cannot be trusted in the omission or disuse of the rites and usages of religion.

The third stage is *œarūf*, signifying knowledge or inspiration; and the disciple who arrives thereunto, is said to have attained superhuman knowledge—in fact, to be inspired; and when he has reached this stage, he is equal to the angels.

The fourth, and final state arrived at, is *ḥaḳīḳat*, or Truth itself, which signifies that his union with the Divinity is perfect and complete.

The dignity of Khalīfah, as the teacher is designated, can only be obtained after long-continued fasting and prayer, and by complete abstraction and severance from all mundane things; *for the man must be annihilated, before the saint can exist.* The preparation for the third stage of Ṣūfi-ism requires a protracted and fearful probation; and many lose their lives in their efforts to attain it. The person who makes the essay must be a devout and godly *murīd* or disciple, who has already advanced, by his piety and abstraction, beyond the necessity of observing religion's forms and usages. He must begin by endeavouring to attain a higher state of beatitude, by a lengthened fast, which should not be less than forty days; and during this period of fasting he remains in solitude, and in a posture of contemplation, and takes no sustenance save enough to keep body and soul together. The character of the votary greatly depends upon the patience and fortitude he may display during this severe ordeal; and when, reduced to a mere skeleton, the disciple comes forth from his solitude, he still has years of trial to endure. He must wander about, companionless, in desert places, or remain in some frightful solitude, and only seeing, occasionally, the Khalīfah, or spiritual guide, whom he follows; for the chief merit of all ranks of Ṣūfis, is complete devotion to their teacher. When he dies, he leaves his *khīrkah*, or patched garment, and worldly wealth, to the disciple he considers the most worthy to succeed him; and when the latter dons the holy mantle, he is invested with the power of his predecessor. *

The most celebrated Ṣūfi teachers have been alike famed for their devotion and their learning, in Persia as well as in other countries; and, in the former, the Ṣūfis have claimed for their own, all who have, by their writings or sayings, shown a spirit of philosophy, or knowledge of the nature Divine, which has elevated them above the prejudices of the vulgar; and, certainly, great numbers of persons, eminent for their learning, genius, and piety, have adopted the Ṣūfi doctrines. Amongst the most distinguished of these are poets; for the very essence of Ṣūfi-ism is poetry. The raptures of genius, expatiating upon a subject that cannot be exhausted, are held to be divine inspirations, by those who believe that the soul, when emancipated by devotion, can wander in the regions of the spiritual world, and, at last, unite with its Creator, the source from whence it emanated. It is the same with all Ṣūfi poets, whatever be their country; but Persia is more generally known as that, in which this species of poetry was supposed to have reached the highest degree of perfection; but it will be discovered, from the following pages, that Ṣūfi-ism has produced, amongst the rough and hardy Afghāns, conceptions equally as sublime. "Human speech, however," to quote the words of a writer already mentioned, †"is too weak and imperfect to convey these lofty experiences of the soul, and hence these can only be represented by symbols and metaphors." For this reason the Ṣūfi poets, to quote the words of Sir William Jones, "adopt the fervour of devotion, and the ardent love of created spirits towards their beneficent Creator; and Ṣūfi poetry consists almost wholly of a mystical, religious allegory, though it seems, to the uninitiated ear, to contain merely the sentiments of wild and voluptuous bacchanals; but although we must admit the danger of such a poetical style, where the limits between enthusiasm and depravity are so minute, as to be scarcely distinguishable;"—for the mystical meaning of their poetry (save in the poems of the Afghān poet Mīrzā) never, or rarely, obtrudes itself;—we may, if we choose, pass it by, confining ourselves to those passages alone, which tell of a mundane passion, and a terrestrial summer and wine. Under the veil of earthly love, and the woes of temporal separation, they disguise the dark riddle of human life, and the celestial banishment, which lies behind the threshold of existence; and, under the joys of revelry and inebriation, they figure mystical transports, and ecstatic raptures. * Still, we must not censure it severely, and must allow it to be natural, though a warm imagination may carry it beyond the bounds of sober reason; "for," to quote the same author, "an ardently grateful piety is congenial to the undepraved nature of man, whose mind, sinking under the magnitude of the subject, and struggling to express its emotions; has recourse to metaphors and allegories, which it sometimes extends beyond the bounds of cool reason, and often to the brink of absurdity." BARROW, who would have been the sublimest mathematician, if his religious turn of mind had not made him the deepest theologian of his age, describes Love as "an affection or inclination of the soul towards an object, proceeding from an apprehension and esteem of some excellence or convenience in it, as its beauty, worth, or utility; and producing, if it be absent, a proportionable desire, and, consequently, an endeavour to obtain such a property in it, such possession of it, such *an approximation to it, or union with it,* as the thing is capable of; with a regret and displeasure in failing to obtain it, or in the want and loss of it; begetting, likewise, a complacence, satisfaction, and delight, in its presence, possession, or enjoyment, which is, moreover, attended with a goodwill towards it, suitable to its nature; that is, with a desire that it should arrive at, or continue in, its best state, with a delight to perceive it thrive and flourish; with a displeasure to see it suffer or decay; with a consequent endeavour to advance it in all good, and preserve it from all evil." Agreeably to this description, which consists of two parts, and was designed to comprise the tender love of the Creator towards created spirits, the great philosopher bursts forth in another place, with his usual animation, and command of language, into the following panegyric on the pious love of human souls towards the Author of their happiness:—"Love is the sweetest and most delectable of all passions; and when, by the conduct of wisdom, it is directed in a rational way toward a worthy, congruous, and attainable object, it cannot otherwise than fill the heart with ravishing delight: such, in all respects, superlatively such, is GOD; who, infinitely beyond all other things, deserveth our affection, as most perfectly amiable and desirable; as having obliged us by innumerable and inestimable benefits; all the good that we have ever enjoyed, or can ever expect, being derived from His pure bounty; all things in the world, in competition with Him, being mean and ugly; all things, without Him, vain, unprofitable, and hurtful to us. He is the most proper object of our love; for we chiefly were framed, and it is the prime law of our nature, to love Him; *our soul, from its original instinct, vergeth towards Him as its centre, and can have no rest till it be fixed on Him:* He alone can satisfy the vast capacity of our minds, and fill our boundless desires. He, of all lovely things, most certainly and easily may be attained; for, whereas, commonly, men are crossed in their affections, and their love is embittered from their affecting things imaginary, which they cannot reach, or coy things, which disdain and reject them, it is with GOD quite otherwise: He is most ready to impart himself; He most earnestly desireth and wooeth our love; He is not only most willing to correspond in affection, but even doth prevent us therein: *He doth cherish and encourage our love by sweetest influences, and most consoling embraces*, by kindest expressions of favour, by most beneficial returns; and, whereas all other objects do, in the enjoyment, much fail our expectation, He doth even far exceed it. Wherefore, in all affectionate motions of our hearts towards GOD; in *desiring* Him, in seeking His favour or friendship; in *embracing* Him, or setting our esteem, our goodwill, our confidence, on Him; in *enjoying* Him, by devotional meditations, and addresses to Him; in a reflective sense of our interest and propriety in Him; *in that mysterious union of spirit*, whereby we do closely adhere to, and are, as it were, inserted in Him; in a hearty complacence in His benignity, a grateful sense of His kindness, and a zealous desire of yielding some requital for it, we cannot but feel very, very pleasant transports: indeed, that celestial flame, kindled in our hearts by the spirit of love, cannot be void of warmth; we cannot fix our eyes on *infinite beauty*, we cannot taste infinite sweetness, we cannot cleave to infinite felicity, without also perpetually rejoicing in the first daughter of LOVE to GOD—Charity towards men; which, in complexion and careful disposition, doth much resemble her mother; for she doth rid us of all these gloomy, keen, turbulent imaginations and passions, which cloud our mind, which fret our heart, which discompose the frame of our soul, from burning anger, from storming contention, from gnawing envy, from rankling spite, from racking suspicion, from distracting ambition and avarice; and, consequently, doth settle our mind in an even temper, in a sedate humour, in an harmonious order, in *that pleasant state of tranquillity, which, naturally, doth result from the voidance of irregular passions*."

This passage, which borders upon quietism and enthusiastic devotion, differs no more from the mystic tenets of the Ṣūfi creed, than do European fruits and flowers from the lusciousness and fragrance of those of Asia, or than the cold skies and sun of the West differ from the gorgeous skies and blazing sun of Eastern lands.

It is to express fervid feelings like these that, by Ṣūfi-ism, poetry is brought into play, which, in its sweetest strains, teaches that all nature abounds with a Divine love, causing even the humblest plant to seek the sublime object of its desire.

"In peace, Love tunes the shepherd's reed;

In war, he mounts the warrior's steed;

In halls, in gay attire is seen;

In hamlets, dances on the green.

Love rules the camp, the court, the grove,

And men below, and saints above;

For Love is heaven, and heaven is love." [*]

Sir William Jones, in his "Essay on the Mystical Poetry of the Persians and Hindūs," [†] has given an excellent description of the Ṣūfis and their doctrine; and I cannot do better here than extract therefrom such portions as may elucidate my present subject. "The Ṣūfis," he says, "concur in believing that the souls of men differ infinitely in *degree*, but not at all in *kind*, from the Divine Spirit, of which they are *particles*, and in which they will ultimately be re-absorbed; that the Spirit of God pervades the universe, always immediately present to His work, and, consequently, always in substance; that He alone is perfect benevolence, perfect truth, perfect beauty; that the love of Him alone is *real* and genuine love, while that of all other objects is *absurd* and illusory; that the beauties of nature are faint resemblances, like images in a mirror, of the Divine charms; that, from eternity without beginning, to eternity without end, the Supreme Benevolence is occupied in bestowing happiness, or the means of attaining it: that men can only attain it by performing their part of the *primal covenant*, between them and the Creator; that nothing has a pure, absolute existence but *mind* or *spirit;* that *material substances*, as the ignorant call them, are no more than gay *pictures*, presented continually to our minds by the spiritual Artist; that we must be aware of attachment to such *phantoms*, and attach ourselves, exclusively, to GOD, who truly exists in us, as we exist solely in Him; that we retain, even in this forlorn state of separation from our beloved, the *idea of heavenly beauty*, and the *remembrance* of our *primeval vows;* that sweet music, gentle breezes, fragrant flowers, perpetually renew the primary idea, refresh our fading memory, and melt us with tender affections; that we must cherish these affections, and, by abstracting our souls from *vanity*, that is, from all but GOD, approximate to His essence, in our final union with which will consist our supreme beatitude. From these principles flow a thousand metaphors, and other poetical figures, which abound in the sacred poems of the Persians and Hindūs, who seem to mean the same thing in substance, and differ only in expression, as their languages differ in idiom." It is the same in Afghān poetry also, as the following pages will amply show.

The modern Ṣūfis, who profess a belief in the Ḳur'ān, suppose, with much sublimity both of thought and diction, that in a prior state of existence the soul had been united with God; and that, at the Creation, the created spirits, and the supreme soul from which they emanated, were summoned together, when a celestial voice demanded from each, separately, "ALASTO BI-RABBIKUM?" "*Art thou not with thy God?*" that is, "*Art thou not bound by solemn contract with Him?*" whereunto the spirits answered, "BALĀ," "*Yea!*" And hence it is that "ALASTO," or "*Art thou not?*" (the question of this primeval compact), and "BALĀ," or "*Yea!*" occur continually in these mystical compositions of Muḥammadan poets, whether Persians, Turks, or Afghāns. "Music, poetry, and the arts," again to quote the words of a modern writer, [*] "are the unconscious aspirations of the soul, as it hurries along in its restless impulses through the world, stung by the echo of "ALASTO," yet ringing in their ears, but with no visible object to claim the passionate adoration which it burns to pour forth."

"The Hindūs," says Sir William Jones, "describe the same covenant under the figurative notion, so finely expressed by ISAIAH, of a *nuptial contract;* for, considering GOD in the three characters of Creator, Regenerator, and Preserver, and supposing the power of *Preservation* and *Benevolence* to have become incarnate in the power of KRISHNA, they represent him as married to Rādhā, a word signifying *atonement*, *pacification*, or *satisfaction*, but applied allegorically to the *soul of man*, or rather to *the whole assemblage of created souls*, between whom and their benevolent Creator they suppose that *reciprocal love*, which BARROW describes with a glow of expression perfectly Oriental, and which our most orthodox theologians believe to have been mystically *shadowed* in the SONG OF SOLOMON, while they admit that, in a literal sense, it is an epithalamium on the marriage of the sapient king with the princess of Egypt. The very learned author of the "Prelections on Sacred Poetry," declared his opinion, that the CANTICLES were founded on historical truth, but involved in allegory of that sort, which he named *mystical;* and the beautiful Persian poem, on the loves of LAYLĀ and MAJNŪN, by the inimitable Niẓāmī—to say nothing of other poems on the same subject—is, indisputably, built on true history, yet avowedly allegorical and mysterious; for the introduction to it is a continued rapture on *Divine love;* and the name of LAYLĀ seems to be used in the *Masnawī* * and the odes of Ḥāfiẓ, for the omnipresent Spirit of God." If reference is here made to the first of the poems of the Afghān monarch, Aḥmad Shāh, at page 294, the force of the words of Sir William Jones will be more fully seen.

According to the interpretation given to these mystical poems, by the Ṣūfis themselves—for they have even composed a vocabulary of the words used by these mystics—by *wine* is meant devotion, *sleep* is meditation on the Divine perfections, and *perfume* the hope of the Divine favour; the *zephyrs* are outbursts of grace; *kisses* and *embraces*, the transports of devotion and piety; *idolators*, *infidels*, and *libertines*, are men of the purest faith, and the *idol they worship* is the Creator himself; the *tavern* is a secluded oratory, where they become intoxicated with the wine of love, and its *keeper* is an enlightened instructor or spiritual guide; *beauty* denotes the perfection of the Deity; *curls* and *tresses* are the infiniteness of His glory; the *lips* are the inscrutable mysteries of His essence; *down* on the cheek, the world of spirits who surround His throne; and the *black mole* upon the cheek of the beloved, the point of indivisible unity; and *wantonness*, *mirth*, and *inebriation*, signify religious enthusiasm, and abstraction from all earthly thoughts and contempt of all worldly affairs.

The poets themselves give a colour to such interpretations as the foregoing, in many passages in their poems; and it is impossible to imagine that such effusions as those of Ḥāfiẓ, Saædī, and their imitators, would, otherwise, be tolerated in a Musalmān country, particularly at places like Cairo and Constantinople, where they are venerated as divine compositions. It must be, however, allowed, that " the mystical allegory, which, like metaphors and comparisons, should be general only, not minutely exact, is greatly diminished, if not wholly destroyed, by any attempt at particular and distinct resemblances; and that this style of composition is open to dangerous misinterpretation." *

The following ode, by a Ṣūfi of Bokhārā, is such an extraordinary specimen of the mysterious doctrine of the sect, although some of the poems of the Afghān poet Mīrzā are sufficiently so, that I cannot refrain from inserting it in this place:—

"Yesterday, half inebriated, I passed by the quarter where the wine-sellers dwell,

To seek out the daughter of an infidel, who is a vendor of wine.

At the end of the street, a damsel, with a fairy's cheek, advanced before me,

Who, pagan-like, wore her tresses dishevelled over her shoulders, like the sacerdotal thread.

I said, 'O thou, to the arch of whose eyebrows the new moon is a shame!

What quarter is this, and where is thy place of abode?'

'Cast,' she replied, 'thy rosary on the ground, and lay the thread of paganism thy shoulder upon;

Cast stones at the glass of piety; and from an o'erflowing goblet quaff the wine.

After that draw near me, that I may whisper one word in thine ear;

For thou wilt accomplish thy journey, if thou hearken to my words.'

Abandoning my heart altogether, and in ecstacy wrapt, I followed her,

'Till I came to a place, where, alike, reason and religion forsook me.

At a distance, I beheld a company, all inebriated and beside themselves,

Who came all frenzied, and boiling with ardour from the wine of love;

Without lutes, or cymbals, or viols; yet all full of mirth and melody—

Without wine, or goblet, or flask; yet all drinking unceasingly.

When the thread of restraint slipped away from my hand,

I desired to ask her one question, but she said unto me, 'SILENCE!'

'This is no square temple whose gate thou canst precipitately attain;

This is no mosque which thou canst reach with tumult, but without knowledge:

This is the banquet-house of infidels, and all within it are intoxicated—

All, from eternity's dawn to the day of doom, in astonishment lost!

Depart, then, from the cloister, and towards the tavern bend thy steps;

Cast away the cloak of the darwesh, and don thou the libertine's robe!'

I obeyed; and if thou desire, with ISMAT, the same hue and colour to acquire,

Imitate him; and both this and the next world sell for one drop of pure wine!"

The tenets of the Ṣūfi belief, as may be judged from what has been already stated, are involved in mystery. They begin by instilling doctrines of virtue and piety, and by teaching forbearance, abstemiousness, and universal benevolence. This much they profess; but they have secrets and mysteries for every step and degree, which are never disclosed to the uninitiated and profane; but I shall now proceed to quote a few passages from the writings of celebrated Ṣūfis, which may tend to throw some additional light upon this dark and mystic creed.

The Persian poet, Shaikh Saædī, in his "Bostan," or "Flower Garden," the subject of which is devoted to divine love, thus describes it:—"The love of a being constituted, like thyself, of water and clay, destroys thy patience and thy peace of mind; it excites thee, in thy waking hours, with minute beauties, and occupies thee, in thy sleep, with vain imaginations. With such real affection dost thou lay thine head at her feet, that the universe, in comparison with her, vanishes into nothing before thee; and, since her eye is not allured by thy gold, gold and dust alike appear equal in thine. Not a breath dost thou utter unto any one else, for with her thou hast no room for any other; thou declarest that her abode is in thine eye, or, when thou closest it, in thy heart; thou hast no power to be at rest for a moment: if she demands thy soul, it runs, instantly, to thy lip; and if she waves a sword over thee, thy head falls, immediately, under it. Since an absurd passion, with its basis on air, affects thee so violently, and commands with a sway so despotic, canst thou wonder that they who walk in the true path are overwhelmed in the sea of mysterious adoration? They abandon the world through remembrance of its Creator; they are inebriated with the melody of amorous complainings; they remember their beloved, and resign unto Him both this life and that to come. Through remembrance of God, they shun the whole of mankind; they are so enamoured of the cup-bearer, that they spill the wine from the cup. No panacea can cure them; for no mortal can be apprised of their malady; so loudly have the divine words, ALASTO and BALĀ, the tumultuous exclamation of all spirits, rung in their ears, from time without beginning. They are a sect fully employed, though sitting in retirement; their feet are of earth, but their breath is like flame. With a single shout they could rend a mountain from its base; with a single cry they could throw a city into commotion. Like the wind, they are gone, and more swiftly; like stone, they are silent, yet utter God's praises. At the dawn of day, their tears flow so copiously, as to wash from their eyes the black antimony of sleep; * though the fleet steed of their conception ran so swiftly all night; yet the morning finds them left, in disorder, behind. Night and day they are plunged in an ocean of ardent desire, until they are, through astonishment, unable to distinguish the night from the day. With the peerless beauty of Him, who adorned the human form, so enraptured are they, that, with the beauty of the figure itself, they have no concern; and whenever they behold a beauteous form, they see in it the mystery of the Almighty's work. The wise take not the husk in exchange for the kernel; and he who makes that choice has no understanding. He alone has drunk the pure wine of unity, who has forgotten, by remembering GOD, all things besides in both worlds."

Jāmī, the author of the celebrated poem of Laylā and Majnūn, defines the principles of this mystic philosophy in the following words:—"Some wise and holy men are of opinion, that when the Supreme Being sheds the refulgence of his Holy Spirit upon any of his creatures, that creature's essence, attributes, and actions, become so completely absorbed in the essence, the attributes, and the actions of the Creator, that he finds himself in the position of regulator or director, with reference to the rest of the creation, the several existences of which become, as it were, his limbs—nothing happens to any of them, that he does not feel it has happened to himself. In consequence of his individual and utter annihilation, the result of his essential union with the Deity, he sees his own essence to be the essence of the One and Only; his own attributes to be His attributes; and his own actions to be His actions;—and beyond this, there is no stage in progression to complete union with God attainable by man. When the spiritual vision of any man is engrossed by contemplating the beauty of the Divine Essence, by the overpowering influence of the Eternal Spirit, the light of his understanding, which is that quality by which we are enabled to distinguish between things, becomes wholly extinguished; and as 'error passeth away on the appearance of Truth,' so is the power of discriminating, between the perishable and the imperishable, at once removed." *

Few orthodox Muḥammadans give a literal construction to the words of the Prophet on the subject of predestination, although the Ḳur'ān inculcates such; for they deem it impious so to do, as thereby God would be made the author and cause of man's sin. All Ṣūfis are fatalists, and believe that the principle which emanates from the Almighty can do nothing without His will, and cannot refrain from what He wills that it should do. Some Ṣūfis deny that evil exists at all, because every thing proceeds from God, and must therefore necessarily be good; and they exclaim, with the poet—

"The writer of our destiny is a fair and truthful writer,

And never did he write that which was evil." Others, again, admit, that in this world the principle of evil doth exist; but that man is not a free agent; and quote the following couplet, from the Persian poet Ḥāfiẓ—

"My destiny hath been allotted to the tavern * by the Almighty:

Then tell me, O teacher! where lieth my crime."

Such is the remarkable doctrine of the Ṣūfis, and still more so their language and allegories, which we have been too much accustomed, in Europe, to consider as the wanton and reckless effusions of Eastern revellers, all devoted to the pleasure of the hour—"effusions bright, indeed, with all the gorgeous hues of Eastern colouring, like unto the skies over their heads, or the gardens around them, but yet transient as the summer's roses, or the nightingale's notes which welcomed them." †

This may be correct as to the outward form of Eastern poetry in general; but most Asiatic poets are Ṣūfis, and if we would attempt to read their poems, we should also desire to understand them; since beneath all this gorgeous and mysterious imagery their lies a latent signification of far different, and more lasting interest, where the ardent longings and fervid transports of the soul find utterance, which we may look for in vain in the venerated literature of pagan Greece and Rome. Their great Molawī assures us that they profess eager desire, but with no carnal affection, and circulate the cup, but no material goblet; since, in their sect, all things are spiritual—all is mystery within mystery:

"All, all on earth is shadow, all beyond

Is substance; the reverse is folly's creed."

Sāhil-ibn-Æabd-ullah, of Shustar, a celebrated Sūfi teacher, states, "That the soul's secret was first revealed when Faræawn * declared himself a god:" and another, Shaikh Muhī-ud-dīn, writes, "That the mighty host of the Egyptian monarch was not overwhelmed in the sea of error, but of knowledge:" and in another place, "That the Christians are not infidels because they consider Jesus Christ a God, but because they deem him *alone* a God." Another author, Aghā Muḥammad Æalī, of Karmānshāh, who, however, is an open enemy of the Ṣūfis, says, that "they ignore the doctrine of reward and punishment," which is as incompatible with their ideas of the soul's re-absorption into the divine essence, as with their literal belief of predestination. Some of their most celebrated teachers, however, deny the truth of this statement, and maintain that sinners will be punished in a future state, and that the good will enjoy a much higher and purer bliss than the sensual paradise of Muḥammad holds out, thus revolting at a literal translation of the on that subject.

Another Persian Author, of high reputation † for his piety and judgment, has given a good account of the Ṣūfis and their doctrines. He conceives, with several other Muḥammadan writers, that some of the principal Muḥammadan saints were of the Ṣūfi belief; but he applies this name to them, apparently, only as religious enthusiasts, and no more. He makes a great distinction between those who, whilst they mortified the flesh, and indulged in an enraptured love of the Almighty, still kept within the pale of revealed religion; and those wild devotees who, abandoning themselves to the frenzied wanderings of a heated imagination, fancied they should draw nearer unto God by departing from every thing deemed rational among men. *

In another passage, this author states, "The Almighty, after his prophets and holy teachers, esteems none more than the pure Ṣūfis, because their desire is to raise themselves, through His grace, from their earthly mansion to the heavenly regions, and to exchange their lowly condition for that of angels. I have stated what I know of them in my Preface. The accomplished and eloquent among them form two classes, the Ḥukamā, or *men of science*, and the Æulamā, or *men of piety and learning*. The former seek truth by demonstration; the latter, through revelation. There is another class called Æarūfā, or *men of knowledge*, and Awliyā, or *holy men*, who, in endeavouring to reach a state of beatitude, have abandoned the world. These are also *men of science;* but as, through Divine grace, they have attained to a state of perfection, their fears are believed to be less than those of others who remain in worldly occupations. † Thus they are more exalted, and nearer to the rich inheritance of the Prophet than other men. No doubt there are imminent dangers along the path: there are many false teachers, and many deluded students pursuing the vapour of the desert, like the thirsty traveller; and these, if they do not rush unto their death, return wearied, grieved, and disappointed, from having been the dupes of their fancy. A true and perfect teacher is most rare; and when he exists, to discover him is impossible; for who shall discover perfection, except He who is himself perfect? who but the jeweller shall tell the price of the jewel? This is the reason why so many miss the true path, and fall into all the mazes of error. They are deceived by appearances, and waste their lives in the pursuit of that which is most defective; conceiving all along that it is most perfect; and thus lose their time, their virtue, and their religion. It is to save men from this danger, that God, through the Prophet, has warned us to attend to established usages, and to be guided by care and prudence. What has been said applies equally to those who live in the world, and to those who have abandoned it; for neither abstinence, nor devotion, can exclude the Devil, who will seek retired mendicants, clothed in the garb of divinity; and these, like other men, will discover that real knowledge is the only talisman by which the dictates of the good can be distinguished from those of the evil spirit. The traveller, on the path of Ṣūfi-ism, must not, therefore, be destitute of worldly knowledge, otherwise he will be alike exposed to danger from excess or deficiency of zeal, and he will certainly act contrary to the most sacred of his duties. A senseless man is likely to exceed the just bounds, in the practice of abstinence and abstraction, and then both his bodily and mental frame become affected, and he loses his labour and his object."

"The Ṣūfi teacher," continues Ḳāzī Nūr-ullah, "professes to instruct his disciple how to restore the inward man by purifying the spirit, cleansing the heart, enlightening the head, and anointing the soul: and when all this is done, they affirm that his desires shall be accomplished, and his depraved qualities changed into higher attributes, and he shall prove and understand the conditions, the revelations, the stages, and gradations of exaltation, till he arrives at the ineffable enjoyment of beholding and contemplating God. If teachers have not arrived at this consummation of perfection themselves, it is obvious, that to seek knowledge or happiness from them is a waste of time; and the devoted disciple will either terminate his labour in assuming the same character of imposture that he has found in his instructor, or he will consider all Ṣūfis alike, and condemn this whole sect of philosophers.

"It often happens, that sensible and well-informed men follow a master, who, though able, has not arrived at the virtue and sanctity which constitute perfection: his disciples conceiving that none are better or more holy than their teacher and themselves, and yet, disappointed at not reaching that stage of enjoyment which they expected to arrive at, seek relief from the reproaches of their own mind in scepticism. They doubt, on the ground of their personal experience, all that they have heard or read, and believe that the accounts of the holy men who have, in this world, attained a state of beatitude, are only a string of fables. This is a dangerous error; and I must therefore repeat, that those who seek truth should be most careful to commence with prudence and moderation, lest they be lost in the mazes I have described; and, from meeting with evils of their own creation, should give way to disappointment and grief;

and, by expelling from their minds that ardent fervour which belongs to true zeal, should disqualify themselves for the most glorious of all human pursuits." *

The Ṣūfis are divided into innumerable sects, as must be expected regarding a doctrine, which may be called an ideal belief. It will not be necessary to the present subject to enumerate them all; for though they differ in designation and some minor usages, they all agree as to the principal tenets of their creed; particularly in inculcating the absolute necessity of entire submission to their inspired teachers, and the feasibility, through fervent piety, and enthusiastic devotion, of the soul's attaining a state of heavenly beatification, whilst the body is yet an inhabitant of this terrestrial sphere.

I have refrained from attempting to give any description of the extraordinary phases the Ṣūfi belief has, from time to time, assumed in Hindūstān, where it has ever flourished, and where it has been beneficial in tending to unite the opposite elements of Muḥammadanism and Hindūism, as shown more particularly in the events of the life of Nānak Shāh, the *gurū* or spiritual guide of the Sikhs, and founder of their religion. On the Bombay side of India, also, it has even taken root among the Gabrs or Pārsīs. Many of the usages and opinions of the Ṣūfis bear a similarity to those of the Gnostics, and other Christian sects, as well as to some of the philosophers among the ancient Greeks. The Ṣūfi writers are familiar with Plato and Aristotle: their more celebrated works abound with quotations from the former. It has often been asserted that the Greeks borrowed their knowledge and philosophy from the East; and, if correct, the debt has been well repaid. Should an account of Pythagoras be translated into the Persian or other Eastern language, it would be read as that of a Sufi saint. "His initiation into the mysteries of the Divine nature, his deep contemplation and abstraction, his miracles, his passionate love of music, his mode of teaching his disciples, the persecution he suffered, and the manner of his death, present us with a close parallel to what is related of many eminent Ṣūfi teachers, and may lead to a supposition that there must be something similar, in the state of knowledge and of society, where the same causes produce the same effects." *

In the same manner as with Ḥāfiẓ's poems in Persian, many of the following odes, particularly those of Raḥmān and Ḥamīd, are commonly sung all over Afghānistān, as popular songs are sung in Europe; but the singers, generally, unless educated men, have little idea of the deep meaning that lies beneath.

Footnotes x:* Ismāæīl the First ascended the throne A.D. 1500, and his family was subverted by Nādir, A.D. 1736.

xi:* Malcolm's History of Persia.

xi:† "The creation proceeded at once from the splendour of God, who poured his spirit upon the universe, as the general diffusion of light is poured over the earth by the rising sun; and as the absence of that luminary creates total darkness, so the partial or total absence of the Divine splendour or light causes partial or general annihilation. The creation, in its relation to the Creator, is like unto the small particles discernible in the sun's rays, which vanish the moment it ceases to shine."—PERSIAN MS.

xii:* E. B. Cowell, M.A.: "Oxford Essays."

xiv:* See 2 KINGS, chap ii., where Elisha dons the mantle of Elijah.

xiv:† E. B. Cowell.

xv:* E. B. Cowell.

xviii:* SCOTT.

xviii:† ASIATIC RESEARCHES, Vol. III.

xx:* E. B. Cowell.

xxi:* A collection of poems, by MOWLĀNA NŪR-UD-DĪN, JĀMĪ.

xxii:* Sir W. Jones.

xxiv:* See note at page 39.

xxv:* CAPTAIN W. N. LEES' Biographical Sketch of the Mystic Philosopher and Poet, Jāmī. Calcutta, 1859.

xxvi:* The sinful world is here referred to.

xxvi:† E. B. Cowell.

xxvii:* PHARAOH.

xxvii:† Ḳāzī Nūr-ullah of Shustar.

xxviii:* MALCOLM: HISTORY OF PERSIA. Some Christians in the extreme west of England have preached such doctrines, but practised the contrary.

xxviii:† It is related that the disciple of a celebrated Ṣūfi, having some money in his pocket when travelling, began to express his fears. "Cast away thy fear," said the old man. "How can I cast away a feeling?" he replied. "By casting away that which excites it," was the answer. He cast his money away, and, having nothing to lose, felt no fear.

xxx:* MALCOLM.

xxxi:* MALCOLM.

ÆABD-UR-RAḤMĀN.

MULLĀ ÆABD-UR-RAḤMĀN is one of the most popular, and probably the best known, of all the Afghān poets. His effusions are of a religious or moral character, and chiefly on the subject of divine love, being, like the poetical compositions of all Muḥammadan poets, tinged with the mysticisms of Ṣūfi-ism, already described in the Introductory Remarks; but there is a fiery energy in his style, and a natural simplicity, which will be vainly sought for amongst the more flowery and bombastic poetry of the Persians.

Raḥmān belonged to the Ghorīah Khel clan or sub-division, of the Mohmand tribe of the Afghāns, and dwelt in the village of Hazār-Khānī, in the *tapah* or district of the Mohmands, one of the five divisions of the province of Pes'hāwar. He was a man of considerable learning, but lived the life of a Darwesh, absorbed in religious contemplation, and separated from the world, with which, and with its people, he held no greater intercourse than necessity and the means of subsistence demanded. He is said to have been passionately fond of hearing religious songs, accompanied by some musical instrument, which the Chastī sect of Muḥammadans * appears to have a great partiality for. After a time, when the gift of poesy was bestowed upon him, he became a strict recluse, and was generally found by his friends in tears. Indeed, he is said to have been in the habit of weeping so much, as in course of time to have produced wounds on both his cheeks. His strict retirement, however, gave opportunity to a number of envious Mullās to belie him; and they began to circulate reports to the effect, that Raḥmān had turned atheist or heretic, since he never left his dwelling, and had even given up worshipping at the mosque along with the congregation—a matter strictly enjoined on all orthodox Muḥammadans. At length, by the advice and assistance of some of the priesthood, more liberal and less bigoted than his enemies, he contrived to escape from their hands, by agreeing, for the future, to attend the place of public worship, and to pray and perform his other religious duties, along with the members of the congregation. He thus, whether agreeable to himself or not, was obliged in some measure to mix with the world; and this, doubtless, gave rise to the ode at page 29, to which the reader is referred.

Raḥmān appears to have been in the habit of giving the copies of his poems, as he composed. them, from time to time, to his particular friends, which they, unknown to each other, took care to collect and preserve, for the express purpose of making a collection of them after the author's death. This they accordingly carried out, and it was not until Raḥmān's decease that these facts became known. It then appeared also, that some of these pseudo friends had, to increase the bulk of their own collection of the poet's odes, mixed up a quantity of their own trashy compositions with Raḥmān's, and had added, or rather forged, his name to them in the last couplets. In this manner two of these collections of odes were made, and were styled Raḥmān's first and second. Fortunately for his reputation, these forgeries were discovered in time, by some of the dearest of the poet's friends, who recognised or remembered the particular poems of his composition; and they accordingly rejected the chaff, retaining the wheat only, in the shape of his Dīwān, or alphabetical collection of odes, as it has come down to the present day. Still, considerable differences exist in many copies, some odes having a line more or a line less, whilst some again contain odes that are entirely wanting in others. This caused me considerable trouble when preparing several of them for insertion in my "Selections in the Afghān Language;" but it was attended with a proportionate degree of advantage, having altogether compared some sixty different copies of the poet's works, of various dates, some of which were written shortly after Raḥmān's death, when his friends had succeeded in collecting the poems in a single volume.

By some accounts, the poet would appear to have been a co-temporary of the warrior-poet, Khushḥāl Khān; * and it has been stated, that on two or three occasions they held poetical disputations together. This, however, cannot be true; for it seems that although Raḥmān was living towards the latter part of that brave chieftain's life, yet he was a mere youth, and was, more correctly speaking, a cotemporary of Afẓal Khān's, the grandson and successor of Khushḥāl, and the author of that rare, excellent, and extensive Afghān history, entitled, "Tārīkh-i-Muraṣṣaæ," and other valuable works. A proof of the incorrectness of this statement is, that the tragical end of Gul Khān and Jamal Khān, which Raḥmān and the poet Ḥamīd also have devoted a long poem to, † took place in the year of the Hijrah 1123 (A.D. 1711), twenty-five years after the death of Khushḥāl. Another, and still stronger proof against the statement of poetical disputations having taken place between them, is the fact of Raḥmān's retired life, and his humble position, as compared with that of Khushḥāl, the chief of a powerful tribe, and as good a poet as himself.

Some descendants of Raḥmān, on his daughter's side, dwell at present in the little hamlet of Deh-i-Bahādur (the Hamlet of the Brave), in the Mohmand district; but the descendants on the side of his only son have long been extinct.

The poet's tomb may still be seen in the graveyard of his native village.

Footnotes

1:* So called from a celebrated devotee named Muæīn-ud-Dīn, who dwelt at a place named Chast, in Arabia. The sect still exists in Afghānistān and the Panjāb.

3:* See Memoir preceding his poems.

3:† See Ḥamīd, Poem XLI. and note.

THE POEMS OF ÆABD-UR-RAḤMĀN.

IN THE NAME OF THE MOST MERCIFUL GOD!

I.

BEHOLD! such an Omnipotent Being is my God,

That He is the possessor of all power, authority, and will.

Should one enumerate all the most mighty, pure, and eminent,

My God is mightier, purer, and more eminent than all.

No want, nor requirement of His, is dependant upon any one;

Neither is my God under obligation, nor beholden to any.

Out of nothingness He produced the form of entity;

In such wise is my God the Creator, and the Nourisher of all.

He is the artist and the artificer of all and every created thing:

My God is, likewise, the hearer of every word and accent.

That which hath neither type nor parallel anywhere,

Its essence and its nature, its material and its principle, my God is.

All the structures, whether of this world or of that to come,

My God is the architect, and the builder of them all.

He is the decipherer and the construer of the unwritten pages—
The unfolder and the elucidator of all mysteries my God is.
Apparent or manifest; hidden or obscure; intermediate or intercalary;
My God is cognizant of, and familiar with, all matters and things.
He hath neither partner nor associate—His dominion is from Himself alone
A sovereign, without colleague or coadjutor, my God is.
Not that His unity and individuality proceed from impuissance;
For, in His one and unique nature, He is infinite, unlimited.
They have neither need nor necessity of the friendship of others,
Unto whom my God is beneficently and graciously inclined.
Wherefore then the occasion that I should seek Him elsewhere,
Since, in mine own dwelling, my God is ever at my side?
O RAḤMĀN! He is neither liable to change, nor to mutation—
My God is unchangeable and immutable, for ever and ever!

II.

My weeping for the beloved hath passed beyond all computation;
Yet the dear one is in no way affected at the sight of my tears.
Though every one of my words should be pearls of great price,
Still she doth not account them at all worthy of her ears.
Were she overcome by sleep, I would arouse her by my cries;
But though fully awake, my loved one is asleep unto me.
Like unto a writing, I speak, though with mouth covered;

But my silence surpasseth my wails and my lamentations?

When is there security for the crop of love in scorching ground!

It requireth a salamander to exist in this desert of mine.

This is not my love that separation hath parted from me:

'Tis my soul, which hath become separated from this body of mine.

I, RAḤMĀN, desire naught else than the beloved of my heart,

Should my prayer be accepted at the threshold of the Almighty.

III.

There is no return for thee, a second time, unto this world!

To-day is thy opportunity, whether thou followest evil or good!

Every thing for which the opportunity is gone, is the phœnix of our desires;

But the immortal bird hath never been caught in any one's net.

The stream, that hath left the sluice, floweth not back again!

The hour, which hath passed away, returneth to us no more!

For time is, alas! like unto the dead in the sepulchre's niche;

And no one hath brought, by weeping, the dead to life again.

If thou hast any object to attain, be quick, for time is short:

Flatter not thyself on the permanency of this brief existence!

Each target, of which, in thy heart, thou considerest thyself sure,

Through pride and vanity, thou wilt surely miss thine aim of.

Over-sanguine hope hath rendered many desponding:

Be not off thy guard as to the deceit and fraud of time!

When thy mouth becometh shattered by the stroke of death,
In what manner wilt thou then offer praises with it?
The bereaved woman, who giveth utterance to her bewailings,
Lamenteth over thee, if thou understandest what she says.
Thou art not a child, that one should teach thee by force:
Thou art wise and intelligent, and arrived at maturity's years.
Exercise, then, thine own understanding as to good and evil,
Whether thy well-being lieth in this, or in that.
Conceal thy face beneath thy mantle, and open thine eyes:
Fly not far away on the winds of vanity and ambition!
Soar not unto the heavens with thy head in the air,
For thou art, originally, from the dust of the earth created.
At the last day, inquiry will not be made of thee,
As to whether thou art the son or grandson of such an one.
To the bride, who may not be handsome in her own person,
What signify her mother's or her grandmother's good looks?
Practise goodness in thine own person, and fear evil!
Presume not on the virtues of thy father or thy mother!
These precepts, O my friend! I urge upon myself:
Be not then grieved that I have made use of thy name.
I use thine and those of others, but speak to myself alone:
With any one else, I have neither motive nor concern.

Whatever I utter, I address the whole unto myself:

All these failings and defects are only mine own.

Had I a place for these sorrows within my own breast,

Why should I give utterance unto these declamations?

Since the racking pains of mortality are before thee,

Why dost thou not die, O RAḤMĀN! before they come?

IV.

No one hath proved any of the world's faithfulness or sincerity;

And none, but the faithless and perfidious, have any affection for it.

They who may lay any claim unto it, as belonging to them,

Speak wholly under delusion; for the world is no one's own.

Fortune is like unto a potter—it fashioneth and breaketh:

Many, like unto me and thee, it hath created and destroyed.

Every stone and clod of the world, that may be looked upon,

Are all sculls; some those of kings, and some of beggars.

It behoveth not that one should place a snare in the world's path;

For the capture of the griffin and the phœnix cannot be effected.

Who can place any dependence upon this fleeting breath?

It is impossible to confine the wind with the strongest chain!

Whether the sun or the moon, the upshot is extinction:

Doth the flower always bloom? Nothing can exist for ever!

Walk not, O RAḤMĀN! contrary to the ways of the enlightened;

Since the love of the world is not approved of by any wise man.

V.

If one seek a charmer in the world, this is the one:

This is the dear one, who is the ornament of the universe.

There will hot be such another lover in it as myself;

Nor will ever such a beloved one be created like thee.

I had shown patience under thy harshness and cruelty;

But, in the place of lamentation, joy and gladness cannot be.

I will never consent to be separated from thee,

So long as my soul is not separated from this body of mine.

Like unto the congregation behind, with the priest before,

In such wise have I imitated and followed thee.

I am not the only one—the whole world loveth thee!

Whether it be the beggar, or the sovereign of the age.

Would that thou wouldst grant me a deed of protection,

Since thou puttest me off with the promise of to-morrow!

'Tis not that of mine own accord I am smitten with thee:

'Twas a voice from thy direction that reached me.

Indeed, from all eternity, I am devoted unto thee—.

It is not that to-day only, I have a beginning made.

When with the sword of thy love it shall be severed,

Then will the neck of RAḤMĀN have its duty performed.

VI.

The godly are the light and the refulgence of the world:

The pious are the guides and the directors of mankind.

If any one seek the way unto God and his Prophet,

The devout are the guides to point out the path.

The alchemist, that searcheth about for the philosopher's stone,

Will find it the bosom companion of the sanctified.

In the society of the enlightened, he will turn to red gold,

Though a person may be as a stone or a clod of the desert.

The ignorant are, as it were, like unto the dead:

Verily, the wise are like unto the saints themselves.

The enlightened are, comparatively, like unto the Messiah;

Since, from their breath, the dead return to life again.

He who may not possess some portion of wisdom

Is not a man: he is, as it were, but an empty model.

I, RAḤMĀN, am the servant of every enlightened being,

Whether he be of the highest, the middle, or the lowest degree.

VII.

Come, do not be the source of trouble unto any one;

For this short life of thine will soon be lost, O faithless one!

No one is to be a tarrier behind, in this world:

All are to be departers, either to-day or to-morrow.

Those dear friends, who to-day bloom before thee,
Will, in two or three short days, fade and decay.
If the sight of any be pleasing to thee, cherish them:
After they wither and die, when will they again revive?
The leaves of autumn, that fall from the branch,
By no contrivance can the sage attach them again.
When the rain-drops fall from the sky upon the earth,
They cannot again ascend unto the heavens whence they came.
Imagine not, that those tears which the eye sheddeth,
Shall e'er again return to the eyes they flowed from.
This is a different sun that riseth every morn:
The sun, that setteth once, riseth not again.
Though paradise is not gained by devotion, without grace;
Still, every man his neck from the debt must release. *
Shouldst thou incur a hundred toils for the flesh's sake,
Not one shall be of any avail to-morrow unto thee.
Shouldst thou gorge thy stomach with the world itself,
Thou wilt not be remembered, either in blessings or in prayers.
Shouldst thou give but a grain of corn unto the hungered,
Verily, it will be hereafter thy provision in eternity.
Shouldst thou bestow but a drop of water on the thirsty,
It will become an ocean between thee and the fire of hell.

Shouldst thou once bow thy head in the road of the Almighty,
Thou shalt, at the last day, be more exalted than any.
This world, then, is the mart, if one be inclined to traffic;
But in that world there is neither barter nor gain.
If friends comprehend aught, to-day is their time,
That one friend may show self-devotion to another.
If there is any real existence here, of a truth 'tis this,
That in some one's society it should in happiness pass.
May God protect us from such a state of existence,
Where thou mayst speak ill of others, and others of thee.
Poison even, is pleasant, if it be in peace and in concord;
But not sugar, combined with sedition and with strife.
The belly, filled with rubbish, is well, if free from sorrow;
But not so, though gorged with confection of the dregs of woe.
The back, bent from toil, is indeed estimable;
But not from a purse of ill-gotten money round the waist.
A blind man, who seeth nothing, is truly excellent;
Better than that he should set eyes on another man's wife.
A dumb person is far better without palate or tongue,
Than that his tongue should become the utterer of evil words.
A deaf man, who cannot hear, is preferable by far,
Than that his ears should be open to scandalous tales.

Demon or devil, that may come upon one, is agreeable;
But let not the Almighty a bad man before thee bring!
Than to bear the society of a fool, it is more preferable
That a fiery dragon should become one's bosom friend.
If there be a real difficulty, it is the healing of hearts;
But the profit and loss of the world are trifling affairs.
Its advantages, or its detriments, are trivial matters—
God forbid that any one become infamous for despicable things!
Forbid that any such desire of thine be accomplished,
Whereby the heart of thy brother or relation be grieved!
Should one eat delicious food, and another be eyeing it,
Such is not victuals, it is mere poison, so to speak.
It behoveth at times to respect other's wishes, at times thine own;
But thine own good pleasure is not to be regarded always.
The wise concern not themselves in such matters,
In which there's constant grief, and not an hour's pleasure.
It is incumbent on judges to administer justice;
But not to give their ears unto venal things.
Thoughts and ideas of all sorts enter into man's mind;
But it is not meet to account them all right and just.
The devout should have a constant eye towards their faith;
For some thoughts are virtues, whilst others are sins.

God forbid that iniquity proceed from any one's hands!

What affinity is there between sin and innocence—evil and good?

It is not that all men are equally on a parity together;

For some are eminent, some indifferent, some vile and base.

The dignity of every one lieth within its own degree:

It idiot meet that the groom should the noble's rank acquire.

I, RAḤMĀN, neither thank, nor complain of any one;

For I have no other friend or enemy but myself.

VIII.

He hath obtained happiness and felicity in this world,

Who in it hath acquired contentment and peace.

The dominion of Solomon, for a thousand years,

Equaleth not an hour's devotion, in this world.

One breath, in remembrance of the Deity, is more inestimable

Than the whole wealth of the universe, in this world.

They have found advantage and emolument in it,

Who occupied themselves in piety, in this world.

If there be any blessing, truly, it is that of devotion:

Consider that there is no greater good, in this world.

If there be any toils and troubles, verily they are religion's:

No other labours and trials are of avail, in this world.

All, all is transitory, and perisheth, save the Almighty,

Whether it be pleasure, or whether it be beauty, in this world.

Even the monarch, he goeth down unto the dust at last:

Then what is glory, and what is.fame, in this world? *

There will be no greater blockhead therein, than he

Who seeketh for happiness or tranquillity, in this world.

Thou, who desirest in this life a short period of repose,

Say, hath any one yet obtained it, in this world?

Relentless fate will make it like unto the shifting sands, †

Whoever buildeth up a structure, in this world.

It is not a whit less than the stumbling of the drunkard,

Man's brief stability and continuance, in this world.

Come near the running stream—here behold life!

There are many such like emblems, in this world.

Every one that approacheth the graveyard of the dead,

Should consider it a sufficient admonition, in this world.

These massive courts, these firm and compact mansions,

Will certainly at last be desolate, in this world.

The insatiable eyes of destiny, indeed, are not such

That they suffer any one to be in safety, in this world.

Whatever cometh into it, departeth from it again:

All creatures are merely travellers, in this world.

When the judgment cometh, austerities cannot be practised:

He is the man, who hath mortified the flesh, in this world.
Since to-morrow he will rise again with the same qualities,
Let not God give any one an evil nature, in this world!
That will, verily, be unto him a harvest after death,
Whatever he may have sown in the field of this world.
Although that world cannot be seen here below;
Yet I can perceive its signs and its omens, in this world. *
There will be no reciprocity of viaticum in the last day;
For I have myself beheld doomsday, in this world.
They will go down into the tomb as a deposit also,
Whoever may exist as a deposit, in this world. †
Virtue is present bliss; but propitious fortune is necessary,
That one may acquire felicity, in this world.
Good habits, virtuous actions, and a noble disposition,
Are paradise and happiness, too, in this world.
Contrariety and opposition plunge a man's life in torment:
Such antagonism is of no avail, in this world.
The hand to the forehead, and on the breast, ‡ to every one:
This, indeed, is greatness and distinction, in this world.
If exalted rank be of advantage unto any one,
A high place is justice and equity, in this world.
No other regrets can be taken out of it by us,

Save those of affection and kindness, in this world.

The whole of that world's traffic is carried on in this,

If one desire to follow commerce, in this world.

If man's good fortune may not have become inverted,

The truth is by no means hidden from him, in this world.

It behoveth that good be rendered for good, evil for evil,

If any one seek after holiness, in this world.

The Almighty hath bestowed sanctity upon them,

Who have shown stedfastness and constancy, in this world.

Should all created beings combine in union together,

They will not be able to change their lot, in this world.

If any one here below can be called a man, verily 'tis he

Who may have neither need nor necessity, in this world.

Since solicitude on its account is the cause of all sin,

How can people show such a hankering, for this world?

Over RAḤMĀN, indeed, this life hath passed away,

Even as a short hour glideth away, in this world.

IX.

Consider not the wise of this world shrewd and sagacious;

For foolish and silly are all the wise ones of this world.

The light of wisdom is prohibited unto those hearts,

On which may rest the dirt and dust of this world.

What one of the world saith, is all nonsense and absurdity:
Emptiness and folly are every word and speech of this world.
They merely play and gambol, after the manner of infants,
Who occupy themselves with the affairs of this world.
Like unto babies, with their mouths filled with milk,
Are all the subtle and the experienced of this world.
He will ever continue to be a dolt and an idiot,
Who may be drunk from the intoxication of this world.
In truth, the toper's inebriation will not be so great
As will be that of the drunken with the wine of this world.
There is a medicine in the world for every sick person;
But, alas! there is no physic for the sick of this world.
The cure of every one that hath been burned can be effected;
But not that of the scorched from the fiery sparks of this world.
Whatever thou throwest into the fire consumeth away;
And satiated will never become the seeker of this world:
He will ever be as a captive, sunk in distress and sorrow;
Then God forbid one should become the slave of this world!
He will be for ever immersed in lurid gloom and darkness,
Whoever may be the captive of the infidel of this world.
Whether it be adoration unto the idol, or unto the world,
Still, idolators all, are the worshippers of this world.

He is the true Muslim amongst the whole of the Faithful,

Who hath burst asunder the Hindū cord * of this world.

Headless behind, his body remaineth, but the head will go;

How, then, is the possessor of a head, a head-man of this world? *

They make their sons and daughters orphans, and desert them—

All are unnatural—the fathers and the mothers of this world.

There will be a load of misery for ever upon his head,

Round which may be wrapped the turban of this world.

All is affliction; whether it be bought, or whether it be sold;

For there is nought else whatever in the bāzār of this world.

They cheat and impose—the whole fraternity are knaves—

All the buyers, and all the sellers of this world.

They will never show the least affection towards it,

Who may be acquainted with the secrets of this world.

He whose regard may be directed to religion and piety,

Fostereth not any hopes or expectations of this world.

He who quaileth at the sight of a precipice or an abyss,

Will never travel upon the dangerous path of this world.

The whole of its friends and associates are impostors—

What dependence can be placed on the deceivers of this world?

Its old and its young, alike, are all rivals of each other—

Where is the true friend in the region of this world?

Whatever may be created, the whole shall fade and perish—
Draw near! behold the raids and ravages of this world!
Unto whom it cometh, from him it again departeth;
For I have well observed the gait and movements of this world.
One hour it may be spring—in another, autumn will come;
For no permanence whatever, hath the spring of this world.
Though thousands of props should be placed to support it,
Without foundation, notwithstanding, is the wall of this world.
Though thou shouldst raise round thyself a fortress of iron,
Still consider but as glass all the bulwarks of this world.
In the same manner as the sun's shadow shifteth,
So likewise there is nowhere permanence in this world.
Entertain thou no hope of pre-eminence by its means;
For incessant and perpetual is the littleness of this world.
Without shears they sever the thread of man's existence,
Both the nights and the days of this world.
After death, an account will be required of every man,
As to the number and magnitude of the sins of this world.
They will be but a mere handful of dust at the last day,
The rosy-cheeked and the rosy-bodied of this world.
They will arise on an equality with the beggar together,
Both the princes and the sovereigns of this world.

There will be a brand impressed upon the miser's breast

By every *darham* and every *dīnār* * of this world.

Let them be an oblation to the contentment of the contented,

All the wealth and the wealthy ones of this world.

Themselves, after death, will become the injured and oppressed—

All the tyrants and the oppressors of this world.

They may enumerate tens and hundreds until doomsday,

But no one hath completed the numeration of this world.

When the time for the winding-sheet and the ablution cometh, *

Unveiled and exposed become the veiled and modest of this world.

They will be brought forth on the bier from their privacy,

Both the coy and the bashful of this world.

More than any other person the Prophet would have enjoyed,

Had there been any thing like propinquity in this world.

One even of its iniquities cannot be fully explained by RAḤMĀN;

For beyond all computation, is the wickedness of this world.

X.

Since thou passest thy days in jollity, and thy nights in slumber,

When, O unfortunate! wilt thou bring the Almighty to mind?

Thy departure, if thou art aware, will be extremely precipitate—

Be not, then, unmindful of the exceeding shortness of life!

Thy breath and thy footsteps here are all, all computed;

Therefore step not on this path inconsiderately and in error.

In the book, the Almighty hath sent a statement of the account:

See, then, thou make thyself with both account and book acquainted.

I am fully aware that, originally, thou art of the earth;

Why then, with thy finger, removest thou the dust from thy person?

Not until thy thirst for this world shall have become quenched,

Shalt thou, at the judgment, become satiated with the water of life.

To the same extent thy inside shall be filled with fire,

As, to-day, it is gorged, with wine and with roasted meat.

Weigh thou, then, with thine own hands, this good and evil,

As to how much thy wicked actions do exceed the good.

In that world, after what manner will thy answer be,

Seeing that in this, thou art wholly unable to reply?

To-day that thou runnest to the shade for shelter from the sun:

When it stands but a spear's height * above thee, what wilt thou do?

Acquiesce not, O RAḤMĀN! in causing affliction unto any one,

If thou desirest salvation from the torments to come.

XI.

In this world, the countenance of the beloved is the object—there is naught else;

Whatever it is, the sight of the adored-one is desired, and naught else.

When I contemplate separation and association with the beloved,

The one is torment, the other a paradise of flowers, and naught else.

Each of the eyelashes of the beloved pierceth me to this degree,

That I declare it is the two-edged sword of Æali, † and naught else.

It requireth a hero to raise the tresses around her face:

The last is a treasure-hoard, the others are snakes; * and naught else.

How shall I recite the praises of the charms of the fair!

I speak briefly—they are innumerable, and naught else.

In whatever direction I listen, with the ears of the heart,

I find it is all love's market in a bustle, and naught else.

The whole of the world's factories, that one seeth around him,

They all belong unto the empire of love, and naught else.

Every physician before whom I present myself saith,

"Thou art sick through love; indeed, it is naught else."

Should poor RAḤMĀN place his affections on any other save thee,

He will assuredly be deserving of death, and naught else.

XII.

From how long since am I a purchaser of thy face!

I am gone beyond life and goods, in the mart of thy face.

There is naught else before mine eyes save the light of it;

To this degree am I sunk, in the refulgence of thy face.

Under the pretext of tobacco, I exhale the smoke of my sighs;

For I burn and emit smoke for ever, in the fire of thy face.

All other folks whatever occupy themselves in the world's affairs;

But I am sunk in expectation of beholding thy face.

Thanks, that thou hast delivered me from obligation to others;

And, head bent in adoration, I am beholden to thy face.

Where'er I, RAḤMĀN roam, for the heart's diversion;

I have no other object—I am the seeker of thy face.

XIII.

If I say aught regarding separation, what shall I say?

Of this agony, without a remedy, what shall I say?

I have no power to breathe in the dear one's presence:

Since I have no power, powerless, what shall I say?

When I gaze upon her, I forget myself entirely—

When I know nothing of myself, what then shall I say?

Of the state of my own heart, unto her I cannot speak—

Of that, without name or vestige, what shall I say?

Of love's mystery, that hitherto no one hath explained—

Of the inexplicable and indescribable, what shall I say?

I am o'erwhelm'd in tears, through grief for my beloved—

Concerning such a flood as this, what then shall I say?

I, who have sunk down upon the furnace of separation—

Of the rose-bower of conjunction, what shall I say?

She plundereth one of life and goods, and stealeth the heart—

Regarding such a heart-ravisher, what then shall I say?

He calleth the crows, and driveth the nightingale from the garden—

Of the gardener of this world, what then shall I say?

She is still far better than all that I can explain—

What then of the loved-one shall I, RAḤMĀN, say? *

XIV.

The garden of existence will not bloom for ever!

The market-place of life will not be in bustle always!

Like as the river Abā Sīnd * boundeth along in its course,

With such like exceeding precipitation is the progress of life.

Just as the lightning, that showeth itself and is no more;

So swift, without doubt, is the swift course of life.

It is violent and impetuous to such a degree,

That no one is able to command the bridle of life.

Since its swift steed hath neither curb nor rein,

The brave cavalier of life must have a fall at last.

In a single hour it severeth the friendships of years—

In such wise, unfaithful is the friend of life.

I will neither leave my house, nor will I travel;

For, without going a journey, I pass over the road of life.

It will, in the end, be severed by the shears of fate—

It will not remain for ever connected—this thread of life.

He should view his own self with the bubble's eye,

If, in his heart, one would compute the length of life.

O RAḤMĀN! there is no opportunity in this world again

For him, over whom hath passed away the period of life.

XV.

This is the adored one—that is the rival:

This is the rose—that is the thorn.

This is the rose—that is the thorn:

This is Manṣūr *—that the gallows-tree.

This is the beloved—that the malicious: †

This is the treasure—that is the snake.

This is wisdom—and that is love:

This is anguish—that the consoler.

This is separation—that is conjunction:

This is autumn—that the fresh spring.

This is devotion—that is sinfulness:

This is refulgence—but that is fire.

This is the wise man—that is the fool:

This is awake—but that is asleep.

This is RAḤMĀN—that is the adored:

This is the sick—that is the physician.

XVI.

So fast our friends depart unto the grave,

As the kārwān, ‡ with speed, returneth home.

So very promptly doth death deal with us,

As the reaper cutteth down the ripe corn.

Like as the moving sand * is quickly commingled,

So speedily is this world together huddled.

The human frame as rapidly decayeth,

As the tulips, in the autumn, wither away.

So swiftly passeth away this sweet life,

As the rapid river boundeth along in its course.

A twinkling of the eye, indeed, will not be so speedy,

As RAḤMĀN'S hasty departure from the world.

XVII.

At times the body burneth from heat; sometimes, it trembleth from the cold:

At others, it dieth from thirst and hunger; at others, from excess of food.

All, all who have come into the world, are in tumult and in uproar:

Neither is that hungry one at peace, nor that cloyed one in tranquillity.

At times, they raise the hand to the head, and act civilly to each other;

Sometimes they stretch out the hand to the dagger and the sword.

When the angels mixed the dust of the first Adam together,

They combined, along with it, all manner of pains and woe.

What matters it, though this very hour one be beaten or be bound?

His time, too, will come likewise, to strike and to pinion others.

For how long will this crazy foundation of our's continue firm?

With plastering and propping it so continually I am quite worn out.

'Tis possible, perhaps, that after death one may laugh in the tomb,

Who may, in this life, have mourned and lamented over himself.

I perceive all are departers—there are none to be tarriers behind:

Travelling upon this road is necessary, alike, for young and for old.

It is the flowing ringlets of the beloved that every one seeketh after,

Whether it be the young or old, the great or small, the rich or poor.

Supremely happy is he who hath been accepted at her threshold;

But woe and misery for him who hath been driven from it.

Like unto me, RAḤMĀN, hundreds were her nightingales;

But which that dark-eyed one hath chosen, God only knoweth!

XVIII.

When the black eye-lashes become submerged in the heart's moisture,

Then both property and effects become engulfed in the ocean of the heart.

Thou speakest vainly of the heart's disquiet unto the "Father of Desire:" *

What know children of the deep, deep sorrows of the heart?

Unto every other countenance than that of my own beloved,

I have permanently closed, altogether, the eyes of the heart.

That the highest canopy of heaven is beneath its shadow,

In the same degree, the more supernal is the banner of the heart.

This sanctuary is more sacred than Abraham's tabernacle,

If one would restore the desolated sanctuary of the heart.

Though others should set itself, feet upon the earth's surface,

I have on the empyrean itself, placed the foot of the heart.

That spot, which lieth midway 'twixt the firmament and world,

Is a place of seclusion—'tis the very staircase of the heart.

From whom, then, shall I crave it, save from thee my God,

Since the world's physicians cannot prepare the salve of the heart?

There are, indeed, very many extrinsic friends in the world;

But RAḤMĀN nowhere findeth, a single friend of the heart.

XIX.

I am ever sitting, with heart dried up, in the moisture of my tears:

Love showed unto me, in my own retreat, both ocean and land.

Like as when, with my lips, I kissed the wound of thy sword,

I have never since, from any salve, such soothing experienced.

Majnūn, that laid his head at the feet of Laylā, his beloved, *

Became exalted in Arabia, and in all foreign lands.

The powerful will always be triumphant over the weak;

And I am preserved from other misery by my grief for thee.

Like unto myself, for thee, thus in wretchedness o'erwhelmed,

Of the whole race of Adam there will be no other similar.

Like as a carcass, that may be fallen amongst the living,

In such wise am I, whilst in it, separated from the world.

From the breathings of the charmers I obtain no alleviation;

For this reason, indeed, that my breath is dependent on thine.

I have neither inquiry nor research to make, save after thee:

Thou art my object every moment, and at every step.

Should it be my good fortune to obtain the platters of thy dogs,

I would no more cast mine eyes, even upon Jamshed's cup. *

So completely have I gambled away my heart upon thy curls,

As when a little button falleth, and, in murky darkness, is lost.

All ensanguined in blood, like unto red roses hang,

A thousand hearts in every ringlet of thy curly hair.

I, RAḤMĀN, withdrawn from the world, was happy indeed;

But looking towards thee, hath brought man's censure on me.

XX.

The fair face turneth like unto a smoky pot in old age:

The upright-statured becometh like a bent stick, in old age.

Like unto the candle in the morning, or the sun in winter,

One turneth pale, and wanteth warmth, in the time of old age.

If a person place his foot in one direction, he goeth in another;

The whole body becometh quite a stranger to us, in old age.

One's limbs are laid out, as if accounted among the dead,

Although he is still palpably beheld alive, in old age.

A defunct is much better off, for after death he liveth again;

But it is not so that one may again grow young, in old age.

If he take any thing, it disagreeth with him, like poison;

For one cannot eat, nor can one drink, in old age.

That is youth, in which one both heareth and seeth something;

But nothing can be heard, and nothing seen, in old age.

O RAḤMĀN! verily, old age is such utter helplessness,

That, were it Rustam * himself, he deserveth pity, in old age.

XXI.

He who placeth any hope upon the fabric of this world,

Embarketh, on a tour of the ocean, in a paper boat.

No one hitherto hath successfully run the steed of the sky †—

How can one practise horsemanship on the back of the wind?

Neither can the wolf be instructed in the art of humanity,

Nor can any reliance be placed on the forbearance of fate.

Fortune revolveth equally with Islām and with idolatry—

When doth the blind make distinction 'twixt white and black?

With mine own eyes have I viewed the portents of destiny:

It createth thousands every moment, and destroyeth them too.

I am unable to place any such trust in fate's revolutions,

As that when its time cometh, it will grant exemption to me.

No one, indeed, will have experienced in his whole lifetime,

Such severity as the beloved-one, hourly, wreaketh upon me.

Should I venture to place in my turban a bud of the rose,

From it, my evil destiny produceth a thorn therein.

If I stretch forth my hand unto gold, it turneth into dust:

If I manifest desire for dust, it treateth me with scorn.

Separation from God is a great calamity, unbearable to me:

My distressed heart ever yearneth for society with Him.

When hath any lover acquired such an amount of patience,

That he putteth off, until to-morrow, the promise of to-day?

O heart ravisher! if thou shouldst even clothe me in fire,

In my sight, the garment will become me like gold brocade.

If, with regard to my love, any one should speak evil of me,

To myself I consider, that he is uttering my praise.

’Tis right that reproaches be heaped on the lover, the rule is such:

It is ever the custom of the healthy to laugh at the sick.

Honour and love are widely separated from each other—

How can one perpetrate a robbery in the light of day?

RAḤMĀN, this ode reciteth in reply to that which Dawlat *wrote—

"Should the beloved present me continually the wine of her love!"

XXII.

If any one should account me an ascetic, an ascetic am I;

If any one should consider me a noble, a noble am I.

I desire the whole world as an oblation unto the beloved:

It is not that, for myself, I care ought about it.

’Tis hard sustaining the dignity of the cowl: were it not so,

Every moment I incline unto the Darwesh's calling.

I take advice from every one, and give counsel unto all:

I am, at once, the disciple of some, and the apostle of others.

In separation the thoughts of the beloved ever follow me:

Along with Yūsuf, * I am a companion in imprisonment.

At the time of laughing, my weeping is like unto the taper's:

In the world, I am totally concealed, yet in fear of my life.

But what freedom, what independence is greater than this?

That I am a captive in the fetters of the locks of the beloved.

What other happiness is there more inestimable than this?

That for the sake of the beloved I am ever plunged in grief.

Khushḥāl Khān and Dawlata † are but slaves of mine;

For, of the Pus’hto tongue, I, RAḤMĀN, am the Æalam-gīr. ‡

XXIII.

Where the lips of the beloved? where affliction of heart and soul?

Where the nightshade's red berry? where the ruby of Badakhshān?

Pure and free is true love from all proneness to carnality

Where is the well of the stomach? where the dimple of the chin?

There is not a little difference ’twixt the libertine and the recluse—

Where are youths and maidens? where are widows and orphans?

They are all fools, who barter their religion for the world—

Where are fifty days? where eternity and everlasting life?

Let ambition and desire be a sacrifice unto contentment

Where is the land of Egypt? * where the Hamlet of the Slaves? †

In one village, the Darwesh and murderer cannot dwell—

Where is Æazīz Khān? where is Mullā ÆABD-UR-RAḤMĀN?

XXIV.

Though kings and princes have made their exit from the world,

It hath not become, in anywise, imperfect or defective thereby.

Though thousands, every moment, perish and pass away,

Thousands, likewise, every instant, are into it brought.

Of their exits and their entrances there is no computation:

They are like unto the fathomless ocean that rolleth along.

At another's sorrows, man doth not become affected:

He is alone sensitive of what happeneth to himself.

One, so illustrious as the Prophet, passed from the world away;

Yet this world did not become ruined by that separation.

When such like eminent people have gone down to the dust,

How shall be remembered, by any one, such dogs as thou and I?

Shouldst thou sift, over and over, the whole world's dust,

Thou wilt not again discover either Dārā or Shāh Jahān! *

Not even a trace remaineth of their names or their records,

Who laid claim unto glory, and sought, from posterity, fame?

Go thou, and see for thyself, if I speak falsely—

Look upon the graves of thy father, and grandfather too!

Behold! what have those mouths and lips become,

Which, on both thine eyes, were wont to kiss thee fondly?

They who used to hail thee with "Thy sacrifice, thy sacrifice," †

Let them now call out unto thee, "Thy sacrifice am I!"

I am quite amazed with the glowing words of RAḤMĀN,

That in the collection of his odes, fire hath not burst out.

XXV.

The chiefs and the monarchs of the world,

At last, abject and confounded, depart.

They are fastened to the link-rope of fate,

Like as captives together are chained.

Sweet existence departeth front him,

And the king hath neither power nor control.

Though he give away wealth and lands,

He obtaineth neither quarter nor mercy.

He hath neither friend nor defender:

Both pain and agony overcome him.

Helpless, in his presence, will be standing,

Both his ministers and his envoys too.

No remedy can be prescribed for him;
And doctors, nonplussed, hang their heads.
His dominions remain behind him;
And from regret and sorrow his heart breaketh.
When the soul hath deserted his body,
His family weep, and bewail his loss.
For an hour or so, they mourn over him;
Then the poor creatures grow calm again.
They then remove him for the ablution, *
And place him naked on the stretcher.
Then of his garments, become covetous,
The washers and the bathers of the dead,
On the return home from the grave,
The heirs share, and carry the effects away.
Both his friends, and his enemies, alike,
To his throne and country lay claim.
His handmaidens and concubines, they
Are carried off by the dead man's compeers.
Both name and vestige of him are lost,
As if, indeed, he had never existed.
Not even a record of him remaineth;
Not even his title, to future times.

The world, verily, is like a running stream,

Upon which no impression can remain.

Though one may people a thousand spots,

Still, all, at last, must desolate become!

Like as the wind cometh and passeth by,

So rolleth away the course of time!

This exposition was long and lengthy,

But RAḤMĀN hath condensed and abridged it.

XXVI.

My black eyes have turned white, from the weeping of separation;

And again, have become coloured, from the blood of the heart.

I was wont to say, "Even yet, I will go and visit my friends;"

For I did not know that the time of their departure was fixed.

Some, like unto the moth, cast themselves into the fire:

Some, alive, like the nightingale, the glowing rose upon.

The abjectness of death hath come before the dead;

And the living become woe-begone, though yet in existence.

The soldiers of destiny have so put forth their hands to plunder,

That a thousand Khasraus and Shīrīns * have been trampled to dust.

They who, in their gaiety, placed their feet upon the heavens—

Such tenderly nourished ones have now sunk into the grave.

They who were wont to repose upon ermine and velvets,

Without bed and without pillow now in the cold earth lie.

Why, then, should not the heart of RAḤMĀN be sorrowful,

When such numbers of his friends have been severed from him?

XXVII.

Whomsoever one's own affections have made abject, contemptible, account not;

For love is sympathy's clouds: as mere clouds of dust, account them not.

At times, the curls become dark spikenards; at others, amber and musk:

Although they are like unto snakes, as such, account them not.

One of its phases is destruction, whilst another is reconstruction:

Indeed, love, radically, is fire; but as such, account it not.

Many awake, are fast asleep, like the statue, with eyes open:

Though it regard thee with staring eyes, awake, account it not.

The object to be conveyed by the faces of the fair, is a certain emotion:

That which produceth not such impression, a face, account it not.

The thorn, which is along with the rose, is among roses reckoned:

What matter though 'tis termed a thorn? as such, account it not.

The wise are those, who confess themselves wanting in wisdom—

They who account themselves sage, as such, account them not.

He, indeed, is sinful, unto whom his own sins are not evident:

Whoever considereth himself evil, as such, account him not.

He, who hath confessed the power of his beloved one's dark locks,

Will be disturbed for ever; then tranquil, account him not.

Let him, who seeketh perfection, practise the lowliness of RAḤMĀN:

That is the expedient: any other plan, successful, account it not.

XXVIII.

Would to heaven that I were the dust and ashes at thy door!

Would that thy foot were, for ever, placed upon my head!

By all means, let thee and me meet face to face;

Then let my breast be the target for thine arrows!

Let my whole body, like antimony, be ground to powder; *

For then, at least, one glance of thy dark eyes will be mine.

Were the society of the fair dependent on gold or silver,

I had acquired it, by my sallowness, and my silvery tears.

Wherefore, indeed, had reproaches been uttered against me,

If any one had been aware of thy heart-ravishing ways?

Should I tell them of the dignity thy love hath brought me,

The angels, all, would cry, "O that we were human too!"

If I were the heart-ravisher, and thou, like me, the heart-ravished,

The spectacle of my condition would then be manifest to thee.

It will not be equal unto the bloody torrent from mine eyes,

Though one's face, all over, might sharp sword-gashes bear.

O that I were the nightingale, or the zephyr of the morn,

That my path might lie amongst thy fragrant bowers!

'Midst the agonies endured for thee, to RAḤMĀN, the physician saith—

"Thou wouldst be better were thy state even worse than it is."

XXIX.

If this, thy heart's affection, be bestowed upon a rival,

For thy sake, this rival shall be my friend also.

He who may be fascinated with one fair countenance,

From that one, a thousand other faces will be acceptable to him. *

Whosoever may have entered into the service of kings,

Must, necessarily, be under obligation unto the janitor.

Against thy malicious guardians, how shall I complain?

It is usual for the thorns to be associated with the rose.

Until a hundred thorns shall have pierced his breast,

How shall the nightingale unto the rose ever gain access?

He will spread the prayer-carpet in the cupbearer's path—

Every Ṣūfi who may be, towards his countenance, prepossessed.

He will lose his senses, entirely, through the phrenzy of love,

Though he may be as wise, indeed, as Iflātūn * himself.

He will, in no wise, cast censures upon RAḤMĀN,

Whoever may be cognizant of thy beauty and grace.

XXX.

Though they may have been a hundred times by each other's side, and in each other's arms;

Still, all the loving-ones of this world will be separated from each other.

They, who, at present, are dwelling together in the same abode;

At the last, will all have separate dwelling places.

These fragrant flowers, whose proper place is in the turban,

All, all of them will fade away, and be trodden under foot.

These fair-faced ones, with bright countenances like the sun's—

The black hair, like a forest, will overspread their cheeks.

This delicious sherbet, which is the society of our friends,

Will, in separation, and in absence, to deadly poison turn.

Through disjunction from a friend, I myself have witnessed,

The wisest of the age become, wholly, of reason bereft.

He setteth not his foot, for dread, on the ground of society,

Who is, already, cognizant of the dread slough of separation.

In what manner shall one devise a fit remedy for this,

Unto which, neither human wisdom, nor conjecture reach?

To such a degree hath anguish rusted RAḤMĀN'S heart;

But the goblet of pure wine will its furbisher become.

XXXI.

The face of the beloved, the sun, and the moon, are all three one:

Her stature, the cypress, and the pine, are all three one.

I have not the least need, either of honey, or of sugar;

For, the lips of the beloved, honey, and sugar, are all three one.

When I am reclining upon my couch, without her by my side,

Fire, thorns, and this couch of mine, are all three one.

When I cast mine eyes toward her dwelling's door and walls,

A garden, a parterre of flowers, and they, are all three one.

When I am soiled with any dust of the alley she dwelleth in,

This dust, and musk, and amber, are all three one.

O God! make no one acquainted with absence from his love;

For invasion, massacre, and such absence, are all three one!

The very moment that man biddeth adieu unto the world,

Dust, and silver, and gold, unto him, are all three one.

Should the monk, in reality, follow a life of austerity,

The sovereign, the chief, and the monk, are all three one.

It is not right that one should roam in foreign lands;

Therein, he who can see, the blind, and dumb, are all three one.

That town, in which there may be neither sweetheart nor friend,

That town, the ocean, and the desert, are all three one.

At the shops of the sightless dealers in jewels,

The kaurī, * the ruby, and the pearl, are all three one.

Let not these saintly monitors hold my love in scorn;

For the true lover, the saint, and the father, are all three one.

Through the despotic severity of tyrannical rulers,

The grave, and fire, and Pes'hour, † are all three one.

What matter, though he may praise himself unto RAḤMĀN?

Still, the fool, the ox, and the ass, are all three one.

XXXII.

Thy fair face, and thy musky mole, are associated together,

Or Maḥmūd and Ayāz are sitting together, bosom friends. ‡

What matter, though thy countenance is hidden by thy curls?

The water of immortality itself is, in total darkness, concealed.

From thy curls, thy ruby lips, and thy face, are produced

The night, the glow of sunset, and the dawn of day.

Is it the teeth, in thy sweet mouth, that shine so lustrously,

Or are there glittering dewdrops in the bud of the rose?

'Tis not that my heart, alone, is pierced by thy glances:

The knife and the flesh, of old, are hostile to each other.

Without floods of tears, the dark eye deigneth not to look on one:

The opening of the narcissus dependeth on the rivulet's humidity.

Peace, without trouble and affliction, no one hath acquired;

But thy cruelty, and thy constancy, are blessings unto me.

Through the good fortune attendant on the meed of thy beauty,

Throughout the world resoundeth the fame of RAḤMĀN'Srhymes.

XXXIII.

If there be any essential duty in this world, verily 'tis that of religion;

And for the followers of this avocation, there is due meed of praise.

Unto whose lot have fallen the gifts of godliness and piety,

The shadow of felicity and happiness ever followeth after them.

Contentment hath so filled their palates with savour,

That, in their mouths, the dry crust is like honey unto.

Without elephants and camels, they wield the sceptre of royalty,

Though a small worn-out piece of mat is their only carpet.

When they, in their necessities, raise their hands in supplication,

The very angels of heaven say, Amen! to their requests.

They, who, in this life, accept indigence and privations,

Their advantage and good in that are infallible indeed.

The lowliness and humility of the meek are, in themselves, dignity:

Their hearts are clean, though their ragged garments be soiled.

The water of the higher ground floweth ever unto the lower—

The Almighty hath raised to perfection, the humble, and the meek.

The heads of the stubborn and scornful reach the heavens now;

But, after a few short days, their place is in the dust!

They, who follow the dictates of presumption and arrogance,

Deserve not mercy—they are abominable and accursed.

What, though their human forms may be termed men?

Men they are not, in reality—they are children of the devil.

Though RAḤMĀN possesseth none of this world's pelf,

Thank Heaven! neither presumptuous, nor self-conceited is he.

XXXIV.

There is a different scar branded upon every one's breast,

Whether he be the beggar, or the sovereign of the land. *

There is no obtaining satiety from this fountain of the world;

And its thirsty-ones are, severally, in dissension and in strife.

A. little peace is obtained, only after much pain and trouble—

A mere straw of this world, without it, is unlawful and unmeet.

This life's joys are not attainable, without bitterness and woe—

From the miser's house, ever so little alms, is a misfortune.

Why then may not tranquillity be prohibited unto them,

Who have entered within the caravansary of this world?

As to the state of Majnūn, why should any one inquire?

The whole world, house by house, is Majnūn and Laylā too! †

Love hath breathed upon the entire universe a spell, so potent,

That the lover, though keen-sighted, is to all things blind.

The Almighty hath accorded unto every one a different lot;

And every man's own portion is, separately, determined.

Giving and taking—buying and selling—all are in others' hands

There is, I perceive, no opening here, either for thee or for me.

All matters, if in accordance with the will of the master,

Though unlawful towards the bondsman, are legal and right.

Willing or unwilling—whether it be one's wish, or whether it be not—

The fulfilment of one's destiny, agreeable, or hateful, is inevitable.

Life and faith, it behoveth to intrust, entirely, unto Him,

Whose decrees have gone out upon every human being.

Into the hands of whomsoever the ruler hath delegated authority,

The whole world boweth unto his wishes and his views.

O RAḤMĀN! if the Most High should not be one's companion,

Though armies may be with him, he still is all alone!

XXXV.

That friend, who is false and faithless, is no friend at all!

The affair, which hath not stability, is no matter at all!

Though laying down one's head is difficult, for thee and for me;

Yet 'tis an easy matter in love, and difficult by no means.

Care and solicitude awaken a man from his slumbers;

And he who hath no anxiety, though awake, is fast asleep.

To the lover, if there is aught in life, 'tis the society of his beloved—

The life of separation cannot be reckoned as existence.

It increaseth and groweth less, in the twinkling of the eye—

Reliance on the revolutions of fortune is no reliance whatever.

If one be the father of a hundred sons, what shall he do with them?

The ignorant, foolish son, is not the son of his father.

Unto their lovers, the beloved ones ever manifest their caprices;

But the beloved of RAḤMĀN causeth him no disquietude.

XXXVI.

In the name of that Deity of mine, this is my meed of praise—

Him, of whose many appellations, one, "The Most Glorious" is.

Those things, which, unto all others, are insuperable,

The whole of these matters are easy, and feasible unto Him.

He is the sovereign over all the rulers of the earth:

Over the head of every monarch, He is also the King.

Is any one able to place a sun in the firmament?

Yet He, in the heavens, hath elevated this glorious orb.

Can any one spread out a veil over the disc of the sun?

But, see! He hath entirely concealed it, in the veil of clouds.

Who is there capable of producing a moon, to light the night?

He hath created many moons, to illumine the nocturnal gloom.

Can any one pour down a single rain-drop from the sky?

Yet He hath rained, upon us, the genial showers of spring.

Who is there-equal to give vitality, even to a mosquito

Yet He hath given life to the whole creation of the earth.

Hath any one the ability to give the red tinge to stone?.

But He hath coloured it with the Arghowān's * rich hue.

Can any one cause a single flower to grow from out the earth

Yet He hath made to bloom gardens of sweetest flowers.

Hath any one the power to produce water from fire?

He, from the fire of summer, hath produced the winter rains.

Hath any one the ability to impart religion unto man?

Yet He, upon all His servants, hath faith and religion bestowed.

Can any one ascend from earth to Heaven?

Yet this potent power, He hath, unto Jesus Christ, assigned.

Who is there. that can hold converse with the Almighty

Yet, to this degree, He hath the patriarch Moses exalted.

Who is mighty enough to place a saddle on the steed of the wind?

Whilst He hath, high in air, the throne of Sulīmān set up. *

What man, with snowy beard, can, unto the Last Day, live?

Yet, upon Khizr, † this great favour hath He conferred.

Hath any one power to produce gems from out the rain-drops?

Whilst He, from out the rain-drops, hath produced pearls.

Who is there can supply food unto all creatures?

Yet He, unto all created things, is the giver of daily bread.

That which He can perform, none else can accomplish:

All the most powerful are impotent, before His omnipotence.

He hath founded the house of stone in the midst of the waters,

In which He hath given, unto fire, security and protection. *

The earth hath bowed down its head in His adoration;

And the firmament is bent over in the worship of Him.

Every tree, and every shrub, stand ready to bend before Him:

Every herb and blade of grass are a tongue to utter his praises.

Every fish in the deep praiseth and blesseth His name:
Every bird, in the meadows and in the fields, magnifieth Him.
All things are occupied in offering thanksgiving unto Him,
Whether mankind, or the genii, or the beasts of the field.
The created things themselves have not held Him in such estimation,
As the great love and regard they are held in by Him.
No one hath discovered the extent of His omniscience—
His knowledge and perception such a boundless ocean is.
Neither doth any one bear likeness or similitude unto Him,
Nor doth He bear likeness or similitude unto any one.
With Him, there is neither deficiency, detriment, nor decline:
He is, wholly, without defect, without decline, or deterioration.
He hath neither simile, nor similitude, nor hath He place:
He is without semblance, without comparison, without abode.
From all form, structure, or configuration, He is exempt;
Yet all figure, lineament, and formation, from Him proceed.
No one beholdeth Him with his eyes, nor can He be looked upon;
And yet, ineffable and inscrutable, He is manifest to all.
If any one should say, He cannot be seen, verily, He cannot:
And should he so say, He is, in truth, apparent unto all.
Without doubt and without distrust, consider Him immaculate
In all things soever, of which people are hard of belief.

No one hath lauded Him equal unto His just deserts;

Neither hath any one-sufficiently resounded His praise.

Out of the thousands of His excellencies and His perfections,

Deem not, that one, by RAḤMĀN, hath been adequately expressed.

Footnotes

11:* See Mīṛzā, Poem VI., second note.

12:* It is customary in the East to carry money in a purse or belt, fastened round the waist.

15:*

"The boast of heraldry, the pomp of pow'r,

And all that beauty, all that wealth e'er gave,

Await alike th' inevitable hour.

The paths of glory lead but to the grave."

15:† The *Reg-i-rawān*, or "Moving sand," situated forty miles north of Kabūl, towards the mountains of Hindū Kush, and near the base of the mountains. It is a sheet of pure sand, in height about 400 feet, and 100 broad, and lies at an angle of 45°. This sand is constantly shifting, and they say that in the summer season a sound like that of drums may be heard issuing from it. See "BURNES'S CABOOL."

16:* That is to say, the signs and omens of the approach of the end of the world.

16:† The deposit or pledge for the observance of faith and obedience unto God. See Mīrzā, Poem VI., second note.

16:‡ The mode of salutation in Eastern countries is, by raising the right hand to the forehead, or by placing it to the breast.

18:* The Brāhmanical cord. Also a belt, or cord more particularly, worn round the middle by the Eastern Christians and Jews, and by the Persian Magi. It was introduced A.D. 839, by the Khalīfah Mutawakkil, to distinguish them from Muḥammadans.

19:* The play upon the words 'head' and 'head-man' here is almost lost in the translation.

20:* Names of Arabic coins. The *darham* is of silver, and the *dīnār* of gold.

21:* Referring to the custom, in the East, of washing the bodies of deceased persons before dressing them out in their grave-clothes.

22:* According to the Muḥammadan religion, the sun at the resurrection will be no further off than a mile, or (as some translate the word, the signification of which is ambiguous) than the length of a spear, or even of a bodkin.

22:† Zu-l-fiḳār, the name of the famous two-edged sword of Æali, the son-in-law of Muḥammad, and which the latter reported he had received from the angel Gabriel.

23:* In the fables and traditions of the East, it is supposed that wherever there is a hidden treasure,-there is a serpent, or serpents, to guard it.

24:* This ode is very popular as a song; but the singers are, probably, not aware of the depth of meaning beneath.

25:* Abā Sīnd, the "father of rivers," the name given by the Afghāns to the Indus.

26:* Al Manṣūr, the name of a Ṣūfi, who was put to death at Bāghdād, some centuries back, for making use of the words انا لحق "I am God."

26:† The Arabic word here used in the original, and very commonly made use of by poets, is scarcely to be translated by an equivalent word in the English language. The Spanish word *duenna* gives the signification, but the Afghāns apply it to both sexes.

26:‡ Commonly "caravan," a company of travellers or merchants associated together for mutual defence and protection, and conveyance of merchandize, in the East.

27:* See *Reg-i-rawān*, note at p. 15.

28:* Desire itself, called also the "Parent of Desire."

29:* The loves of Majnūn and his mistress Laylā are the subject of one of the most celebrated mystic poems of the Persian poet Niẓāmī, and famous throughout the East.

30:* Jam or Jamshed, the name of an ancient Persian king, concerning whom there are many fables. The cup of Jamshed, called *jām-i-jam*, is said to have been discovered, filled with the Elixir of Immortality, when digging for the foundations of Persepolis, and is more famous in the East than even Nestor's cup among the Greeks. It has furnished the poets with numerous allegories, and allusions to wine, the philosopher's stone, magic, enchantment, divination, and the like.

31:* The Persian Hercules.

31:† The steed of the sky—the firmament, the revolving heavens, fortune, destiny, fate, etc.

32:* The name of an Afghān poet, a cotemporary of Raḥmān's. His poems are not to be met with in the present day.

33:* The patriarch Joseph.

33:† The name of Afghān poets.

33:‡ Æalam-gīr—"The world-conquering"—the name assumed by Aurangzeb, Emperor of Hindūstān.

34:* Muḥammadans consider the land of Egypt the peculiar country of presumptuous and ambitious rulers, who, like Pharaoh, laid claim to divinity.

34:† The name of a village near Ḳandahār, on the Tarnak river, and, for centuries past, in ruins. It is proverbially used in reference to a place utterly desolate and deserted.

35:* Dārā, the Persian name of Darius; Shāh-i-Jahān, "the Emperor of the Universe," the title assumed by the fifth Mughal, sovereign of Hindūstān.

35:† Equivalent to the reply of "Thy sins be upon me" of Scripture, a common mode of reply in Afghānistān and Persia.

36:* See Raḥmān, Poem IX., second note.

37:* Khasrau, King of Persia (contemporary with Muḥammad), having been driven from his kingdom by his uncle, took refuge with the Greek Emperor Maurice, by whose assistance he defeated the usurper, and recovered his crown. Whilst at Maurice's court, Khasrau married his daughter Irene, who, under the name of Shīrīn, signifying 'sweet,' is highly celebrated in the East, on account of her singular beauty; and their loves are the subject of the celebrated Persian poem by Niẓāmī.

39:* Black antimony, ground to powder, is commonly used in the East, as a collyrium for the eyes.

40:* "There are such wild inconsistencies in the thoughts of a man in love, that I have often reflected there can be no reason for allowing, him more liberty than others possessed with phrenzy, but that his distemper has no malevolence in it to any mortal. The devotion to his mistress kindles in his mind a general tenderness, which exerts itself towards every object as well as his fair one."—STEELE, Spectator, No. 336.

41:* Plato.

43:* Cypræa moneta.

43:† Pesh̲āwar, sometimes written as above.

43:‡ Maḥmūd, Sulṭān of Gh̲aznī, who was much attached to his servant Ayāz.

45:* "There is a skeleton in every house."

45:† See note, page 29.

47:* The name of a tree, whose fruit and flowers are of a beautiful red colour—the *Cercis Siliguastrum*, of botanists, probably.

48:* According to the Muḥammadan belief, Solomon succeeded his father David when only twelve years old; at which age the Almighty placed under his command all mankind, the beasts of the earth and the fowls of the air, the elements, and the genii. The birds were his constant attendants, screening him from the inclemencies of the weather, whilst his magnificent throne was borne by the winds whithersoever he wished to go.

48:† The name of a prophet, who, according to Oriental tradition, was *Wazīr*, or Minister, and General of Kaykobād, an ancient King of Persia. They say that he discovered and drank of the fountain of life or immortality, and that, in consequence, he will not die until the sounding of the last trumpet, at the Judgment Day.

49:* As fire can be produced by striking stones together, the Muḥammadans suppose that fire is inherent in stone, and that water protects it.

MĪRZĀ KHĀN, ANṢĀRĪ.

MĪRZĀ KH̲ĀN, ANṢĀRĪ, was a descendant, probably a grandson, of Pīr Ros’h̲ān, the founder of the Ros’h̲ānīān sect, which made a great noise among the Afgh̲āns, about the year 1542-3 of our Era. He appears to have commenced writing poetry in the year A.H. 1040; and these effusions were afterwards brought together in the form of a Dīwān or Collection of Odes, bearing his name. Some parties contend that his real name was Fat'ḥ Khān, and that he was of the Yūsufzī tribe of the Afghāns, and that the term Mīrzā is an assumed name, usually taken by Oriental poets. Mīṛzā, however, is a Persian word, signifying a prince or a nobleman, and also a secretary or writer, and would never be assumed by an Afghān, it being a distinctive appellation applied to persons of Persian descent, by the Afghāns. This statement, however, is also fully disproved, from the fact, that several old copies of his poems, which I have examined or have in my possession, end in these words: "Here ends the Dīwān of Mīṛzā Khān, Anṣārī."

Ḳāsim Æalī, Afrīdī, an Afghān poet of Hindūstān, in one of his odes, states, that Mīrzā Khān was of the family of Bāyazīd, or Bāzīd, Anṣārī, who assumed the name of Pīr Ros'hān, or Saint of Light, as already mentioned. Bāzīd himself (of whom it will be necessary to give a brief account, as Mīṛzā's subsequent misfortunes were chiefly owing to his being a descendant of that impostor) was, altogether, a remarkable man; and the Anṣārī tribe, to which he belonged, is an offshoot of an Arab tribe of Madīnah, mentioned in the Ḳur'ān, which received the prophet Muḥammad after his flight from Makkah; and hence the name Anṣārī, from the Arabic word *anṣār*, signifying aiders, or assistants. People of this tribe are to be found, even now, scattered over Afghānistān, the Panjāb, and some parts of India.

Bāzīd's religion, which he instituted in the year A.D. 1542-3, spread rapidly amongst the Bar Pus'htūn, or Eastern Afghāns, till, at length, he was able to assemble armies, and oppose the Mughal government. He held the same tenets as the Ṣūfis (of whose mysticisms some account has been given in the Introductory Remarks), but having been a disciple, for some time, of the notorious Mullā Sulīmān—known in the East as Jālandharī Sulīmān, from the town of Jālandhar, in the Panjāb, where he dwelt—Bāzīd became initiated in the tenets of the Jogīs, a sect among the Hindūs, and became a fast convert to the creed of the Metempsychosis, or Pythagorean system of the transmigration of souls. On these doctrines, however, he engrafted some of his own, the most remarkable of which was, that the most complete manifestations of the Divinity were made in the persons of holy men. * The great opponent of Bāzīd was Akhūnd Darwezah, the greatest and most venerated of all the saints of Afghānistān, who, in derision of the title of Pīr Ros'hān, or Apostle of Light, which Bāzīd had himself assumed, conferred on him the name of Pīr Tārik, or Apostle of Darkness, by which name he is now chiefly known.

Mīrzā, was a great traveller, and was well known from Herāt to Agra, throughout the Afghān country, and also in India; for he himself had numerous disciples in the mountainous parts of Afghānistān—from Suwāt and Bājawrr, north of Pes'hāwar, as far as Ḳandahār and Herāt. He dwelt for a long period in the Rājpūt state of Rājwārrā or Rājpūtānah, in Hindūstān, the Rājā of which country, although a Hindū, ever treated him with great veneration and liberality. The Mughal Emperor, Aurangzeb, also, in whose reign Mīrzā flourished, allowed him a regular stipend. The Emperor, however, was a great bigot, and, as is well known, was entirely in the hands of the priesthood; and, consequently, on more than one occasion, at the instigation of some of them more ignorant and bigoted than others, Mīrzā was summoned by the monarch, to answer accusations of heresy and blasphemy, preferred against him at their instigation. The Emperor, with all his bigotry, appears, however, to have had some scruples of conscience; and, generally, had some plausible excuse to save Mīrzā from their clutches, and himself from a bad name. The only reply the Mulls, or priests, could draw from the monarch, who is famous for personally administering justice, was, that they should enter into disputation with the accused, and if anything contrary to the lip orthodox laws of Muḥammad could be drawn from him, he would then consent to punish Mīrzā, but not otherwise. Notwithstanding Mīrzā's enemies were thirsting for his blood, still they could not succeed in drawing him into the snare they had spread for him; and the poet, very prudently, retired from the scene, fearing lest, at some time or other, they might be more successful in their machinations, and bring him to destruction; for, according to the well known Oriental proverb—"Kings and rulers have neither eyes nor ears; and between truth and falsehood they are incapable of discerning; for the words of a few designing men being sufficient to make the innocent guilty, the unfortunates are plunged into the calamity of destruction." Mira, on this account, generally confined himself, when in India, to the territories of the independent or tributary Hindū princes, by whom he was honoured and respected.

The poems of Mīrzā contain many Arabic and Persian words, which most Oriental poets freely use; but his Pus'hto is very ancient, particularly in words used amongst the hill tribes of

Eastern Afghānistān, in his day, and which are not generally understood by the people of the present time, together with some words purely Sanskrit; but these latter usually occur in the last words of a line, when at a loss for a rhyme, in which very great licence is taken and allowed, by poets, in all Oriental countries, without such words being common to the language, or used in conversation by the people. Some of the philosophers of the present day, in their blind rage for comparative philology—the hobby they ride for the time being—based merely on their own superficially theoretical, and not practical knowledge of Oriental languages and subjects—would probably consider this use of some pure Sanskrit words as conclusive and undeniable evidence to prove the Pus'hto or Afghān language, of the Sanskrit family of tongues. They seem to forget that all those parts of Central Asia, now called Afghānistān, from Kabūl eastward, were, even in the days of Alexander, peopled by a Hindū race, remnants of whom, existing even at the present day, lived as Helots among the Greeks, to their various Muḥammadan conquerors, of whom the Afghāns are the most recent, the Afghān tribes of the Pes'hāwar district, and its northern vicinity more particularly, having arrived in those parts as recently as the beginning of the sixteenth century. They, as will also be seen from the languages of many other conquering tribes, adopted, for convenience sake, some few words of the people they conquered. However, the Sanskrit in Mīrzā's poems may be accounted for, from the fact of his long residence amongst Hindū people.

The poetry of Mīrzā is deeply tinged with the mysticisms of the Ṣūfis, and, to some extent, with the religious tenets of his ancestor Pīr Ros'hān. His effusions are, certainly, more difficult than that of any other poet, from the fact of their being (as I think will be allowed) more sublime, and grander in conception.

It is said that Mīrzā, in the latter years of his life, married and settled in the Tī-rāh district, lying immediately to the south of the famous Khaibar Pass, and ignored the Ros'hānīān faith, which in his more youthful days he had adopted, and manifested great repentance for every thing he had written or said, contrary to the *sharœ*, or orthodox canons of the Muḥammadan creed. On this account, he soon became great with the ecclesiastics of Pes'hāwar—a city, in those days, as famous as Bokhārā itself for theological learning—and thenceforth was held in high estimation by them. His descendants, on this account, are still greatly respected by the Muḥammadans of those parts, whether Afghāns or others.

Nothing is known, for certain, regarding the death of Mīrzā; for he passed a great portion of his life in Hindūstān, and must have ended his days in that country. * His descendants still dwell in the Tī-rāh district, amongst the clan of Mī-ān Khel, and have the repute of being quiet and well behaved. There is generally one of the family who follows the life of an ascetic; and is allowed, by the simple people, to have the power of working miracles.

Footnotes

52:* ELPHINSTONE: Caubul.

55:* A person named Mīrzā, son of Nūr-ud-Dīn, one of the sons of Pīr Roshān, lived in Shāh Jahān's reign, and was killed at the battle of Dawlatābād.

THE POEMS OF MĪRZĀ KHAN, ANSĀRĪ.

I.

O THOU, in heart ignorant concerning thine own soul!

O man, seek thou the nature of it, from the reality itself!

From the refulgence of religion, acquire thou comprehension:

Bear away, unto the desert, this darkness of infidelity!

Sin abandon; and set out towards devotion and piety!

This is the road, without anxiety, and from danger free.

This secret praise is the lamp of truth and orthodoxy;

Therefore, from the Immaculate's hand, the lighted lamp take.

Should perception's light become enkindled in thine heart,

Thou wilt, altogether, acquire life's happiness and felicity.

The penetrating, and the enlightened, are spectators of both worlds;

But the bat flieth about in the dark, without seeing.

What do I, blind that I am, know of the state of the sublime?

How wilt thou, from the deaf, ask the import of sound?

Thou wilt comprehend, forthwith, the language of all things,

Shouldst thou, sagacious one! make thine heart's ear to hear.

Err not, regarding the amount of attributes and properties;

And unto the source of the essence, bear the essence itself.

About their own materiality, the enlightened are in torment;

But there can be no dread of mortality from corruption itself.

Every attainer * who hath passed beyond this nature frail,

Assuredly discovereth the signification of immortality.

He wandereth about in the boundlessness of infinity:

He arrived even unto his home, that he might unity behold.

That fruit, which on its own branch acquired ripeness,

This brief claim of its own perfection, made to the parent tree—

"Notwithstanding there is not much excess in thy greatness;

Still, within this body of mine, do I see thee, entirely, O tree!

From the first, thy root germinated from me, and flourished:

The development of thy purpose devolved, wholly, on me."

Answer, to this effect, on the part of the tree, proceeded—

"Colour and flavour, O fruit! whence didst thou acquire?

From one fruit, naught but a single tree is produced;

And the fruit of that tree is renewed, year by year."

The reply from the tree, however, is here sound and wise,

Though the observation of its fruit is, of attention, worthy.

From that, which possesseth no kernel, no corn groweth:

It is not advisable that any one should sow husked seed.

The reputation of the servant lieth with his master;

And without the servant, the master's dignity is not.

Invoke, then, within thine heart, the sayings of MĪRZĀ,

If the page of thy mind be unblotted, and unstained.

II.

When, with the mind, I examined the shoulder-bone of prediction, *

I saw that, within unity's area, the community of plenitude dwelleth.

In what manner shall I describe the infiniteness of the Omniscient,
When all that's inscrutable, He hath drawn, like a veil, over His face?
I behold, floating upon the surface of the waters, the ship of the earth; †
And on all sides, I perceive, cones of stone have protruded therefrom.
For how long shall the heavenly bodies, in the firmament, revolve?
By what art, profound, hath the Great Sage suspended them therein?
The conception of the intellect of the wise is unable to penetrate
Unto where the hand of, "Let it be," and "It was," ‡ hath reached.
These unadorned heavens became arrayed with embellishments,
Which He, with the diamonds of omnipotence, carved out.
The lamp of the sun and the moon became enkindled therein—
He assented not that, unrevealed, His own skill should remain.
From the clouds, He caused the genial rain to descend on earth;
And herbs and plants of every kind he disseminated thereon.
On its face, the phenomena of spring and autumn, so admirable, arose;
And the gradations of heat and cold were diffused throughout.
From the whole achromatism of colour, that manifesteth itself,
The face of nature is with every tint and hue emblazoned.
On all sides, where'er I cast mine eyes, of every tinge and dye,
The chequered carpet of the Great Chamberlain is spread out.
The countless creatures that, in all directions, meet the eye,
Are the army of this great chess-board, in order arranged.

Here, the destiny of every one, whatever he may be, is fulfilled—
From the game's commencement, the knights are mounted, the footmen on foot.
And mankind themselves, originally, are of one origin and race;
Yet some rule empires, whilst others beg from door to door!
Though the beasts of the field exist, from inconvenience free,
The whole burden of "Do" and "Refrain" is laid upon mankind.
Unto every man his own private interests are the most agreeable;
But the decrees of the Great Judge are separately meted unto all.
The mercy of the All-merciful is equally extended to all men;
Though some have chosen to deny Him, whilst others have obeyed.
For the use of mankind were all living creatures produced;
And man himself created, to acquire knowledge of the truth.
He, who in this life, acquireth not a perception of the nature divine,
Hath naught of humanity in him; and 'tis just to term him a beast.
Whosoever giveth ear unto the inordinate promptings of carnality,
Though, in outward appearance, he liveth, yet his soul is annihilated.
Wherefore doth he give himself airs about this short existence;
Since, without an aim, he is standing like a sign-post in the path?
Like unto the hare, with eyes wide open, he for ever sleepeth:
In what manner, as though entranced, shall the sleep-overcome awake?
He hath abandoned the path at the counsel of the Accursed:
His mind is misled by hypocrisy's manifold deceits.

The poor, ignorant creature is accounted a demon, and beast of prey:
Even worse still—he is amongst decayed carcasses numbered.
His dark, confined heart is as a tomb, for his soul is dead:
His decked-out body, a grave, on which the mould is beaten down.
His distressed and distracted mind is the emblem of the worm:
His sepulchre is intact: it is his soul that is devoured.
He hath no peace nor tranquillity: nought else save torment:
Every moment overwhelmed in misery: driven away as one unclean.
He possesseth not strength sufficient, the human form to support—
He took the deposit on his head, without calculating its weight. *
Like unto the mule, it is expelled from its own kindred race,
That, which being one by nature, hath become, with another, mixed.
Tyrant and fool that he was, he should have acted in this way—
He should have cried with piercing cries, and have dashed his head. †
Such a ponderous load, as neither Heaven nor earth could bear,
By what strength could the weak, helpless, ignorant, sustain
It behoveth to call for aid, with all speed, unto the perfect,
That they may consign the burden into the hands of the Master.
Unto every wise man, who hath become released from the debt,
Therefrom, the hereditary gift of knowledge divine hath fallen.
The gravity and importance of such knowledge the saints know;
Since they have sought it in the mind, and unto the world's limits.

His laws and His edicts go out upon every person and thing:

He hath built up a wall from this crude and untempered dust.

He made the inanimate to be counted among the living,

When He, the Immaculate, with His own breath, breathed on them.

He will live for ever and ever, and death shall affect him not,

Through whom the Eternal hath drawn the thread of vitality.

What blessed one became purified from ungodliness and scepticism?

He, whom the Lord of Holiness hath, with sanctity's water, cleansed.

Upon the face of the waters, his lamp effulgent burneth;

And, like straws, infidelity and mistrust consume thereon.

At his entreaty, from the stars, was ill-presage wholly removed;

And, thro' his good offices, no hour is accounted portentous.

O MĪRZĀ! of the praises due unto the perfections of the saints,

Who, commensurate with their infinity, hath a tittle rendered?

III

خ is the vanity * of thine own doubt and mistrust;

And, thro' scepticism, thou sustainest injury exceeding.

Fall not into error, concerning thy outward appearance;

Since, after spring passeth away, the autumn cometh.

Set out in pursuit of the great object of solicitude,

Whilst thou thy command upon the bridle retainest.

The Omnipotent is, by no means, distant from thee;

For He is nearer unto thee, than even thine own self.

Whether on the earth, or whether in the heavens,

The Omniscient there also is present in the midst.

He became, in unity and individuality, unique:

In immensity, and in infinitude, He is diffused.

From His divinity, He departed and advanced towards it;

And now, throughout the whole universe, He moveth.

The limits of His boundless infinity cannot be discovered;

And in mankind is His abode, and His place of sojourn.

He himself inflicteth, and He himself performeth;

And man He hath made, the motive and the plea.

From every saint that hath commenced his mission,

Some sign, or some indication becometh manifest.

The scepticism of MĪRZĀ hath vanished, and is no more;

But whatever is by him spoken, Mī'ān Ros'hān * speaketh.

IV.

س standeth for the pilgrim *—in this path let him proceed:

Let him, in all sincerity, become a seeker after Him.

From the sleep of negligence and remissness awake!

Follow now in pursuit of thy well-wisher and friend!

Tho' the object thou seekest be obscure and invisible,

Ride lightly, and without baggage, in following it.

Its acquirement is attended with much trouble and toil:

Determine thou, therefore, a dauntless spirit to show.

Since the lamp of love and affection is become lighted,

Like the moth, to-day, become thou the sacrifice thereon.

He hath bestowed upon thee the cup of vitality;

Then let the largess be upon the cupbearer scattered! †

Seek not to discover the faults and failings of others;

But become the mirror of thine own acts and ways.

The desired object of thy attainment is near unto thee:

Then, in sincerity and piety, towards it draw near!

Thou art, from the beginning, one and indivisible:

Become now, therefore, the narrator of those hidden things!

God is one—without partner, and without associate:

Forbear thou, then, from all, contrary thereto.

In this, O MĪRZĀ! the choice lieth with thee, entirely;

Therefore, in the qualities of the tranquil, be thou stedfast!

V.

ص is significant of faith's straight and narrow path; *

And, after much terror and danger, its goal is attained.

The artifices and deceits of the Devil are manifold in number;

But far, far worse than those, is that enemy the flesh.

Follow thou not, in pursuit of the lusts of the world:

The state is evil, and their promptings are pernicious.

The Devil spread out for man, the snare of posterity;

And wealth, and various pleasures, are the baits thereon.

Distinction, and fame, one of its ramparts became,

Whilst another of its attractions were silver and gold.

He layeth out separate snares quietly, and with caution;

But the whole are like unto embroidery upon the carpet.

He will neither be prosperous nor happy, in this world,

Who giveth ear unto the temptations of the Accursed.

Though a whole region should fall beneath his sway;

Still, that man's heart will long, another to acquire.

They who give way unto the promptings of the flesh,

For them, especially, there is torment excruciating.

But they who have passed safely this dread ordeal,

For them are the perfect gifts of the patient and the meek.

Unto MĪRZĀ, His beneficence and His kindness are vouchsafed;

For He alone, is the All-merciful, and the Accepter of penitence.

VI.

ع signifieth the great evil * of mistrust, and scepticism,

Through which, all the world is, in bewilderment plunged.

That mind cannot rest assured, or be at peace,

Which is constantly distracted in pursuit of nothingness.

It cannot partake of the advantages of unity;

For it is in the infiniteness of infinity dispersed.

The elaboration of its counsels and reflections is great;

But 'tis like unto a cloud, that containeth no rain.

Verily, he will not be able to attain unto perfection,

Whose looks are directed unto detriment and defect.

The ignorant wreaketh tyranny, merely upon himself,

Who is the sponsor of the onerous deposit of faith. †

A worshipper of himself, sunk in egotism and vanity,

He is, like the first Adam, in amazement and perplexity lost.

The soul contained in the human form, is like unto Joseph;

And the body's nature and disposition are its prison-house.

When it hath become, from this thraldom, liberated,

It is then in safety, and Heaven is its dwelling-place.

With transports filled, and mounted upon the steed of love,

Enraptured, it is come forth unto the Choukan * of its desire.

Draw near, O MĪRZĀ, and lift up thine eyes!

See! this is the ball, and this is the arena too!

VII.

غ—All that may be contrary to nature change: †

Make the soul king, and wisdom its minister.

Give not ear unto the flesh, for it is ignorant;

And with wisdom, understanding regard.

The deceits of the Devil are without number;

Therefore, consider as a fetter each of his spells.

There are five robbers ‡ in thine own house,

Each of which, in separate places, chain up.

Deprive them of all evil appetites and desires;

And, in thy heart, give place to reliance on God.

Draw thou near unto truthfulness and piety;

And from thee, drive all deceit and guile.

I have spoken unto thee without disguise;

Therefore, guide all thy actions accordingly.

Shouldst thou seek to be with these gifts endowed,

Then go, seek the society of thy spiritual guide.

Guard well the heart from the Evil One;

And upon it, register the remembrance of God.

The mundane things of this world are a dream:

Now give thou the interpretation of the truth.

Subtile and profound are the words of MĪRZĀ:

In their elucidation, do thou thy perception show!

VIII.

The loved-one is not concealed from thee,

O thou obstruction, round about thy soul!

Thou thyself hast become thine own veil,

Standing obdurate, in scepticism's path.

Thou becamest visible—the beloved, invisible;

But like unto thee, a perfect counterpart.

Spotless and pure, on every side and surface—

A simple lineament, but substance without.

Shouldst thou behold her, thou art blest:

How long, then, O forlorn! wilt thou gaze upon thyself?

When doth grain shoot up and flourish

In arid soil? O thou, of hard earth, a clod!

When a clan pitcheth its tents upon a plain,

Forthwith the grass thereon entirely disappeareth.

The black bee * buzzeth lightly around the lotus;

Whilst thou, O beetle! hast sunk under thy load.

The flame, full soon, consumeth the straw;

But thou burnest, clumsy block! with many groans.

From love alone, is the heart's existence:

What were the callow brood, without the parent bird?

O MĪRZĀ! the compact of affection and love,

The moth, with the lamp, hath adjusted.

IX.

The anguish of love, alas! is incalculable.

It is, alas! without antidote, without cure.

Without its thorns, the rose will never be;

And friendship, alas! is with absence coupled.

The beloved, happy, and in her own heart, at peace,

Is, alas! unconcerned—a ravisher of hearts!

He will undergo the pangs and agonies of love,

Who may be, alas! reckless and regardless of life.

I live but in the remembrance of my dear one:

Alas! indeed, I cannot exist, without my life.

The only regret of the ascetic MĪRZĀ, alas! is this—

That his passion's object is without indication.

X.

How amazing is the sublimity of the mind of the adorer!

Unto whose throne, there was no access, even for the giant Æūd. *

This stage of it is more contracted than Ṣarāt's narrow bridge: †

How, then, did the army of love accomplish its ascent?.

His passion became like unto a vast and boundless ocean,

Which, by its first swell, o'erwhelmed him in the billows.

The sword of unity, from between, He removed altogether; ‡

And upon infinitude, He conferred the name of spouse.

The boundless ocean, O MĪRZĀ! hath encompassed all things;

But the Ganges merely floweth to Shamsābād and Kanouj.

XI.

If it be thy wish to pass through life, from hatred and malice free,
From the longings of covetousness deliver this spotless breast.
Thro' heedlessness of heart, like what wilderness art thou grown?
Account the Devil's temptations a monster, not a gnat!
The expecting heart is one only—its cares and anxieties many:
The term, too, of thy existence, long or short, is nothingness.
The spiritual guest is an inestimable one: cherish him carefully—
Broken rice possesseth not the fitness for the tables of kings.
Covetousness tottereth like one with ophthalmia stricken;
But by perfect reliance upon the Almighty, cure thou the disease.
Change sinful arrogance for meekness and humility;
And the sword of thy vanity and pride return unto its sheath.
Become pliant, and bending, like unto the tender twig;
Not of thine own accord, like a hard, dry log of wood.
The five fingers once had an astonishing dispute together,
At which time the little finger acknowledged its own littleness.
There is dignity, in the very insignificance of form;
Hence fitness for the ring went unto the little finger.
Outwardly, become the spectator of the heart's internal things,
O thou, from truth's source, great—by scepticism, contemptible!
O MĪRZĀ! behold thou the infinite greatness of unity;

Since such delicious honey, is from the bee produced.

XII.

Thou art the vitality of my soul, O Thou, than soul itself, more precious to me!

Thou art the whole universe's existence, O Thou, than the world, more precious to me!

Thy comprehension hath embraced all things; yet all things have not comprehended Thee:

Thou hast possessed Thyself of the seat of faith, O Thou, than faith, more precious to me!

Whence shall there be aught of bliss in Heaven, if that sight of Thee, be not for me?

My heart is carried away in yearnings for Thee, O Thou, than Heaven, more precious to me!

Wherefore should I rehearse the world's praises? unto whom repeat them, when Thou art not?

Thou, nightingale! gayest me hue and fragrance, O Thou, than the parterre, more precious to me!

The bower is the hearts of the worshippers, and the heavenly Paradise of the recluse;

And the beholding of Thee, The Inscrutable, beyond all indication, precious to me!

Thou art without similitude; infinite; indubitable; without ambiguity:

And hence, the mine of all things, O Thou, than every mine, more precious to me!

Thou art, moreover, the vitality of the universe; the breath of every living creature:

Thou art the inspiration of this Adam, O Thou, than inspiration, more precious to me!

Thou art the repository of vitality, that hast pervaded all and every living thing:

At times invisible, at others visible; but whether hidden or apparent, precious to me!

Thou art a voice, after many kinds; encompassing all things; without indication:

Thou art without lineament in every respect; but, in every way, precious to me!

Thou art wholly inscrutable in all things: the invisible in the manifest:

Thou art the signification in description, O Thou, beyond description, precious to me!

Concerning the soul, what shall I say? verily, it is an attribute of unity itself:

MĪRZĀ, without the soul cannot exist, O Thou, than soul even, more precious to me!

XIII.

Shouldst thou once become an inmate of the house of God's love,

Thou wilt, forthwith, become a stranger unto the world, entirely.

From out of entity, nonentity will come upon thee;

Thou, by this inexistent, in all existent, shalt unique become.

This perfect knowledge will be with thee, entirely;

But thou wilt be mad in the sight of the weak-minded.

The whole arrows of calumny will be poured upon thee;

And thus, thou wilt become the butt of great and small.

From the world's unworthy, thou shalt the heart's concerns withdraw:

Thou wilt be like a hidden treasure in a wilderness.

Shouldst thou change this, thy well-being, for misfortune,

Thou wilt become the whole prosperity of all adversity.

Shouldst thou cast this heart of thine on that consuming flame,

Thou wilt, the self-sacrificing moth become thereby.

A pure, unadulterated wine shall fill thy mouth;

From the effect of which, thou shalt be ever inebriated.

Thou wilt not hold, in any consideration, either world,

Shouldst thou grow rich from the treasury of contentment.

Thus thou wilt shower mercy's genial rain upon the world,

And become the seed, through the universe disseminated.

The all-knowing, concerning thy condition shall speak;

And by truth, thou wilt become the parable of the truthful.

On speaking, thou wilt give reply worthy of being spoken;

And become, of every harp and every melody, the harmony.

The eloquent, who shall enter on the praises of the Almighty,

Shall, like unto MĪRZĀ, be remembered throughout all time.

XIV.

He, who placeth reliance on the lying and deceitful,

Maketh firebrands out of nothing, by such utter folly.

It is the senselessness of fools, in opposition to wisdom,

That, in the heat of summer, raiseth a tower of snow.

His prosperity is trouble—he groweth down-hearted thereby:

And his fresh adversity addeth twofold misery his sorrows unto.

Every man, who seeketh fidelity from the perfidious world,

Taketh it, in lease, for much bitterness, and many woes.

Success and disaster good and evil—are with the act coupled;

But fools suppose such things influenced by the stars.

I am amazed, beyond measure, at such like people,

Who place any reliance upon the bubble's permanency.
The ocean's waves will, one day, dash against each other;
And will, full speedily, the garment of the bubble rend.
When the pious and devout view this running stream,
They perceive, in its flowing, the scene of their own existence.
The wise enter upon the search of the object of their desires:
The beasts of the field, about food and sleep, themselves concern.
When the adorers awake from the slumber of remissness,
They take due heed of the fleeting of every breath.
That the traveller may, from his sweet repose awaken,
The warning bell of departure, tolleth at the dawn of day. *
The delight of the Darwesh is in fervour, and in study:
The pleasure of Chieftains is in their banners and drums.
That country cannot be exempt from confusion and ruin,
Whose army indulgeth in grossest tyranny and rapacity.
If a friend should lend ear unto the secret of the stranger,
Friends will, themselves, ruin their own affairs, thereby.
When the mandate of the All-powerful shall reach him,
From whence shall MĪRZA'S strength a remedy obtain?

XV.

How shall I define what thing I am
Wholly existent, and non-existent, thro' Him, I am.

Whatever becometh naught out of entity,

The signification of that nothingness am I.

Sometimes a mote in the disc of the sun;

At others, a ripple on the water's surface.

Now I fly about on the wind of association:

Now I am a bird of the incorporeal world.

By the name of ice I also style myself:

Congealed in the winter season am I.

I have enveloped myself in the four elements:

I am the clouds on the face of the sky.

From unity I have come into infinity:

Indeed, nothing existeth, that I am not.

My vitality is, from life's source itself;

And I am the speech, every mouth within.

I am the hearing-sense within every ear;

And also the sight of every eye am I.

I am the potentiality in every thing:

I am the perception every one within.

My will and inclination are with all;

With mine own acts, also, satisfied am I.

Unto the sinful and vicious, I am evil;

But unto the good beneficent am I.

In the lot of the devoted, I am the honey:

In the soul of the impious, the sting.

I am with every one, and in all things.

Without imperfection—immaculate I am.

'Tis by the mouth of MĪRZĀ that I speak:

An enlightened heart, without similitude, I am.

XVI.

The tresses of this impassioned loved-one, are all dishevelled:

They are spread all around her face, like a shadow unto.

She hath prepared every separate hair as a snare—

Each one laid for the capture of wounded hearts.

Within those hearts how can there be aught of tranquillity,

When she hath held them in check, by the reins of love?

Since from such an abode of their own they are exiled,

Where is the land of their sojourn, in which peace may be found?

They, who have their reason lost, thro' such a charmer's love,

Have now renounced both the rosary and the Brahmanical cord. *

All things have happened through their own affection;

And those without it, are useless, in all respects.

They have no place, either in the closet or the wine-shop:

Neither in the Muslim's regard, nor the infidel's sympathy.

With regard to such like eyes, what caution can I use,

When their glances are prepared for piercing me?

Her lovely person she hath transformed to a sandal tree; *

And those tresses, like unto snakes, are around it fallen.

He, who nourisheth the desire of such a sight as this,

On him, are the whole miseries of the universe heaped.

The hearts of lovers ever kindle, at the loved-one's glance;

For 'tis a flame; and her eyes are like firebrands unto.

To-day she hath again lighted the lamp of her beauty;

And her adorers' hearts, like the moth, are oblations thereon.

The names, nightingale and wooer, are one and the same;

And conscious hearts, in her praise, are melodious songsters. †

Her eyes are lotuses, and the pupils, they are black bees; ‡

And their gaze, like the gazelle's, is free and unrestrained.

Her eyebrows are bows, and her eyelashes, the arrows;

And to launch upon her lover, she hath raised them.

The pure and sincere, in both worlds, enjoy liberty:

'Tis a tower, whence to gain a good sight of the beloved.

Than this supreme felicity, what greater can there be,

When, every moment, they expect the adored to behold?

This infinity, on the water-wheel § of unity she placed;

And each water-pot, in its own turn, cometh and departeth.

She hath endowed every one with her own understanding;

And every one's perception is, in proportion, according.

O MĪRZĀ! behold thou those languid, sleepy eyes,

That, for the love of the adored, beam with phrenzy ever!

XVII.

What inquiry makest thou concerning the lover's condition I

No one hath hazarded a conjecture of the interminable road!

Wherefore had I been afflicted with misery such as this,

Had I guarded the heart from hearing the sight's promptings?

How can there be any peace or tranquillity for them,

Whose hearts, the ardent glances of the beloved have abducted?

Love, she hath made the chain of a distracted breast;

And, by the power of her glance, draweth the bond unto her.

A wondrous state of affection hath come over them—

Without seeing, they are disturbed, and in pursuit tired out.

Without any will of their own, they search for liberty:

With such a death impending, the dead yearn after life.

When the ripe fruit falleth to the earth, in its perfection,

The seed, with gladness, boweth its head to the ground.

This bubble, even now formed by the water, is by it again broken;

But what is carried away by the flood, floateth, its surface, upon.

They of little sense, are at their good fortune perplexed;

And this wind, like unto chaff, carrieth them before it.

One, here and there, comprehendeth the reality's purport—

The lightly equipped travelleth, easily, along the narrow path.

Cast, O MĪRZĀ, thine eyes upon the burnished mirror!

There is no particle of iron-dross in the steel thereof.

XVIII.

Upon them, that journey on the road of love,

New assaults, incessantly, are made.

How can there be any peace in those hearts,

That have beheld the splendour of the beloved?

Though, at first, she showed her face in its splendour,

A part of her mantle is now drawn o'er it again.

She hath made each of those eyelashes an arrow;

And her eyebrows are the ambush with bended bow.

The pilgrims, she hath ripened by separation's heat;

And now her preparations are for the reaping of them.

Care and anxiety are the motives of existence;

But what is life unto them, that before death die?

Since from sweet existence, they have, their hearts withdrawn,

The world is a barleycorn in the sight of their resolve.

The truly beloved is, by no means, distant from thee:

Thine own insensate scepticism is the abyss in thy front.

To that godly one, who entered the transient abode,

The whole universe is God, and he followeth Him.

It behoveth to acquire love from both the eyes,

That, apparently separate from each other, are but one sight.

Since thou wanderest not far from thy abode,

Surely thy heart, O MĪRZĀ! is pledged unto thy beloved.

XIX.

When that rose, out of nothingness, a form assumed,

The violet fell down, in adoration, at its feet.

Thou shalt drink from the cup of the perfect-one,

If to the melody of flute and harp, thy intellect respond.

Make thine heart the pleasant meadow of Abraham!

And become thou, as the scorching fire of Nimrūd therein! *

Behold the fidelity and sincerity of the world!

See how it deserted the tribes of Thamūd and Æād! †

Like as the rose bloometh, so it fadeth away;

As its short life, so is mine also computed.

Where is the rose, and where, too, is the thorn?

For all things soever there is a purpose fixed.

Let the idea of a partner with God perish:

The Indivisible is one only, and Omnipresent.

He hath entered into the emporium of infinity:

He is the attestor, and He is the attested become.

The adored, from His countenance hath raised the veil;

And the fortune of MĪRZĀ become propitious and august.

XX.

How long wilt thou wander, O covetous one! in the world's pursuit?

This very avarice, in itself, is an impediment in thy design!

For far fiercer than fire, is the flame of covetousness:

As much more as its food may be, so much is its voracity.

New cares and anxieties about it, every moment increase:

It hath taken all zest and pleasure from its bondsmen.

It coquets and toys, separately, with every one:

To the whole creation it is the seller, and they its buyers are.

Neither did Shaddād, in his arrogance, enter his paradise, *

Nor did Ḳārūn † derive any profit from its pursuit.

It concealed religion from the children of profanity;

And the straight-path, mere rites and ceremonies termed. *

It hath spread out a great net in this universal road;

And no wise man, save the contented, escapeth from it.

The pious and devout, thro' contentment, peace of mind acquire,

When unto the Consoler, they their distressed hearts turn.

From head to foot, the devout shall become illumined,

When they, thro' their hearts' courage, to the Creator draw nigh.

He, who hath died unto the world, obtaineth all things—

This is the great axiom of the Sower of bygone times.

The advantages he will acquire, will exceed all computation,

Who, in his necessities, becometh the acquirer of the Giver of Good.

Both states of being he vieweth, upon every respiration:

In truth, he is absorbed into the Shining Bright.

On the foot of the spirit, he ever soareth upon them,

However sublime the highest heaven, or the empyrean boundless.

His ice-like scepticism becometh thawed, by unity's sun:

He neither speaketh, nor acteth, save with the Creator's assent.

The felicity of the wise is after this manner recounted—

That its signification relateth unto the reality itself.

If adoration unto the Almighty is a divine command,

Bow thine head, unto the good and perfect too.

How long wilt thou have occasion for MĪRZĀ, as the medium?

Distinguish thou thyself, O auditor, the speaker's voice!

XXI.

I continually call to mind this sweet and charming friend,

Through this exalted name of whom, I acquire the heart's good.

How then can I be patient, severed from such a dear one,

When I perceive no sign of resignation in my heart?

Through this anxiety about her, I am ever miserable,

As to what remedy I shall devise; of whom, inquiry make.

In its eagerness for a look, it hath wholly left its seclusion:
With what chains shall I restrain this incomparable heart?
Except I make a snare of the ringlets of the faces of the fair,
And place for the bait, their musky moles therein.
I will put forth the whole wisdom of the enlightened,
If I may, this wayward heart, by any means, entrap.
Verily, it is become so utterly scattered to the winds,
That I find not the least vestige of it, in any direction.
It hath abandoned the universe, in search of the beloved:
How then shall I quit the world, in the pursuit of it?
No tidings thereof can be obtained, in any quarter:
I sit not down, abstaining, nor do I follow, in pursuit.
The body's vitality is the heart; and the heart's, the soul;
Then, without heart, and without soul, how shall I exist?
Of life, not even a dying breath remaineth unto me:
Frantic and beside myself thereat, I beat my hands and feet.
Still, this my death, is far better for me, than life itself,
Since, my soul I have abandoned, for the loved-one's love.
Regarding the putting off of mortality, MĪRZĀ thus testifieth—
When from this being, I cease to be, I shall entity become.

Footnotes

57:* One who has attained a certain stage in the Ṣūfi mysticisms.

58:* ولي, *walaey*, The shoulder-bone of an animal, or more particularly that of a sheep, used by the Afg͟hāns in divination.

58:† "The ship of the earth" here referred to is the earth itself, and the "cones of stone" are the mountains protruding from its surface. According to the ideas of Muḥammadans, the earth is placed upon the waters, in the midst of which it floats.

58:‡ فيكون *kun fa-yakūn*, "Be! then it is," a phrase attributed to the Creator at the creation of the world.

60:* The conditions which Adam accepted from the Creator regarding the duties for which he was created. See Mīrzā, Poem VI., second note.

60:† Referring to Adam.

61:* خ *k͟h*, is the first letter of خودي *k͟hūdī*, vanity, pride, etc.

62:* Mī'ān or Pīr Ros͟hān, the founder of the Roshāniān doctrine, and ancestor of Mīrzā. See page 51.

63:* س stands for سالك, of which it is the first letter, signifying a pilgrim, a traveller, and, metaphorically, a devotee.

63:† A custom of scattering money, by way of largess, amongst the people on festive occasions.

64:* صراط المستقيم—the direct and narrow path—the way of religion and orthodoxy.

65:* The first letter of عيب, sin, evil, fault, infirmity, etc.

65:† By faith is understood here, entire obedience to the will of God, on the observance or neglect of which, no less than eternal happiness, or misery depends; and so difficult in the performance, that when God proposed it to the vaster parts of creation, on the conditions annexed, they declined to undertake as a duty, that, the failing wherein must be attended with such terrible consequences. God made the proposal to the heavens, earth, and mountains, which, at their first creation, were endued with reason; and made known to them that he had made a law, and created Paradise for the recompense of such as were obedient to it, and Hell for the punishment of the disobedient; to which they answered, they were content to be obliged to perform the services for which they were created, but would not undertake to fulfil the divine law on these conditions, and therefore desired neither reward nor punishment. When Adam was created, the same offer was made to him, and he accepted it, notwithstanding man's weaknesses, and the infirmities of his nature. Jellāl-ud-Dīn, al Beidāwi's COMMENTARY ON THE KUR'ĀN.

66:* Choukān or Chougān is the Persian name of a game resembling tennis or cricket, but played on horseback by many Asiatic tribes. It also signifies the crooked bat used therein.

66:† غ the first letter of غير, contrary, different, etc.

66:‡ The five robbers or enemies here referred to, as in the house of the body, are the five senses—hearing, seeing, touch, taste, and smell.

68:* A bee enamoured of the lotus.

69:* Æūd is the Arabian name of Og, the son of Anak, concerning whose enormous stature, his escaping the Flood, and the manner of his being slain by Moses, the Muḥammadans relate numerous fables. See NUMBERS, xxi. 34, 35.

69:† The bridge over the infernal fire, and over which those who are to be admitted into Paradise, as well as those who are destined to Hell-fire, must pass. It is described as finer than the thread of a famished spider, and sharper than the edge of a sword.

69:‡ "In remotest time, the sword was emblematic of chastity. When the Emperor Maximilian married Maria of Burgundy by proxy, he enjoins the knight, who is to be his representative, to lay him down in the bridal bed, to which he is to lead the princess, in full armour, and to place a drawn sword between himself and her."—CHAMBERS' JOURNAL, Vol. XI. From this it would appear to have been also practised by the nations of the East.

74:* It is usual to ring a bell at the dawn of day, to arouse the people of a caravan to prepare to set out.

76:* See note at page 18.

77:* The sandal-wood tree is said to be the favourite haunt of black serpents.

77:† The mūsīkār is a bird, said to have numerous holes in its beak, from which as many melodious sounds issue.

77:‡ A species of bee, enamoured of the lotus.

77:§ The Persian wheel is a contrivance for drawing water for irrigation, etc., round the rim of which a string of earthen pots revolves.

80:* The commentators on the Ḳur'ān relate, that by Nimrūd's (or Nimrod's) order, a large space was enclosed at Kūtha, and filled with a vast quantity of wood, which being set on fire, burned so fiercely that no one dared to venture near it. Then they bound Abraham, and putting him into an engine (which some suppose to have been the Devil's invention) shot him into the midst of the lire, from which he was preserved by the angel Gabriel, who was sent to his assistance; the fire burning only the cords with which he was bound. They add, that the fire having miraculously lost its heat, in respect to Abraham, became an odoriferous air, and that the pile changed to a pleasant meadow; though it raged so furiously otherwise, that, according to some writers, about two thousand of the idolaters were consumed by it.—SALE'S KUR'ĀN, note to page 269.

80:† "And unto the tribe of Thamūd *we sent* their brother Sāliḥ. He said, Oh my people, worship GOD: ye have no GOD besides him. Now hath a manifest proof come unto you from your LORD. * * * Those who were elated with pride replied, Verily, we believe not in that wherein ye believe. And they cut off the feet of the camel, and insolently transgressed the command of their LORD, and said, Oh Sāliḥ, cause that to come upon us which thou hast threatened us with, if thou art *one* of those who have been sent *by God.* Whereupon a terrible noise from Heaven assailed them; and in the morning they were found in their dwellings prostrate on their breasts, *and dead.*"—AL KUR'ĀN.

81:* Shaddād and Shaddīd, the two sons of Æād, who reigned shortly after the death of their father, and extended their power over the greater part of the world; but the latter dying, his brother became sole monarch; who having heard of the *celestial paradise*, made a garden in imitation thereof, in the deserts of Aden, and called it Irem, after the name of his great-grandfather. When it was finished, he set out, with a great attendance, to take a view of it; but when they were come within a day's journey of the place they were all destroyed by a terrible noise from heaven. SALE'S KUR'ĀN, page 488, and note.

81:† Kārūn, the son of Yeshar (or Izhar), the uncle of Moses, and consequently the same with Korah of the Scriptures. Ile surpassed every one in opulence, so much so, that the riches of Ḳārūn have become a proverb. God directed Moses to punish him; and the earth having opened under him, he was swallowed up, along with his palace, his riches, and his confederates.

82:* That is to say, that the sacred book of the Lawgiver Muḥammad has been called a mere collection of rites and ceremonies.

ÆABD-UL-ḤAMĪD.

ÆABD-UL-ḤAMĪD, the author of the following poems, was born at Māshū Khel, a small village belonging to the Kudrīzī clan, or branch, of the Afghān tribe of Mohmand, one of the purely Afghān tribes at present dwelling in the Pes'hāwar district. Hence, Ḥamīd, like Raḥmān, was a Mohmand, but of a different clan. The exact year of his birth I have been unable to discover, but it was certainly about the middle of the last half of the seventeenth century. He was brought up to the priesthood, and is said to have been endowed with a considerable amount of learning, which he acquired at Pes'hāwar; and students from all parts of the surrounding districts sought his instruction.

He is the cynical poet of the Afghāns—the Shaykh Sāædī of the Pus'hto language—and the beauty of his compositions is fully acknowledged, even amongst a nation so rich in poets as the Persians, by whom he is styled "Ḥamīd the Hair-splitter." His poetry, though generally of a moral tendency, and breathing contempt of the world and its vanities, is still tinged with Ṣūfi doctrines, as all Muḥammadan poetry, in whatever language written, more or less is. He was the author of three works—a poem entitled "Nairang-i-Æishḳ," or "Love's Fascination;" "Shāh Gadā," or "The King and the Beggar;" and a Collection of Odes, entitled "Dur-o-Marjān," or "Pearls and Corals," from which the following translations have been selected.

The year of the poet's decease is, like that of his birth, somewhat uncertain; but the people of his native village account his death to have taken place about the year A.D. 1732; and his descendants, on inquiring of them, state, that four generations have passed since that event occurred, which, at the usual computation of thirty years for each generation, agrees within five years with the period mentioned. An aged man of the same village, who died about twenty years since, in the 107th year of his age, had been, repeatedly, heard to say, by the people of the hamlet, that he had, in his youthful days, seen Mull Ḥamīd frequently, who, at that time, was upwards of fifty years old. Another patriarch, Malīk Æazīz Khān, who is about a century old, states, that he had heard his father and grandfather relate, that they remembered Ḥamīd well; and that he was just coming into notice as a poet, towards the close of Raḥmān's life; and some of Ḥamīd's odes having reached the ear of Raḥmān, he sent for the poet to come and visit him; and was so pleased with his modesty and humility, that he gave him his blessing, and prayed that his verses might be sweet unto all men, and that no one might ever excel him in Afghān poetry. Up to the present day, certainly, Ḥamīd has not been surpassed.

The poet's grave is still pointed out by the people of his native village. Some of his descendants continue to dwell at Māshū Khel, and some are dispersed in other villages. The dwelling in which Ḥamīd was born, lived, and died, is now in ruins.

THE POEMS OF ÆABD-UL-ḤAMĪD.

I.

O THOU, for ever, with the cares of the flesh, distracted!

Why awaken for thy soul, sleeping misfortune and calamity?

The wise act not according to the counsels of their enemies:

Then why takest thou the advice of the devil, carnality?

Have some degree of shame for this white beard of thine!

And, moreover, in broad day, robbery cannot be effected.

Look thou well to this thine own fast fleeting breath;

Since to depart, every respiration raiseth the cry—Begone!

For what evil are worldly goods accumulated with thee?

When the bees fill the comb, they are of the honey deprived.

In the sight of God, as a man among men, thou art well;

But not, in the world's eye, a self-made Shaykh * and Mullā. †

When the pus exudeth from the sore, the invalid ease obtaineth;

But thou, at the passing away of this world, bewailest.

The hand of despair he will soon place upon his hip, *

Who girdeth up his loins, in the world's people confiding.

O ḤAMĪD! the fostering of the flesh's lusts is improper;

For no one, surely, showeth affection for an inveterate foe!

II.

This world, O friend, is neither mine nor thine!

It is to be left behind, and to endure after every one!

Fallen into the arms of one, it laugheth and flirteth with another:

What an immodest, wanton harlot, indeed, is this world!

Although it seemeth pretty and attractive, what then?

Intrinsically, and inherently, this world is a black calamity.

Since there is no generous, no disinterested friendship in it,

Though it may seem a friend, it is an enemy, in reality.

It will very speedily dash from the mountain's summit

Them, with whom ’tis hand in glove, and cheek by jowl.

It ridiculeth to their faces, its own followers, at all times;

For ever practising mockery and derision, is this world.

In any one place of it, there is never, either rest, or tranquillity;

For like unto a mere shadow, and naught else, is this world.

No one's affairs can be brought to completion by the light of it;

For this world is as the lightning, and the light of the sky.

Absurdly, thou attachest thine heart to the sounds of its drum;

For the world is a bridal procession—the mere guest of an hour.

No one hath become a gainer, by its trade and its traffic;

For the world is a seller of barley, though an exposer of wheat.

It is not meet, that the good and great bend their steps towards it;

For this world is a spectacle—a mere children's show.

Ḥamīd, who laugheth and is merry therein, but laugheth at himself;

For, indeed, the world is only a place of sorrow and of grief.

III.

I know not, in the least, whether this is love, or whether fire:

Do I consume in it of my own choice, or is this compulsion?

Is this the incurable agony of the tender passion, that thus killeth me,

Or a viper, for whose sting, there is neither antidote nor charm?

Since I have no pretty and lovable companion by my side,

This is, in reality, no dwelling; it is, verily and truly, a grave!

Be not disturbed, shouldst thou be reviled, on love's account;

For such like abuse is the acme of all greatness whatsoever.

Since thou severest my heart's fibres, and leavest none sound,

Are these the arched eyebrows of the beloved, or a reaping-hook?

Is it, indeed, the stigma attendant upon the dark-eyes' glances,

Which, notwithstanding loss of life and goods, leaveth me not?

Do not be in any way abashed, by the censure love bringeth on;

For it is the embroidered decorations of existence itself.

Since it hath preserved me safely, from mine own sorrows,

Is this love's anguish, or is it my sympathizing consoler?

Whoever entereth on love's path must, indeed, endure its pangs;

For this is an excellent present to send after the bride.

When I beheld Ḥamīd over head and ears in love's affairs,

I found him mad—in sooth, Majnūn's * elder brother.

IV.

Love, assuredly, is both profit, as well as traffic,

Hence, why the candle yieldeth its head with a smile.

The chikor hath dyed red its legs, † and laugheth heartily,

Because, alone in its roost, it found happiness and joy.

Inasmuch as life and goods are staked upon it,

This trade is, certainly, constituted to some advantage.

Though, the lover's appearance seemeth wretched, what then?

This beggar in rags, swayeth the sceptre of dominion.

Where is wandering in the desert? where sauntering in hamlets?

Where the hale and healthy? where the crazy and mad?

Zulīkhā ‡ abandoned, entirely, the cushion of sovereignty,

When the first inception of love's passion she acquired.

Those lovers who, from affection, openly, weep and wail,

Merely conceal, by so doing, their transports and their joy.

When the beloved accordeth her society with willingness,

The lovers say, unto themselves, now are we repaid!

Because thou, O Ḥamīd! hast made but a beginning in thy love,

Hence, towards me, thy endearments thus so trifling are.

V.

In such wise have the fair made away with my heart,

As if, indeed, it had never, at any time, been mine own.

Though I summon back, this stag-eye captured heart;

Yet, like the deer, it heedeth not any calling of mine.

Whereas my beloved inflicteth one wound upon another,

The medicine-chest of the physician is useless unto me.

Since thoughts of the rosy-cheeked, are the light of my eye,

It is objectionable, unto the rose, this gazing of mine.

Whatever part shall be found, free from headaches for the fair,

There's the befitting spot where my head should be smitten.

Whether I die or live, my head is laid at the portal of the beloved;

Save that threshold, there is no other place of existence for me.

Should I draw the whole of the world's beauties to my side,

I could not derive from another, the good I gain from thee.

There cannot exist between any lover and his beloved,

Such cruel treatment as thine, and endurance like mine.

If other folks groan under the tyranny of the Mughals,

The Almighty hath made my grief for thee, the Mughal to me.

Both the moth and the taper have often consumed themselves;

But they have no conception, O ḤAMĪD, of this consuming of thine!

VI.

How shall I stroll in the garden, without thee at my side?

What shall I do with the jasmine and the lily, without thee?

Since thou art the light of mine eyes, when thou art absent,

How shall I, the view of the parterre and its fragrant flowers, enjoy?

When every tulip, to a live coal turneth, and I burn thereon,

Let me not see them; for what were Yaman * without thee?

No one yearneth after Paradise, save the Deity's face to behold:

What then is home, or hamlet, or country to me, without thee?

Forasmuch as it cannot reach the dimpled well of thy chin,

What shall I do with the short thread of life, without thee?

As a mendicant monk, in the dust at thy door, I am happy;

But what were Khuṭan's sovereignty † to me, without thee?

Since I am carried to the fire, perpetually, like meat for the roast,

Of what use to me is existence, like slaughter, without thee?

Say then unto me, ḤAMĪD, whom thou, so cruelly, leavest—

Unto him of the sightless eyes say, what shall I do without thee.

VII.

Do not become, like the bubble, wholly vain and inflated;

For, from such vanity thou wilt, to ruin and perdition go.

Ask not from the Almighty, the rank and dignity of man;

Since, like the brutes, thou art occupied, in eating and drinking.

Even the beast, in the plough, goeth uniform to the furrow;

Wherefore then, quittest thou, thus sinfully, the Law's precepts?

Every breath thou drawest, without remembering thy Creator,

Consider, that thou swallowest a live coal, by the same computation.

Seeing that thou knowest nothing, save sleeping and eating,

In what respect art thou superior to the beasts of the field?

Why writhe in agony, at the bare thoughts of Hell's pangs,

When thou wanderest about tormented by carnality's cares?

Follow not, thus presumptuously, the vanities of the world;

For in this, like the lightning, thou wilt soon lose thyself.

If, in the accounts here below, there shall no errors be,

There will be none, in those, of the account-book above.

Be not concerned, O ḤAMĪD, regarding thy daily bread;

For that Causer of Causes, the Infinite, existeth!

VIII.

A spoiled son taketh not to discipline and instruction;

And a shaded palm-tree yieldeth not ripe dates.

Let not that boy be ever taken unto thy embrace,

Who may not take, also, to his lessons and his school.

Certainly, the ass and mule are in their place, in the stable;

But not a blockhead, without application, in the house.

When one degenerate creature appeareth in a family,

He bringeth disgrace on his lineage, both present and past.

"According to the son's good or bad actions, the father is remembered,"

Is a saying that hath been verified, throughout the world.

The finger is pointed towards the rider, and to him only,

Whose horse, the bridle's guidance doth not properly obey.

In heart, affection—on tongue, asperity; it behoveth, with the son:

What an excellent axiom—"Where the blow is, there is respect."

Joseph, then, became fit for the exercise of sovereignty,

When he received the blows of displeasure, and of wrath.

Like the flies, every worthless creature buzzeth about him,

When sugar-lipped ḤAMĪD reciteth his sweet strains.

IX.

I am sunk in care, to this degree, on account of the fair,

Like unto a stone, submerged at the bottom of Æmān's sea. *

For this reason, all peace and tranquillity are lost unto me,

That my tears have engulphed the goods and chattels of patience.

Those unacquainted with the case, call it the sunset's redness,

Though by weeping blood, I even, the sky itself, submerge.

Be not misled by the honied words of the deceitful fair;

For they, by this witchery, have whole peoples o'erwhelm'd.

Thus, under the mask of fondness, they slay and destroy one,

Like as though Khizr * were drowned, in immortality's fount.

In such wise, they keep me at a distance, when in their presence,

Like one thirsting for a draught of water, in solicitude drowned.

The pearl of the ocean of their coyness cannot be found,

Though I engulph, without number, the ships of patience therein.

Love's lighted taper, unto the tomb, he hath borne away,

Who carried the arrow of separation, embedded in his heart.

The paper boats of ḤAMĪD'S cares and anxieties,

The world hath, in the fathomless ocean of amazement, o'erwhelmed.

X.

In what manner shall I hush the sighs of this seared heart?

The nightingales will not be mute, among the roses of the parterre!

The tongue becometh again extricated, like a hero from the melée,

However strongly I seize it with my teeth, that it may silent remain,

Through crudeness and rawness, fermentation, from the vessel ariseth;

But the wise, from their own shrewdness, will taciturn be.

With water only, shall the lamp of thy desire become lighted,

Shouldst thou, like the pearl-oyster, silence, with patience, thy tongue.

When the seed is concealed in the earth, it becometh an ear of corn;

Therefore, lock up thine anguish, within the recesses pf thy breast.

The nightingale's wailings, about the rose, are not befitting;

For the moths consume themselves, in silence, on the red flame.

Like as the straw and the yellow amber * attract each other,

Thus, with silent tongue, do loving friends, each other invoke.

As the mother, the innocent cause of her infant's death, mourneth silently; †

So, inaudibly, the heart-enamoured utter their sighs and wails.

How could he entertain honourably his sugar-mouthed guest,

Should ḤAMĪD'S sweetness-raining, thoughtful strains be hushed?

XI.

My heart hath gone out, as a help in the fight, a look to obtain;

And to the right and to the left are discharged the arrows of sight.

With the ardour I am filled with, my heart throbeth and beateth,

Like as the infant springeth and boundeth, in its mother's arms.

By the hand of the forsaken, peace of mind cannot be grasped—

When do the heart-scorched, from a handful of water, find relief?

The stars, in their gladness, at my union with the beloved,

The tamborine beating, have thrust their fingers through.

By the recollection, every moment, of the mole of my beloved,

A musk-pod, as it were, becometh broken upon my head,

The Rustams * of patience and abstinence, like little children,

Take shelter, in retirement, from the crushing blow of love.

At the fountain of union's attainment, I die, with lips parched,

From the burning fever of the dread of separation.

Since the self-willed, like ḤAMĪD, they have made humble,

Love's pomp and grandeur are not without mishaps and blows.

XII.

From the fire and fever of separation defend us!

Preserve us, O God, from the fierce flames of Hell!
They make earth and heaven tremble on man's account
Shield us, alas! from the great tyranny of the fair!
Evil destiny made it my grievous lot, unto life's end,
To be ever departing, alas! from the sweet-lipped ones.
Though I, through reverence, cannot look upon her face;
Yet, for the courtesy of the ungracious ones, alas! alas!
The lot of the love-born, in comparison with the damned,
Is, alas! very many times more horrid and abominable.
Who deem the tormenting of lovers to be a virtuous act—
O, guard us, and defend from this creed of the fair!
Who cannot utter, with the tongue, what the heart wisheth—
From the desires of such lovers, O save and rescue us!
The morning, whose dawn is called the morn of doom—
From the night of such morning, O save us, and preserve!
Thou sayest, that ḤAMĪD should be debarred from the fair—
Alas, O monitor, that thou shouldst speak such monstrous words!

XIII.

O necessity! what a terrible calamity art thou,
That changest man's nature into that of the dog!
The Muḥammadan, thou makest follow Hindū rites,
And the Hindū, the usages of the Faithful to observe,

Kings and Princes thou makest stand at the door,

Of their crowns deprived, and from their thrones driven.

Even the free and unrestrained birds of the air also,

Thou entanglest, helpless and paralyzed in the net.

The tutor likewise, in the sight of his own scholar,

Thou makest even more contemptible than the fowl.

Since by them, man cannot be exempted

From the tax of necessity's urgent demands,

Say then, from all power and dominion soever,

And in empire's sway, what advantage is there?

Unto the opulent, infinite Deity, this is exclusive,

That He is wanting in nothing, whatsoever it be.

The raising up of ḤAMĪD, too, shall be effected,

From out of the waves of affliction, and of grief!

XIV.

The friendship of this world's friend is false and hollow:

From the tulip thou seekest permanence, unavailingly. *

Like unto one who vainly calleth to a goose for a porringer, †

So absurd, hath become, the hope of any constancy.

Since no one is the gainer from a friend's friendship,

Let not this unprofitable, gainless trade be entered on.

He, who in his necessities, craveth aught from fate's revolutions,

Unavailingly, runneth after the lightning's bright gleams.

To-morrow, thy manliness will be, from thy acts, seen;

Therefore, in boasting, raise no foolish noise, to-day.

Speaking, without acting, is mere trouble and vexation:

The kernel of desire, by this absurdity, cannot be obtained.

He, who may open his mouth unto the mean and base,

Rendereth the pearls of his own speech worthless, altogether.

When, thereby, its own rent garment it cannot gather together,

The rose, unreasonably, laugheth, at the weeping of the dew. ‡

Since, in the flame, O ḤAMĪD! the moth uttereth no cry,

The wailing of the nightingale for the rose, is utterly vain.

XV.

Keep thy face for ever wet with the water of thy tears;

For in these waters can be seen, the lustre of the pearl.

The lamp of Joseph's countenance at that time became lighted,

When his brethren made it red, by their cuffs and blows.

The tree that is obscured, will be backward in giving fruit,

Until it shall be brought, face to face, with the sun.

Like the rose, thy face shall glow before every one,

If thou but wash the face of the heart with blood.

The darksome stain of thy eagerness will not disappear,

Till, with patience's pearl-powder, thou cleanse not the face.

The patient and submissive, from prudence and bashfulness,
Are unable to look upon their own faces, the mirror within.
He who beareth the blister of toil and labour, upon his hand,
Will gaze, without apprehension, on the surface of the gem.
Unto the wise, a display of knowledge is a great defect
The lustre of the gem changeth the mirror to an earthen plate.
If thou seek after distinction in the court of the adored,
Like as the mirror, smear over thy face with ashes and dust.
The ardent longing of ḤAMĪD containeth naught of sinfulness;
It only seeketh everywhere, for that which it hath lost.

XVI.

Since the world's pomps and vanities are accounted nothing,
Only the worthless man will boast of such nothingness.
The existence of the transitory world is as the lightning's flash;
And by the light of a meteor, no affairs can be disposed of.
The world's lusts and vanities, are but the phantoms of a dream;
For when the sleeper again awaketh, they will be naught.
From this world, every man departeth, mouth filled with gall;
For it hath never yet made sweet any one's disposition.
Notwithstanding they fought and struggled so together,
Neither Alexander nor Darius carried the least thing hence.
He, who is acquainted with the world's deceptions and deceits,

Neither tradeth nor trafficketh in its markets, in the least.

Since the integrity of friendship cannot be preserved,

The friendship of this world's friends is, than nothing, less.

This embryonic thing, no one hath brought to perfection;

For its permanence is no longer than the lightning's flash.

O ḤAMĪD! he who is free from its cares and vexations,

Is perfectly indifferent regarding the world's people too!

XVII.

Shroud well the sight from the black eyes' glances!

Arise not, but, from drawn swords, guard well thine head!

Before love, the asceticism of a century is as nothing:

From a thousand bales of cotton, keep off a single spark!

Unto thy human form, a road of dire peril is affection:

Guard well thyself: on the path of danger enter not!

Love hath made reprobates of many simple devotees:

Mountains on mountains of ice, from the sun's face screen!

No other attainment will avail thee, in love's affairs,

Save one—the gift of madness—of which, be then beware!

Like as the naked man, from sharp swords himself shieldeth,

Do thou, from the morning curses * of the afflicted, thyself guard!

Cold sighs are not good for the novice in ardent love—

Keep the pinching wind, carefully, from the fresh wound!

Love and affection, with conceit and vanity, cannot exist:

Guard well the guide's breath and footsteps, in this path!

Shouldst thou, O Zephyr! go in the direction of the beloved,

Be mindful of the message, respecting ḤAMĪD'S aspirations!

XVIII.

When black antimony is applied unto dark eyes, †

From one dark calamity, another hundred spring.

Black eyes, and sable locks, and dark eyebrows—

All these are gloomy misfortunes—man-devourers.

No one is able to guard himself; even from one ill;

Yet on me, a hundred misfortunes are heaped, one on the other.

I am neither accounted among the living, nor the dead;

For love hath placed me, absolutely, the two states between.

What now, indeed, is either name or fame unto me?

Wherefore doth the bare-headed, woe-begone, beat his breast?

If thou, O monitor! tallest thyself as wise as Plato,

Unto me, in sooth, thou art but Majnūn's crazy brother. *

I will now embrace the paganism of sable ringlets,

If thou givest any of thy admonitions unto me.

O fool! love hath vanquished many powerful ones:

Why then, on the strength of thy hypocritical austerity, so elate!

What idol is it, O HAMĪD, that is resting on thy heart,

Unto which, thou art ever, in adoration, bent down!

XIX.

Were the looks constantly directed to every fair one's face,

How long, in love, would the saint's sanctity stand?

"As thou eatest of every tree, one, at least, will be poison"—

This axiom hath been tested throughout the world.

In one short moment, love turneth into ridicule

The saint's century of piety, and the empire of the prince.

It will drag him away disgraced to the market-place,

Though the hermit be sitting, a hundred seclusions within.

Love's affairs cannot be conducted by the wisest counsels—

The body cannot be cast into the fire, by any safe plan.

The languid eyes, far-reaching, have my heart reached,

Though the arrow of the lax bow but tardily striketh.

It is ever, either the jingle of the anklets of the beloved,

Or the clanking chains of love's distracted ones.

Though the mart of the fair be crowded with misfortunes,

They are not, by rebuke of saint, or ascetic, restrained.

Every breath, every step, it placeth at the breast malediction's sword;

And separation from the beloved, sick unto death, hath ḤAMĪDmade!

XX.

The fragrance of the flowers of this world's garden is gone;

And the kind disposition of its fair ones hath, also, departed.

Neither the nature of my love for the idols leaveth me,

Nor hath the proneness to tyranny left them either.

How will love, O monitor! leave me now,

When, from head to foot, it hath entered at every pore?

My soul would make efforts to depart and leave me,

If the pursuit of the fair were to leave my heart.

The heart, gone forth in the search of the youthful, cannot be found:

He is lost, who, at night, towards the distant fire, proceedeth.

This river Abā Sind, * which appeareth to our view,

Is but a small rivulet, exuded from the ocean of my tears.

My friend, I conceive, hath gone over to my rival's counsels;

Since observance of that vow, ’twixt her and me, hath ceased.

To obtain justice on them lieth in no one's power, ḤAMĪD!

The blood of the slain, by the dark-eyed, is shed and gone!

XXI.

Soften, O God, the heart of the guardian * with benevolence!

Make this Hindū, somewhat of a Muslim unto me!

My patience, make into a sharp sword, for love's sake;

And the marplots, with their own doubts, cut to pieces therewith!

Since the hearts of the fawn-eyed take fright therefrom,

Change the whole of my prosperity to a desert wild!

Apply fire unto the dwelling of my faith and worldly goods!

On this plea, at least, make me a guest, for love's own sake!

Give unto destruction the goods and chattels of my existence,

That may not be illumined with the lamp of the dear one's face!

Either, for me renew the period of union with the beloved,

Or, in separation, let my term of life but a moment be!

Since she acteth, at all times, on giving ear unto my enemies,

Make my friend somewhat ashamed of conduct like this!

My adversaries cast me into the burning flames of separation—

Preserve me, O God! like as Abraham, † save Thou me!

O ḤAMĪD! to-day, look stedfastly on the face of the beloved;

For to-morrow, thou wilt wring thy hands, and grieve for her.

XXII.

To thyself thou speakest well, but actest not rightly:

What is this thou sayest—what is that thou doest?

Thou wouldst reap wheat, where thou didst barley sow;

But the good cometh when thou actest worthily.

Day and night, for the sake of the flesh's lusts,

Thou takest the trouble to count the hairs of thy head;

But in seeing the truth, like unto the hare,

With eyes wide open, thou puttest thyself to sleep.

Shouldst thou, upon the impaling stake, be placed,

Or shouldst thou be precipitated into a well,
Thou hast neither those eyes nor those ears,
By means of which, thou mightest hear or see.
The very branch, actually, on which thou sittest,
Thou cuttest off—thou actest like one that is blind:
Thou plantest thorns in the midst of that path,
On which, every moment, thou thyself journeyest.
If any worldly loss should come upon thee,
Thou lamentest thereat, and makest thine eyes red;
But though faith and religion should leave thee altogether,
Thou makest that a matter of not the least concern.
For the sake of sweet-flavoured and dainty victuals,
Thou, willingly, acceptest a hundred heats and colds:
No dog, even, for the sake of its belly, would practise
Such despicable acts, as those that thou committest.
Sometimes, thou usest force; at others, entreatest
At times, actest with humility; at others, with pride:
This one body, for the sake of the world's lusts,
Thou now makest a dog of; and now, a wolf.
At that time, brightness cometh upon thee,
When thou causest darkness in another's house:
The funeral entertainment is, unto others, sorrow;

But thou turnest it into a joyous bridal feast.

Any matter, however vile and base it may be,

Meeteth with entire approval, thy heart within.

Thou neither feelest shame, nor accountest it a fault,

However improper the act that thou committest.

Now, thou becomest a monk; now, turnest priest:

Sometimes, blackenest the eyelids; * at others, dressest in green. †

At times, a strolling singer, with hand to forehead, bowing:

Sometimes, a soldier, thou takest to sword and dirk.

At times, thou heavest sighs; at others, weepest:

Sometimes, speakest choleric words; at others, cold ones.

All these are caused through the promptings of the flesh—

Thou turnest water into fire, O thou sensualist!

Though the worship of God is incumbent upon all,

Neither do these things constitute it, nor dost thou perform.

Say then, in what employment wilt thou delight—

Wilt thou, with an ox, or with an ass, amuse thyself!

If the favour of the Almighty be essential unto thee,

Thou wilt renounce for thyself all vanity and pride.

Thou wilt, thyself, tread carnality under thy feet;

And wilt, upon another spot, thine eyes direct.

Thou wilt seize contentment with thy hands:

Thou wilt consider carnality and the devil thieves.

Thou wilt follow in the steps of the good, always:

With heart, and with tongue, thou wilt imitate them.

What canst thou by thine own evil disposition against others effect?

Thou wilt merely bring injury and calamity, upon thyself!

Thou fallest into a well of thine own free-will:

Then what complaint against Ḥamīd bringest thou?

XXIII.

Although free from grief and sorrow, am I never;

Still, that I meddled in love's affairs, regret I never.

Though my goods be plundered, and my neck stricken,

The one to turn from the moon-faced, am I never.

In the acquirement of a single straw's weight of love,

To be obstructed, by either faith or religion, am I never.

Whether my head be firmly placed, or be it severed,

The one to rejoice or grieve thereat, am I never.

Though I stake both life and goods, on the heart-ravishers,

Reproached therefrom, the world before, am I never.

Like one bereaved of his senses, in love's affairs,

Thinking of mine own profit or injury, am I never.

To me, O monitor! say naught regarding patience;

For the ear-giver, unto such speeches, am I never.

Whose sweet face hath not, thus, amazed me ever,

On such a charmer yet, set eyes have I never.

Why should my dear one, on HAMĪD a kiss bestow,

When, of such beneficence as this, worthy, am I never.

XXIV.

Though I have become crushed by the multitude of my sorrows,

I cannot be patient, nor can I, from the fair abstain.

Let all the offerings and sacrifices of the world, be an oblation,

Unto the reproaches, upbraidings, and coquetry of the fair.

When I cast my eyes on their beauty, sweetly blooming,

The fresh-blown flowers of spring are nothing to me.

Before the sleepy, languid glance of my love, I wonder,

That with a lax-strung bow, they, so sharply, strike.

She raiseth uproar in the privacy of the secluded,

When this peace-disturber displayeth her charms, unto them.

She dischargeth a thousand darts, right into my heart,

When, in anger, she turneth her eyes, sharply, on me.

Why would any one, entreatingly, ask aught of them,

Were not the upbraidings of the fair, with honey mixed?

The sweet creatures, by their duennas, * avert the evil eye;

For in front of the melon-bed, the black shard will be placed. †

If he hath not pressed the lips of the sugar-lipped ones,

How hath ḤAMĪD'S tongue become a scatterer of sweets?

XXV.

Patience and forbearance, turn man's nature into fire:

The malevolent and the ill-willed, on its flame, shall be straw.

Fire reacheth the evil-minded, from their own persons—

The Phœnix maketh its own nest, a furnace for its body.

The arrows of the pangs of the oppressed, strike home—

None of the discharges are harmless—none miss the mark!

The world-enamoured are, of all fools, the greatest;

For, like the baby, they show eagerness for the flaming fire.

Every man, who, after a pestilence, desireth a market,

In his eagerness for physic, the worthless fellow, poison taketh.

They, who look for perfection out of arrogance, are fools;

For, in foul water, the necessary ablutions cannot be performed.

No one can restrain the passions from manifold wickedness:

No one can prevent fire from consuming straw.

When one benefit, out of a thousand such, thou hast not realized thereby,

Out upon such shameless, such execrable longings as those!

The world, slumbering in the sleep of negligence, heareth him not,

Though ḤAMĪD shouteth, as loud as the peal of a bell.

XXVI.

Be not grieved at the departure of this world's wealth!

Be not sorrowful if out of thy foot cometh a broken thorn!

The flesh's lusts and vanities, God hath given captive unto thee;

Then do not thou, the captive of thine own slaves, become!

Godliness and piety cannot exist with conceit and egotism:

In this matter, without a guide or instructor, be thou not!

There is no bridle that can be placed in the mouth of passion;

Then let it not be trained up, as a reprobate and robber, by thee!

Where is the scar of a single brand? where that of a thousand?

Enter not, then, into schemes for increasing worldly wealth!

Say, is the light or the heavy load, the best for the head?

Indigence, for thee, is good: do not thou a lordling become!

The Almighty hath given thee ears to hear, and eyes to see;

Then do not, wittingly, like one, blind, from the precipice fall!

With smiling face and unclouded brow, unto the world become

Its injustice-receiving target; but, the arrow, become thou not!

All other bonds soever, O ḤAMĪD! are easy to be borne;

But, at least, let thy neck be, from the chain of avarice, free!

XXVII.

My friend observeth none of the usages of affection towards me!

Alas, my dark, dark destiny! shine out a little on me!

Let me some day, at least, to mine own, that lip press,

That every hour sippeth up the very blood of my heart!

Through her unkindness, even yet, thou rubbest thine eyes with thy hand:

Then why, after the fair, runnest thou again, poor wretch?

My friend, through coquetry or playfulness, speaketh incoherently to me,

Or her lips adhere together, from the sugar of their sweetness.

The load of love, which neither earth nor heavens can bear—

With what strength wouldst thou raise it, thou improvident one?

Alas, that I had not become enamoured, when I first fell in love!

Now, whatever it is, this must be, with a good grace, borne.

Gazing upon the countenances of the beautiful, is ḤAMĪD'Scalling;

The eyes of the coward only, become dazzled at the gleam of the sword!

XXVIII.

Really, this existence, so to say, is altogether worthlessness,

Since, in the world, I pass my life away, absent from my friend.

I cannot imagine what unfortunate, hard grain I am,

That I do not become ground, between the mill-stones of absence.

The sable locks and fair countenance of my beloved,

I behold in every thing, white or black, in the world.

I use my tongue in such a manner, through helplessness,

That I may my friend regain, either by falsehood or by truth.

If other folks, by alchemy, transmute dust into gold,

I, by the alchemy of love, have turned gold into dust.

Where is love? and where too, shame and modesty's fear?

Where there is shame or modesty, dancing cannot be. *

If thou seekest a dear-one, for her, shed thou rivers of tears;

For, in the waters of this ocean, that pearl can be found.

From the door of worthy and base, he preserveth both breath and step

Whoever wandereth about frantic, in desert and in wild.

Ḥamīd styleth that person a mere worshipper of idols,

Who, with manifest hypocrisy, performeth his duty unto God.

XXIX.

When the dear friend who departed, unto her friend returneth,

In truth, 'tis as if the Messiah drew near unto the dead!

Disjunction from the adored is a dire, and a black calamity;

God forbid any follower of Islām, into such affliction fall!

In such wise, hath separation caused my confidence to fail,

As when, all at once, a fiery dragon might one confront.

Through bashfulness, I am unable to look upon her sweet face—

Bleared eyes become wholly dazzled by the lightning's flash.

Neither will the promises of the fair be, hereafter, fulfilled,

Nor will the Phœnix fall entrapped, in any one's snare.

Do not become altogether hopeless of desire's attainment;

For the Almighty bringeth to the ground the birds of the air.

Since I have taken up my residence, the city of sorrow within,

For me, there is no laughter or joy, without sorrow after.

Through excessive fear of the dread morn of separation,

In the presence of the rosy-cheeked one, I like the taper weep.

By this, thy non-appearance, thus, full-well, I know,

That, either to-day or to-morrow, unto ḤAMĪD, bringeth death.

XXX.

O thou constant endurer of misery in the cares of the flesh!

O thou, happy in this affliction, and in doing injury unto others!

No one obtaineth the slightest benefit, or advantage from thee:

Indeed, thou art like a thorn ever buried in the side of others!

Thou wilt, one day, become a captive, like unto the hawk;

Since, day and night, thine own species' flesh, hath thy food become.

Let not the sighs of the afflictions of the oppressed strike one;

For, from their gasps and sobs, whole regions to perdition go.

The execrations of the oppressed pass not harmless, ḤAMĪD

The shaft of the archer striketh the target unerringly!

XXXI.

At the present time, extinct is the principle of sincerity!

That which is taken now, is but the empty name of sincerity!

I discover nought else, whatever, save duplicity and deceit,

Though I have carefully examined the horoscope of sincerity.

Let any one, with the finger, unto me a single man point out,

Whose acts are in accordance with the usages of sincerity.

As though folks, festive songs, over a dead bride, should sing;

So entirely hollow and doleful are the drum sounds of sincerity.

When the occupation of father and son, is dissimulation,

What then remaineth of the colour and odour of sincerity?

Because hypocrisy hath destroyed the taste of the world's mouth;

Hence poison of the infernal tree * is the sweet savour of sincerity.

Examine closely the cottages and the mansions of the world:

Say, hath any one laid on their walls a single layer of sincerity?

The world containeth none sincere; but should such be found,

Then, ḤAMĪD is the special and obedient servant of sincerity.

XXXII.

Every rebel is brought to submission, by sincerity:

Every shameless one is made ashamed, by sincerity.

Like the sun, its brightness shall become world-irradiating—

Every brow, that uprightness and sincerity may illumine.

I will be answerable if it come not, and crouch at his feet,

If one act, with sincerity, unto the most ravenous beast.

No shears soever can, with its mouth, any bond sever,

That shall have been made strong and durable, by sincerity.

Like as when, on the rising of the sun, light appeareth;

Thus sincerity life bestoweth, at every breath and footstep.

Like as the morning dawneth, so shall the bud blossom,

When sincerity, its smiling mouth, to laugh shall incline.

Those things, which the sorcerer by his enchantments effecteth,

Are as nothing, compared to what is effected by sincerity.

Forthwith, the hardened old infidel of a thousand years,

Is made a seeker of Islām's true faith, by sincerity.

From the race of hypocrites, O Ḥamīd, guard thyself,

Lest, with their deceit, they turn rotten thy sincerity!

XXXIII.

To this degree, art thou become absorbed in thine own selfish objects,

That the interests of others are good for nothing, in thy sight.

When the feasible wishes of others are so difficult unto thee,

What remedy wilt thou devise, as to thine own impossible ones?

Until, of thine own free will, thou carry out the wishes of others,

How, by the means of them, shall thy ends be effected?

"Where there is no object, what is the object?"—so the proverb runneth;

Hence, for the lamp, the nightingale no solicitude showeth.

Dost repeat a prayer, that with such vehemence thou criest?

Calling upon the Almighty, is not the object of thy invocations!

Without being summoned, folks around the lamp assemble,

Because, with silent mouth, it mentioneth its aims and wishes.

In all this amount of trouble, that he taketh on himself,

The giving of advice and admonition is the only object ofḤamīd.

XXXIV.

Were there any chance of thy exhortations taking effect on me,

Then, O monitor! unto me, thou wouldst have given admonition.

Love hath made my eyes more wanton, even, than the locust's, *

Whilst thou, unjustly, stirrest about in them the rubbish of advice.

I had not been o'erwhelm'd to this degree, in the ocean of grief,

Had admonition, whether little or much, into my heart entered.

Like as the state of the dead, past all remedy, becometh;

So the heart, by love despoiled and ravaged, giveth not ear to advice.

When, O counsellor! will they become acceptable unto lovers—

These monk-and-hermit-approved expostulations of thine?

From counsel, what alleviation doth the poor lover obtain?

To the snake-and-scorpion-stung, what availeth admonition?

'Midst the uproar and tumult of the assembly of reprobates,

Can a secret and whispered homily, at any time, be heard?

Love hath ever condemned me to far worse punishment,

Whenever I have listened, the admonitions of others unto.

I will not then, O mentor! unto thy counsels give ear;

For, as fate will have it, I, HAMĪD, hold advice unlucky.

XXXV.

When men covet, from their fellow-men, any worldly object,

Their human nature, from this covetousness, that of a dog becometh.

The foot of their modesty trippeth and stumbleth, perpetually,
When they, by the flesh's lusts incited, upon covetousness seize.
Thro' covetousness for the grain, the free bird becometh ensnared;
And this thy covetousness also, will, speedily, bring calamity on thee.
The bitter words of rectitude and truth, will all be left by them,
Who sweeten their mouths with the confection of covetousness.
The colour of their friendship will, speedily, be demolished,
When one friend hath any want requiring to be satisfied by another.
This single drop of water becometh a pearl within its breast,
When the oyster, towards the ocean, all covetousness escheweth. *
The difference between royalty and beggary, ceaseth, altogether,
When the king satisfieth not the beggar's craving covetousness.
The stranger leave out; for, verily, though it were father or mother,
God forbid, that any one should be under necessity to another!
Pestilence is far preferable, O ḤAMĪD! than that covetousness,
Which, for the sake of the flesh's lusts, coveteth aught from others.

XXXVI.

Be not captivated by the friendship of this world's people—
This shameless, this faithless, this barefaced world!
Like unto dogs, that snarl and fight over a rotten carcass,
Thus, in the world, its insolent people squabble and contend!
They neither inquire about, nor cast a look upon each other—

Back to back, pass along the world's acquaintances and friends.

The peevish, ill-tempered, disagreeable ones, are left behind;

Whilst cruel fate hath removed from us the sweet and charming!

Thine eyes, indeed, will not be pleased with a single one of them,

Shouldst thou bend thy looks upon the people of this age!

Since their hands are wholly withdrawn from what is right,

Wherefore may not the world's folks be, in calamity, immersed?

Lying and duplicity have become sweeter to them than sugar;

But like poison, the world's people have spitten out truth!

They will not leave thee, O ḤAMĪD! in thy decency, and repute;

Since the base and infamous have become the great ones of the age.

XXXVII.

I perceive in friendship together, the vile, deceitful world;

By which means its people have forfeited the country of truth.

It appeareth unto me, merely poison mixed with sugar,

This, than honey or than sugar, more seemingly, loving world.

Be mindful never to sit in the assembly, at any time soever,

Of this, without hurt, and without detriment, woe-begone world!

When is the brightness of any one's face agreeable or pleasing,

In the dark eyes, of the unto-justice-blear-eyed world?

Let it be an oblation on the altar of a single grain of modesty,

The hundred-weight-lascivious, wanton, shameless world!

In reality, it is but a useless shell, without a kernel,

The present race of mankind in comparison to the past.

The hand, from toil blistered over, is, truly, Yaman * in itself;

Then why, in search of rubies, doth the scabby world wring its hands?

From the vile and base, it behoveth well, the heart's secret to guard—

In the flower-garden, the foul and filthy world is not admitted.

What do the sound and healthy ken of ḤAMĪD'S heart's pangs?

Only the afflicted know, the state of the suffering world!

XXXVIII.

When my love for thy sweet face became noised abroad,

The love of Majnūn and of Lailā, † became an empty jest.

That, which appalled, even Majnūn, within the tomb,

Such a grievous calamity, unto me, hath love assigned.

Tho' his head, like the taper's, disappeareth at every respiration;

Still, no one should consider himself, from this love, exempt.

In the hands of the sorrow-stricken, it placeth harp and rebeck,

When, in the court-yard, love seateth the bridal train.

Fire, kindled by way of jest, blazeth up in real earnest;

And love, made in sport, hath brought many unto tears.

The brokers of sense and reason, lose their occupation, entirely,

When love, on its own account, beginneth to traffic and trade.

Like as by applying fire, one setteth dry straw in a blaze,

In the same manner, doth love, piety and austerity unto.

Doth any one, a false claim and a true, in one breath, prefer?

How then shall sincere love, remain concealed one moment?

He never again obtaineth a smile from the rosy-cheeked ones,

Though love caused ḤAMĪD to weep, like unto the dew.

XXXIX.

If kings have a liking for the throne and the sceptre,

Lovers have a partiality for ruin and desolation.

There is no such injurious effect, in the agony of love,

That those afflicted with it, desire any cure.

Like Joseph, he will descend into the well of grief,

Who hath a desire for the ascension unto gladness.

My heart hath now grown cold with regard to passion:

It hath a yearning towards the waves and billows of woe

Wittingly, the prince of reason engulpheth himself,

Who hath a longing for the taxes of the country of love.

What compassion do the amorous eyes of the fair possess,

When they always have a desire for an occasion to slay?

ḤAMĪD will, at all events, bear the burden, notwithstanding;

Since he nourisheth a fondness for thy capricious ways.

XL.

O, when are the sorrows of love so easy to be borne,

That they shall suffice for any one's food and raiment!

Speak not unto me, O monitor! regarding modesty or shame:

From any apprehension of water, what have the naked to dread?

Love placed me as far from patience, as earth from heaven;

And, unto the firmament, no one's comprehension can reach.

Affection hath completely set free my heart from control:

With it, I am unable to exercise any power over patience.

Thro' the roofed building, the sun's rays penetrate not—

The heart, by one sorrow rent and torn, is good indeed.

When will he find peace of mind, even seated on a throne,

Whose heart may be always pining after some fair face?

The association of the beloved, with a rival, is the same to me,

As though one should, together, purity and impurity mix.

How shall ḤAMĪD obtain any relief from the fair,

When, over him, power of life and death, God, to them, hath given?

XLI.

Though thou mayst speak with warmth or anger;

Or, though thou mayst, to staff, or to bludgeon take;

With all this useless absurdity, O blockhead!

Thou wilt not be able to effect aught against fate.

That which was to happen to thee, hath come to pass,

Whether the matter of a straw, or of a hundred thousand.

Save resignation, there is no remedy soever,

For this pain and trouble, beyond all doubt.

Whoever sayeth aught about that which hath occurred,

Nonsense talketh—he striketh at a fly, the water upon. *

Do not, O fool! become, from a trifling of success,

Like unto the drum, for announcement inflated.

There will not be grief and sorrow upon man for ever,

Nor will there be mirth and gladness every moment.

A person may, sometimes, be gay and cheerful;

At others, from care, he may be melancholy and distressed.

At times, starving, with intestines doubled up;

At others, gorged with food, even up to the throat.

At times, he becometh a lion, appropriating the plain;

At others again, he becometh the mere rat of a burrow.

Where is lamentation? where is the song of gladness?

Where the plundered? where the Uzbak * that harried him?

Were the actions of fate, ever of one uniform colour,

The firmament would not be thus spotted with stars.

The tyranny and injustice are not upon thee alone,

Of fortune's ever changing, inconstant revolutions.

In these troubles and vicissitudes, many other folks

Are thy companions, and are, hand in hand, with thee.

Ever unto distance remote, direct thou thy sight:

Even from the heavens, the earth-supporting-fish unto. †

There is a dart embedded in the heart of every one,

Discharged therein by the ruthless hand of fate.

This fearful pestilence, indeed, hath reached

Every house, and every dwelling-place, unto.

It, however, behoveth, that in this net of calamity,

The prudent bird should be careful not to flutter.

ḤAMĪD'S resignation hath to songs of gladness turned,

Through the tyranny and oppression of every dastard.

XLII.

Every chieftain, who contemplateth the injury of his clan,

Should make the ease of Jamāl, ‡ a mirror for himself.

From beneath his own feet, he cutteth away the branches,

Who nourisheth, in his heart, evil towards his friends.

That chieftain, in the end, shall abominable remain,

Whose envy exciteth him to the injury of his own kin.

He who coveteth the lives and goods of other people,

Ere his desire be fulfilled, shall lose his own life and goods.

Indeed, he will himself fall into it—such is the proverb—

Who is guilty of the crime of digging a well for others.

Strife and bloodshed shall first arise in their dwellings,

Who long to see others, in contention and slaughter engaged.
Whoso may be powerless over his own hands and feet,
With what power against his foes, shall he contend?
"By strangers' aid, without one's own, bravery cannot be shown"—
This howl raise Jamāl and Jalāl from the tomb.
Should the hawk pounce upon the quarry of the falcon,
It effecteth nothing, but tireth itself in bootless tugs and pulls.
Hundreds cannot take the victory from thousands;
Save the All-Powerful should, specially, the advantage decree.
Whoso advanceth his foot beyond his own bounds,
Destiny will trample him, like Jamāl, under foot.
He, who, by force, decketh himself out, in others' garments,
Shall use them, all soiled and dirty, to bandage his own wounds.
No one hath yet won over the good fortune of strangers to himself;
Moreover, by entertaining such ideas, he throweth his own away.
Every moth, that flieth about, upon this flambeau;
Like unto Jamāl, will only consume itself thereon.
The base man, who is ambitious of acquiring reputation,
Plagueth himself to thread a needle by the lightning's flash.
A result such as this will, upon himself, return,
Whosoever, in requital of good, giveth evil back.
Neither goodness, nor virtue, is manifested by the base;

Nor doth the sweetest water affect the bitter fig. *

"If thou bringest up a wolf's whelp, it springeth upon thee"—

To our state, and that of Jamāl's also, this saying applieth.

As Yazīd was infamous, on account of Ḥasan and Ḥusain;

So was Jamāl a disgrace unto us, were any one to ask.

That which hath happened, is from the same necessity,

As maketh the timid hare spring on the dog, to terrify it.

Whatever those unacquainted with the case say, let them say:

The informed, however, take our plea into due consideration.

Other people will always get burnt * on their account,

Who abandon the sword's defence, for the shelter of walls.

Truly, the Almighty hath made the Khudrzīs infamous by Jamāl:

Indeed, whatever happeneth to mankind, their own acts bring about.

Since in traffic, profit and loss have, from the beginning, existed,

Wherefore, upon the broker, do mankind thus cast blame?

These, O ḤAMĪD! are the customs and usages of the time,

That one showeth his grief at another's death: the other, his joy.

XLIII.

Until thou, against the belly, makest a determined stand,

By mildness thou wilt not escape from the Uzbak's hands. †

Neither doth a stone, forsooth, grow soft, nor an enemy, a friend;

Then do not be beguiled, O mean one! into the belly's servitude.

It is not advisable to show ever so little kindness to the belly—

The pilfering hostess satisfieth herself by a snack from each dish.

How can there be a place therein for the remembrance of thy God,

When thy belly, with eatables, is constantly crammed?

If thy heart desire, that thy body should be resplendent,

Take example of the pinched-up belly, from the firmament, itself. ‡

Crave not, for thy belly, aught soever from fortune,

For it will merely give thee the new moon in thy bowl. *

From a slight blow, this turban will fall unto the ground,

Which, from pride, thou placest so jauntily, one side of thy head.

Consider the belly more contemptible than all else besides,

If thou desire the standard planted, on Heaven's pinnacle.

That thou shouldst show no affection towards the world's people,

Is, beyond all doubt, the safe and the peaceful side.

Thro' this thine own meekness and humility, O ḤAMĪD!

Thou art dust in the eyes of the conceited and the proud.

XLIV.

Many, many times have I rent my garment before thee;

Still thou hast not removed thy guardians † from my path.

Save causing thee to upbraid, and set thy face against me,

Of no other use, to me, my offerings and oblations became.

The child playeth not thus with shards and with stones,

Like as I gamble away, upon thee, my religion, and my faith.
When to such a pitiless one as thou art, I gave up my heart,
I, certainly, thrust my own self into calamity's jaws.
There are none of constancy's or fidelity's wares therein;
For the fair, in their shops, barter naught but hollowness itself.
When I come upon the paraphernalia of the heart-ravishers,
The goods and chattels of my self-control become naught to me.
Should I erect a hundred castles of patience round my heart,
I see no safety for myself, from the inroads of the fair-faced ones.
A thousand times over, they will be thankful for their condition,
Should I narrate, unto the damned, the way my life passeth.
Shouldst thou, O ḤAMĪD! come under the aspersion of love,
Account as profit, not yet acquired, this mulct of thine.

XLV.

Thy face hath shamed the rose, and thy tresses, the spikenard:
The nightingale forsaketh the parterre, and flieth unto thee.
From how long since, indeed, dost thou inflict, and I endure?
Bravo unto thy tyranny, and unto this resignation of mine!
My heart, thro' jealousy, becometh lacerated within my breast;
When the senseless comb runneth its fingers thy ringlets thro'.
When smiling, thy rosy lips reveal their beauties,
Exactly like unto the rose-bud, when it unfoldeth its leaves.

The whole world, through injustice, had become desolate,

Had kings shown such arrogance and indifference as thou!

Though I observe a thousand fasts of patience and austerity;

With a single glance towards me, thou subvertest them all.

How long shall I dry thy tyranny's tears with my sleeve?

Wherefore is the bridge not constructed on the waters of the flood?

For with love, as with quicksilver, there is no repose, save in death! *

How long then am I to live, when I am in agitation ever

O ḤAMĪD! the fair maids of the Sarraban * tribe have no equals;

Whether it is in Egypt, or in Kanæān †—in Kabūl or Kas͟hmīr.

XLVI.

Wherefore doth the possessor of beauty boast of loveliness?

It will, of itself, become the pointed at, like the new moon.

Though one should call it a ruby a thousand times over,

The crowfoot's red berry ‡ therefrom, doth not to a ruby turn.

Whoever aspireth after the beauty of the Scythian-like fair, §

Like the ant, merely for his own destruction, acquireth wings. §§

Just as the child playeth and gamboleth with earth and mud;

So sporteth the poor lover, with his property and his life.

Expel selfishness from thy heart, if thou wouldst love pursue;

For without that deficiency, this perfection existeth not.

This doctrine of love is an ecstacy, from beginning to end;

And for the utterance, even of a word, there is no power here.

Is this a black mole upon the forehead of my beloved?

Or is it Bilāl ** arisen, the summons unto prayer to sound?

Defend us from the patronage of the self-conceited, be he ever so liberal:

The mouth gasping thro' hunger, is good; but not opened, to beg.

Envy not, O possessor of riches, the poverty of ḤAMĪD!

This poor blanket, for that shawl, I will not exchange with thee!

XLVII.

Though I adjure thee again and again, a thousand times,

Or give counsel unto thee, in a hundred different ways,

Neither my monitions, nor my entreaties touch thee—

What calamity am I? what abomination fallen in the path?

If these are not the marplot's counsels, what then are they,

That my admonitions make no impression on thy ear?

Such joy as thou displayest in cruelly torturing me,

Such delight the nightingale showeth not, even for the rose.

In love, since I live on less than half of a dying breath,

Death is a hundred times preferable, to such existence as this.

Since they talk to me of patience, when separated from thee,

The admonishers chew, out of place, these cuds of monition.

Ask no promises of me regarding the affairs of love;

Else, why is it, that poison is not with relish swallowed?

As one, that from the sheath, half draweth a sword on another,

In such wise, do thy white arms daunt and terrify me.

A nightingale, like ḤAMĪD, there would not be among them,

Were not the Sarrabans * a garden, thro' their maidens fair.

XLVIII.

How unseemly, how culpably, thou pratest, O addle-head one!

Wherefore from the Almighty, askest thou not pardon for this.

Thou grievest long enough about thy modesty and good name;

But, in the affairs of the world, who more dastard than thou?

Thou showest no concern about religion, though it should be destroyed—

Thou misguided—thou shameless—thou unworthy creature!

Just as the child giveth pearls and jewels, in exchange for bread;

In such wise playest thou, for the world, thy faith away.

What! thou, who givest thy heart to the world, seekest grace!

Thy life passeth bootlessly away, thou sifter of the wind!

The foolish man yearneth after the goods of the world;

And the baby capereth along, astride the cane horse. *

Nothing unlawful, is a whit more pleasant than the lawful;

But thy own sister and daughter are foul-nosed, † in thy sight.

Thou hast not, in the least, swept it with the broom of repentance—

The path of death, thou hast left, in the same thorny state as before.

Since thou hast kept the field against men, good and brave,

Unto the smiting-sword of ḤAMĪD'S intellect be all praise!

XLIX.

Though thou canst manage to give it good food, and fine clothes;

Still, thou wilt not be able to exempt the body from the fire of hell.

Until thy body shall be decked out in the garments of piety,

Plume not thyself on the mere adornment of the person.

These acts, which passion, to-day, prompteth thee to commit,

I perceive in them, for thee, death and destruction to-morrow.

Since by death, thou becomest like unto a putrid carcass,

Do not become, in life, like unto a musk-deer of Khuṭạn. *

Fools, that they may gain the world thereby, their faith barter;

But such like buying and selling as this, the wise practise not.

Save thee, by whom both grave and resurrection are forgotten,

Know, that every stranger seeketh his own country to reach.

From the goblet which is full, no sound proceedeth ever;

But thro' deficiency and emptiness only, thy notoriety ariseth.

Since here thy sitting is among the wicked, and the unworthy;

Flatter not thyself, that there, thou shalt, with the just, arise.

Unto thee, O ḤAMĪD! the wise and the prudent will give ear;

But what know the ignorant, concerning thy stringing of pearls. †

L.

How many lions hath fortune made a spectacle of,

Into whose dens, both dogs and cats, now fearless enter!

When destiny, in its own dire pitilessness, cometh,

It casteth down stones, upon the furnace of glass.

Destiny maketh that head a plaything for dogs,

Within whose domain, the lion dared not place his foot.

In the conflict with fate, they fled far away,

Whom the world feared to enter into contest with.

The teeth, by which those iron-like pulse were masticated,

God knoweth what acids have rendered them thus blunt.

By the tears of what unfortunate, was that fire quenched,

That, enwrapped in its flames, distant hills and dales?

Like unto a scorpion, insignificant and contemptible dieth

That man, whose envenomed sting, maketh others weep and wail.

The skilled in language must have arranged the rhymes ofḤAMĪD;

Otherwise, no one would have entered them upon any page.

LI.

Since thou confessest unto ignorance, it proveth thy sense is good;

But when thou boastest of thy wisdom, thou art then unwise.

When thy comprehension reacheth not unto thine own faults,

How then knowest thou aught about the shortcomings of others?

If thou hast preserved thy heart from the deceits of the flesh,

Then mayest thou say unto it, verily thou art wise!

Seeing that thou hast no conception of religion in thy heart,

Thou, foolishly, pleasest thyself—thou art but lip-wise.

But wherefore is not the thief of thine own abode seized by thee,

When thou pointest out others' stolen goods, and knowest the robber too?

First repair thine own ruined and dilapidated affairs,

If, in truth, thou knowest a plan for restoring them.

Since, O heart-ravisher! all my wishes, thou fulfillest,

How wonderfully well must thou, the heart of ḤAMĪD know!

LII.

Whom love may make lighter, even than a feather,

Consider that person heavier than the mountain of Ḳāf. *

When, with the ashes of abjectness, it shall become daubed,

The mirror of their hearts, shall clear, and bright become.

Though the fool may prate and vapour before the wise;

The roasting grain will not, in the least, crack the pan.

With eyes that see, and ears that hear, thou showest thy malice:

Art thou not, unto the breath and footstep of the Messiah, blind?

If a person shut not his eyes, purposely, on what is unlawful,

The stranger's shoes can be easily recognised upon his feet.

Since ḤAMĪD stretcheth forth his hand to the chin of the beloved,

O! would that the branch of the willow did apples yield!

LIII.

Thou shouldst not take amiss, O beloved! my gazing upon thee;
For the nightingales fly and flutter, continually, about the rose.
Any worthiness of association with thee, in myself, I see not;
Hence have the pupils of mine eyes, from looking, wholly ceased.
Those eyes of thine, at last, carried away my heart from me,
Notwithstanding with endurance and patience I guarded it.
Art thou aware of thy raids and onslaughts, or art thou not,
Seeing that thou hast pillaged the abode of my resignation?
The stones of resentment and hatred, rain down upon my head,
When I behold my rivals, around the door of thy dwelling gathered.
Let Khizr * be the gate-keeper of those gates, and those walls,
Whence thy coming and going—thy exit and entrance, may be.
When that smile of thine, in thy chin, a well-like dimple dug,
Then was it, that I perceived my own falling helpless therein.
I would, at that time, have concealed this dejection of mine,
Had I any idea, that from thee I should have comfort received.
Throughout the whole world there is quiet and tranquillity;
But the Mughal † of sorrow for thee, hath, against ḤAMĪD, risen.

LIV.

Whereas I discovered the science of the alchemy of love,
Therefore, this earthy form of mine hath sallow become.
When the fair, their spells and incantations commence,

They cast burthens upon the back of forbearance and control.

With prayers upon my lips, I fell in love in my heart

Verily, the lion hath devoured me, whilst seated by the hearth.

It heareth not the wails of the nightingale in the parterre;

For this reason the mountain partridge laugheth so loudly.

I have sunk down, to this degree, in the ocean of love,

That I remember not whether I am of the sea, or of the land.

So sore distressed am I, with dried up heart and humid eyes,

That Majnūn seemed insignificant and contemptible to me.

The bitterness of separation will not pass down my throat,

Notwithstanding I eat, along with it, the sugar of association.

Tears too, in the time of adversity, severed themselves from me

Alas, one's own, as well as strangers, are but prosperity's friends!

How wonderfully gorgeous thou makest simple things, OḤAMĪD!

May thy penetrating conceptions never come under the evil eye!

LV.

When a superior entereth into contention with an inferior,

Through folly, he exchangeth a shawl for a woollen blanket.

He who calleth another, the son of a dog, is, himself, a dog;

For the son of a man affiliateth not another on a dog.

Than this, that at a dog thou shouldst fling a stone or a clod,

It is far better, that thou shouldst throw him a cake of bread.

Now, out upon such like name and indication,

That may set up for thee the staff of injury and ill!

The acts of youth cannot be practised in old age

Therefore, old woman! with gilded paper ornament not thy head. *

Every proceeding harmonizeth with its own proper season—

White hair suiteth not for side locks, nor for back ones either. †

Plodding about in the world, is of no advantage whatever—

Then what have I to do with the embraces of this old hag?

Let not the inferior sit in the dwelling of the superior!

Let not wool be vended at the market price of silk!

Since, unto such pure white admonitions, it giveth utterance,

God forbid that the tongue of HAMĪD should falter ever!

LVI.

Since thou art occupied in giving ear unto envy and covetousness,

Tho' thou shouldst the possessor of treasures become, a poor beggar art thou.

Sovereignty and dominion shall follow thee, like a shadow,

If thou art content, like the Ḥumā, upon dry bones to live. *

Wherefore then, cast away life and faith, for the sake of the belly?

Why, O why! dost thou, broken-down-asses, upon roses graze?

Like unto dogs, that circle round about the putrid carcass,

Thus thou, for protection, to worthy and unworthy payest court.

Thy human nature will become that of the dog by this covetousness;

Therefore, guard well thy integrity by patience, if thou art wise.

Greediness and envy will bring such calamities upon thee

As may never have befallen any one—so hereafter wilt thou say.

Safety from Hell's burning flames, cannot be effected by this,

That thou shouldst gay clothes don, eat delicacies, and extol thyself.

In this world, restrain thy violent passions by devotion and piety,

If thou entertain the desire of salvation, in the world to come.

Since in love, thou endurest such an amount of affliction,

Thou form of ḤAMĪD! what a terrible calamity art thou!

LVII.

God forbid that the mouths of affliction be opened on any one;

For these mouths, in agony, are the very mouths of dragons!

That which, very speedily, levelleth the strong fortress with the plain,

Is either the evil mouths of cannon, or the mouths of enmity.

Tremble at the words from a single mouth of the oppressed,

Tho' a thousand tongues may offer prayers for thy long life.

When the blast of the sigh of the woe-begone reacheth them,

It filleth, with ashes and dust, the mouths of flattery and deceit.

Whom the inflammation of deep-drawn sighs shall strike,

The mouths of that person's wounds shall never, never close.

Have those folks made sweet with words those speaking mouths,

Which, to charm, have the power of the mouṭh of the Messiah?

When it receiveth the blow of the injuries of the oppressed,

The soundest mouth is more useless made, than a hole in a wall.

O, where are those tongues, so enchanting and bewitching,

Which make the mouths of denial, in confession, to assent!

Now, thou hast laid the hand of silence upon thy tongue,

Since thou, O mouth! didst feel the blow of the fist of reply.

The morning shall not dawn upon their night of sorrow,

Against whom, every morning, mouths maledictions utter.

ḤAMĪD hath thus torn to pieces the slanderous world,

Like the hungry dogs, when they place their mouths to the game

LVIII.

Thou meltest me, every moment, in a hundred ways;

But thou showest not, unto me, the tinge of attachment.

All unprofitably, during the reign of thy tyrannical beauty,

Anchorites bring under cultivation patience and austerity.

To the sight, become manifest, in every wrinkle of thy brow,

The signs and portents of the torments of the judgment-day.

Who, with thy sanguinary eyes, may contract acquaintance,

In their families will be woe and misery for evermore.

Whereas, I go about searching every portal and gateway,

I seek the threshold of the door of thy dwelling to find.

How shall I bring myself before the sword of thy countenance,

When the mirror, itself, recoileth from the edge of it?

Since, the "Night of Power" of thy curls became its portion, *

What night-watching is fallen to the good fortune of the comb!

I, ḤAMĪD, twist and twine myself about, unavailingly,

Like unto a serpent on the treasure of the faces of the fair. †

LIX.

Although on thy sitting and rising thou mayest be hailed "Thy sacrifice;" ‡

Yet, when thou sittest at another's door, thou sprawlest on the stake.

Account not this lowliness humiliation; for it is, truly, wealth,

That upon thine own mat, poor and distressed, thou reclinest.

Out upon that rising, and that sitting, though it be upon a throne,

That ever sitteth down in enmity, and, in animosity, ariseth!

From the head of that *masnad*, * thou wilt contemptible arise,

Shouldst thou press, like a burden, on the heads of the poor.

By pity and sympathy, strive to gain the hearts of people,

If, like the taper, thou wouldst sit pre-eminent, all others above.

Wherefore dost thou not tremble at seeing the tears of the oppressed?

Why sittest thou tranquil and undisturbed, on the face of the flood?

Regard him not, who neither himself consumeth, nor bestoweth on others,

That thus, like unto a serpent, upon a hidden treasure reclineth.

This world is neither the abode of stability, nor of peaceful repose;

Yet still, foolishly, thou standest fast at the bridge's head.

The ruby of honour and fame, O Ḥamīd! thou wilt acquire,

If, in meekness, with the poor and humble, thou sittest in the dust.

LX.

Like as thou art all powerful over me, so is thy guardian;

For although he is the dog of thy door, he is the master of me.

Though he may do me a thousand injuries, I will not return them—

For thy sake, civility towards him, is expedient unto me.

Whatever wrongs thy heart desireth, heap them upon my head;

Since every thing improper of thine, is meet and proper for me.

Though thy coldness drew out the very breath from my body,

What matter, since solicitude for thy love, is a substitute for it?

At the yearnings of this maddened heart, I am confounded;

For I know not, in the least, what thing it desireth from thee.

Even in association, it weepeth on account of separation

What wonderful dignity hath it been the heart's fortune to acquire!

Now, taking thy love into account; again, considering its tyranny;

At one breath the heart is impetuous, and at another it is repentant.

May the Almighty keep the thoughts of thee, ever present in my breast!

Then what mattereth it, whether thy face may present, or absent be?

Though Ḥamīd, from the beloved, desireth the hand of society;

Yet what poor beggar hath a patent of nobility acquired?

Footnotes

87:* A prelate, a doctor learned in the law, a venerable old man.

87:† A priest, a learned man.

88:* The term "placing the hand on the hip," is similar to one's scratching his head, or putting his finger in his mouth, when entirely at a loss what to do.

90:* See Raḥmān, Poem XIX., first note.

90:† The chikor is the bartavelle or Greek partridge; and the redness of its legs refers to the custom amongst Muḥammadans of dyeing the hands and feet, by young people, on festive occasions; and is a symbol of joy.

90:‡ Potiphar's wife.

91:* Referring to the hateful rule of the Mughal Emperors of Hindūstān, from the days of Bābar to the foundation of the Afghān monarchy by Aḥmad Shāh, which all Afghāns cry out against.

92:* Yaman—Arabia Felix, celebrated throughout the East for its tulips and its rubies.

92:† A country of Chinese Tartary, famous for its musk, and the beauty of its women.

94:* The Persian Gulf.

95:* See note at page 48.

96:* Oriental anime, or species of amber, which has the virtue of attracting straws.

96:† This refers particularly to Afghān mothers very often becoming the innocent cause of the death of their infants, from falling asleep whilst giving suck at night, and the nipple being in the infant's mouth, the weight of the breast itself suffocates the child.

97:* Rustam—the Persian Hercules, and the hero of the celebrated epic poem of the Shāh Nāmah by Firdousī.

99:* The tulip is considered the frailest flower of the garden.

99:† Children, in Afghānistān, when they see wild geese, run after them crying out to give them a cup.

99:‡ The rose is said to be laughing when it is wet with the drops or tears of dew, which is unreasonable; for by the dew's moisture, the rose's garment, which, as a bud, was gathered together, becomes rent or full- blown.

102:* It is supposed that the complaints and the curses of the oppressed are most effective at the dawn of day.

102:† See note at page 39.

103:* See note at page 29.

104:* The Father of Rivers—the Afg͟hān name for the Indus.

105:* See second note at page 26.

105:† See note at page 80.

107:* Anointing the eyelids with antimony on festive occasions, and also to increase their blackness.

107:† Green is the mourning colour of Muḥammadan countries.

109:* See second note at page 26.

109:† It is the custom to stick up a piece of a broken black pot in melon grounds, to avert the evil eye, in the same manner as they raise up scarecrows in England to keep the birds away.

112:* Referring to public dancing in the East, the occupation of a certain class of females, and confined to them only.

114:* The infernal tree mentioned in the Ḳur'ān, the fruit of which is supposed to be the heads of devils.

116:* The fixed, staring eye of the locust, is an emblem of immodest eyes, that never look down.

118:* They say, in the East, that pearls are formed by the oyster receiving a single drop of rain-water in its shell.

119:* Yaman—Arabia Felix, said to be famous for its rubies.

119:† See note, page 29.

122:* There is a certain fly or beetle that skims along the surface of the water, and is difficult to strike; hence the doing of any absurd or useless thing, is like attempting to strike it.

123:* The name of a tribe of Tartars, residing to the north of Bālkh, notorious robbers.

123:† From the pinnacle of heaven to the bottom of the uttermost abyss. According to Muḥammadan theories, the earth is supported by a fish.

123:‡ Jamāl Khān, of the tribe of Mohmand and clan of Khudrzī, about the year H. 1122 (A.D. 1711), during the governorship of Nāsir Khān, Ṣūbah-dār of Kābul, was raised to the chieftainship of his clan, during which time he plundered and destroyed the village of Æsau, one of his own tribe. About this time, the marriage of Jalāl, son of Jamāl, was about to be celebrated; and the Ṣūbah-dār himself sent the sum of two thousand rupees towards its expenses. Æsau, however, bent upon taking revenge, and Jamāl's clan being weak in proportion to his own, he sent his spies to bring him intelligence when his enemy should be occupied in his son's nuptial ceremonies, to fall upon him. On the night of the marriage, therefore, he assembled his friends and clansmen, and came upon Jamal's village. Jamul, though totally unprepared for such an attack, came out to meet his enemies; but having been badly wounded, he had to seek shelter within the walls of his own dwelling. On this, Æsau set it on fire; and Jamal, with his son and family, and the parties assembled at the celebration of the wedding, to the amount of upwards of eighty men, women, and children, were consumed. According to the Poet Hallman, Gul Khān was the only friend who stood by Jamal on this occasion, and was burnt to death along with the others; thus proving his friendship by the sacrifice of his life. Æsau was of the same tribe as Ḥamīd himself; and the poem above seems to have been written in reply to one by Raḥmān, who takes the part of Jamal, by way of defending Æsau.

125:* The name of an Indian tree (Ficus Indica.)

126:* Alluding to Gul Khān and others, mentioned in preceding note.

126:† See note at page 123.

126:‡ Referring to the hollowness of the heavens, as apparent to us.

127:* Darweshes and Faḳīrs carry a bowl, in which they receive alms.

127:† See second note at page 26.

128:* What chemists term "killing mercury."

129:* The name of one of the two grand divisions of the Afghān tribes, inhabiting the tracts about Peshāwar, and to the north.

129:† Canaan.

129:‡ A plant bearing a red berry, the ranunculus or crowfoot.

129:§ The Turks or Scythians have generally fine countenances and large dark eyes, hence the Muḥammadan poets make frequent use of the word to express beautiful youth of both sexes.

129:§§ There is an insect called an ant by the Afghāns, which, on its wings appearing in the spring, comes forth and falls a prey to the birds.

129:** The name of the negro *mu'aẓẓain* or crier, who announced unto the people when Muḥammad prayed.

130:* See first note at page 129.

131:* Children in Afghānistān ride on a long reed for a horse, as they do in England upon a stick.

131:† That is to say, what is foreign is good.

132:* A district of Chinese Tartary, famous for its musk.

132:† The composition of poetry is termed, stringing pearls.

134:* A fabulous mountain, supposed to surround the world, and bound the horizon.

135:* See note at page 48.

135:† Figuratively, a tyrant. See note at page 91.

136:* Women in Afghānistān ornament their hair by sticking patches of gilt paper in it, on festive occasions in particular, if they do not possess ornaments more substantial, in the shape of golden ducats.

136:† The hair of young females is either plaited into numerous small plaits, or divided into three large ones, one on each side of the head, and the other hanging down the back.

137:* The Humā is a fabulous bird of happy omen, peculiar to the East. It exists on dry bones; never alights; and it is supposed that every head it overshadows will, in time, wear a crown. See ATTILA, by the late G. P. R. James, Chap. VI.

139:* Laylatu-l-ḳadr, or shab-i-ḳadr—the night of power—is the 27th of the month Ramaẓān, and is greatly revered on many accounts, but more particularly as being the night on which the Kur'ān began to descend from heaven. On its anniversary, all orthodox Muḥammadans employ themselves throughout the night in fervent prayer, imagining that every supplication to the Omnipotent, then put up, will be favourably received.

139:† Every buried treasure is supposed to be guarded by a serpent or a dragon.

139:‡ "I am thy sacrifice"—a respectful and endearing form of answer, in use amongst the Afghāns, Persians, and others.

140:* A carpet and cushion at the upper part of a room, and accounted the seat of honour; but it generally refers to the large cushion which kings sit on as a throne.

KHUSHḤĀL KHAN, KHATTAK.

KHUSHḤĀL KHĀN, the renowned chieftain of the powerful Afghān tribe of Khattak—alike a warrior and a poet—was born in the year 1022 of the Hijrah (A.D. 1613). Shāh-bāz Khān, his father, having received a wound in a battle with the Yūsufzīs—one of the most numerous and powerful of all the Afghān tribes—from the effects of which he shortly after died, Khushḥāl, who had also been severely wounded in the head and knee, in the same battle, in the year H. 1050 (A.D.1640), with the unanimous consent and approbation of his relations and friends, became chief of his tribe. His father's fief was confirmed to him by the Mughal Emperor, Shāh Jahān, together with the charge of protecting the royal road from Attak, on the Indus, to Pes'hāwar; and other duties were entrusted to him by that sovereign, in whose estimation Khushḥāl stood high. He accompanied Ṣulṭān Murād Baksh, the son of that monarch, on his expedition to Badakhshān in 1645, and was also engaged in other wars of that period.

On the death of Shāh Jahān, Khushḥāl continued to serve his son and successor, Aurangzeb, in the same capacity as formerly; but after some time, through the machinations of his enemies, among whom was Amīr Khān, Ṣūbah-dār, or governor of the province of Kabūl, he fell under the displeasure, or rather suspicion of the monarch, and was sent prisoner to the strong hill fortress of Gwalior, in Upper India, where he remained in captivity about seven years; and there it was that many of the following poems were written. At length, at the recommendation of Muḥabbat Khān, the second of that name, Aurangzeb released

Khushhāl, and sent him, along with the noble just referred to—who had been lately appointed Ṣūbah-dār of Kabūl—for the purpose of settling the affairs of the Pes'hāwar district, which had fallen into a very distracted state. But the iron had entered the soul of Khushhāl, and on reaching his native country, he kept as retired as possible; ceased to hold any intercourse with the governor of the province, and other subordinate officers; and declined rendering any assistance to the troops of the Emperor.

Khushhāl's tribe had been long at feud with many of the other Afghāns around Pes'hāwar, amongst whom were the Yūsufzīs—fighting against whom, as before mentioned, his father lost his life—and was generally engaged in hostilities with one or other of them; but with the Afrīdīs, who were also powerful, the Khattaks maintained a close alliance. Matters, at length, went so far between the Khattak chieftain and the Mughal authorities, as to produce an open rupture. Khushhāl now girded his loins with the sword of courage; and in concert with Ae-mal Khān, and Dar-yā Khān, chiefs of the Afrīdīs, carried on, for seven or eight years, a determined and destructive war with the Mughals, in which the latter were generally defeated.

The whole of the Afghān tribes from Banū to Jalālābād, seeing the success of their countrymen over the hated Mughals, had been drawn, by degrees, into the confederacy, which now aimed at no less than the total expulsion of the Mughals from Afghānistān. But the Yūsufzīs, who could have aided so effectually, held aloof; mid would render no assistance to their countrymen, through enmity to the Khattaks, notwithstanding that Khushhāl went in person, even as far as the Suwāt valley, to endeavour to instil into them some of his own and his confederates' patriotic spirit, but without effect—they were deaf to the voice of the charmer. These events he refers to, in the first of the following poems, written on that occasion.

Affairs at Pes'hāwar had assumed such a serious aspect, that Aurangzeb considered it necessary to appear in person on the scene; and for about two years he remained encamped at Attak, superintending the prosecution of the war; and that wily monarch, finding force unavailable in such a difficult country, began to try the effect of gold. In this he met with the success he desired; and some of the petty clans of the confederacy became fascinated with the gold of the Mughals, and submitted to the government; whilst others of Khushhāl's friends began either to desert him, or to give him cause to doubt their sincerity; and Ae-mal Khān and Dar-yā Khān, his most powerful, and most trusty supporters, having previously been removed, by death, from the scene, such an effect was produced upon the fine spirit of Khushhāl—as the following pages testify—that he became disgusted, and sought to find peace in retirement.

At length, he resigned the chieftainship of the Khattak tribe, in favour of his eldest son Ashraf, and devoted himself to books and literature. On Ashraf's becoming chief of the clan, Bahrām, another son, who appears to have been always regarded with aversion by his father for his degenerate acts, succeeded in gaining over a considerable party to his side, and appeared bent upon bringing misfortune upon his brother. They met in battle several times; and on one occasion, Bahrām was taken prisoner, but succeeded, by his artfulness and duplicity, in exciting the pity of his injured brother, who set him at liberty. Khushḥāl, well aware of the disposition of Bahrām, was highly incensed with Ashraf for allowing him to escape so easily, and, as it turned out, not without reason; for no sooner was Bahrām free, than he again commenced his intrigues against Ashraf; and at length, in the year H. 1093 (A.D. 1681), he succeeded in betraying him into the hands of the Mughals. Aurangzeb sent him prisoner to the strong fortress of Bejāpūr, in Southern India, where, after lingering in captivity for about ten years, he died. A further account of this unfortunate chieftain, will be found prefixed to his poems; for, like other sons of Khushḥāl, as well as numbers of his descendants, he was a poet as well as his father.

Afẓal Khān, the young son of Ashraf, now took up arms in his father's cause, and was installed in the chieftainship by his grandfather, who was still regarded as their natural and rightful chief, by the majority of the tribe; but the youth and inexperience of Afẓal—for he was only seventeen years of age—could not yet cope with the wily Bahrām, who was also aided and upheld by the Mughals. Khushḥāl, therefore, taking Afẓal's youth into consideration, and in order to prevent his clansmen from shedding the blood of each other, interfered between the contending parties, fearing that the tribe might hesitate to obey one of such inexperience, and allowed Bahrām to enjoy the chieftainship, advising Afẓal to bide his time, and not lengthen his father's captivity by opposition for the present. Afẓal, therefore, retired with his family into the friendly country of the Afrīdīs.

Not content with this success in all his schemes, Bahrām would not allow his aged father to end his days in peace. Several times he made attempts upon his life. He once despatched his son Mukarram Khān, with a body of troops, to endeavour to secure the old man's person. Mukarram went, as directed, against his grandfather; but the brave old chieftain, who had attained his 77th year, having discovered the party from the place of his retreat, advanced to meet them with his drawn sword in his hand, at the same time—to quote the words of Afẓal Khān, his grandson, already alluded to, who subsequently wrote a history of these events—exclaiming, "Whoever are men amongst you, come to the sword, if you dare; but veneration for the aged chieftain was so predominant in every one's breast, that no one would make any attempt to lay hands on him;" and Mukarram, ashamed, returned as he went. Bahrām, his father, enraged at his son's failure, ordered him to return, with directions to kill Khushḥāl with his own hand, if he should refuse to deliver himself up. On Mukarram's return, to carry out this inhuman order of a degenerate son, the old chief again advanced from his place of shelter, and taking his stand upon the crest of the hill, with his good sword in his hand, again dared them to approach; and in this manner is said to have remained on the watch for several days. But no one amongst the party had either the inclination or the courage to face him, whom they still regarded as their natural chief.

Bahrām, however, thinking the prey in his toils, had despatched a message to the Mughal governor at Pes'hāwar, to the effect that the old lion was at length at bay; and requested him to send a sufficient escort to take charge of him, and conduct him to Pes'hāwar. Khushḥāl, however, having been warned, as soon as night set in, made his escape, after two of Bahrām's party had lost their lives, and by the next morning succeeded in reaching the boundary of the Afrīdī tribe—who had always been his friends—a distance of 90 miles from Akorrah, the scene of the occurrences just related.

Khushḥāl took up his residence in the Afrīdī country, and returned no more to the home of his fathers, which he loved so well. He died as he had lived, free, among the mountains of his native land, in the 78th year of his age. Before taking his departure from a world, in which he had drunk so deeply of the bitter cup of treachery and unfaithfulness, he particularly charged those few of his children and friends, who had remained faithful to him through all his trials and misfortunes, that they should bury him where—to use his own words—"the dust of the hoofs of the Mughal cavalry might not light upon his grave;" and that "they should carefully conceal his last resting-place, lest the Mughals might seek it out, and insult the ashes of him, at whose name, whilst in life, they quailed; and by whose sword, and that of his clansmen, their best troops had been scattered like chaff before the gale." A third request was, that in case any of his faithful children should succeed, at any time, in laying hands upon Bahrām the Malignant, they should, divide his body into two parts, and should burn one half at the head of his grave, and the other at the foot. He was buried, accordingly, at a place named I-surraey, a small hamlet in the Khattak mountains, where his tomb may still be seen; and, according to his dying request, his last resting-place was kept concealed, till all danger of insult from the Mughals had passed away.

Khushḥāl Khān was the father of fifty-seven sons, besides several daughters; but, with the exception of four or five of the former, they do not appear to have been particularly worthy of their parent's affection.

Khushḥāl, from all accounts, was a voluminous author, and is said to have composed about three hundred and fifty different works. This, however, must be greatly exaggerated; nevertheless, he is the author of numerous works, which I have myself seen, both in Persian, and in the Pus'hto, or Afghān, consisting of Poetry, Medicine, Ethics, Religious Jurisprudence, Philosophy, Falconry, etc., together with an account of the events of his own chequered life. It is greatly to be regretted, however, that his descendants, after his death, had not the opportunity to collect all his writings together; and the upshot is, that many are known only by name. Amongst those which have thus been lost or dispersed is, I fear, the autobiography I have referred to.

Some of Khushḥāl's poetical effusions, written during his exile in India, and whilst struggling against the power of Aurangzeb, will, I think, be considered highly of, even in the form of a literal translation, and in an English dress, as coming from the pen of an Afghān chief, cotemporary with the times of our Charles I., evincing, as they do, a spirit of patriotism, and love of hone and country, not usual in the Oriental heart, but such as we might look for in the Scottish Highlander, or Swiss mountaineer, of bygone days, whom the hardy Afghāns strongly resemble. A more extended account of Khushḥāl's writings, and those of his descendants, will be found in the Introductory Chapter to my Afghān Grammar, published last year, together with an account of the Afghāns and their literature.

Up to the time of Khushḥāl's chieftainship, the bounds of the Khattak country were not well defined; that is to say, each family of the tribe had no fixed lands allotted to them.Khushḥāl caused a survey to be made of all available land; fixed the boundaries; entered them in a register; and, according to the number of each man's family, assigned a corresponding quantity of land for cultivation. This arrangement is still in force, and hitherto has not, that I am aware of, been deviated from; and many small towers of stone, erected to mark the different boundaries, still remain.

THE POEMS OF KHUSHḤĀL KHĀN, KHATTAK.

I.

AN ODE TO SPRING.

FROM whence hath the spring again returned unto us,

Which hath made the country round a garden of flowers?

There are the anemone and sweet basil, the lily and thyme;

The jasmine and white rose, the narcissus and pomegranate blossom.

The wild flowers of spring are manifold, and of every hue;

But the dark-red tulip, above them all, predominateth.

The maidens place nosegays of flowers in their bosoms;

The youths, too, fasten bouquets of them in their turbans.

Come now, musician! apply the bow to thy violin:

Bring out the tone and the melody of every string!

And thou, cupbearer! bring us full and overflowing cups,

That I may become fraught with wine's inebriety!

The Afghān youths have again dyed red their hands,

Like as the falcon dyeth his talons in the blood of the quarry.

They have made rosy their bright swords with gore:

The tulip-bed hath blossomed, even in the heat of summer.

Ae-mal Khān and Dar-yā Khān—from death preserve them! *

Were neither of them, at fault, when opportunity occurred.

They dyed red the valley of Khaibar, with the blood of the foe:

On Karrapah, † too, they poured forth war's din and tumult.

From Karrapah, even unto Bājawrr, ‡ both plain and mountain,

Time after time, as from an earthquake, quaked and shook.

It is now the fifth year, since in this neighbourhood,

Every day heareth the clashing of glittering swords.

Since I arrived in this part, § I have become a nonentity—

Either I am despicable, or this people are infamous grown.

I cry out unto them, "Troops, troops," until I am weary;

But deaf to all, they neither say "Die," nor "Thy sacrifice." §§

When the state of the Yūsufzīs became known unto me,

Lowāghar was then my better place, not Damghār.

The dogs of the Khattaks are far better than the Yūsufzīs,

Though, in disposition, the Khattaks are more worthless than dogs.

The whole of the other Afghāns, from Ḳandahār unto Attak,

In honour's cause, both secretly and openly, are one.

See how many battles have been fought on all sides;

Yet still, amongst the Yūsufzīs, there is no sense of shame.

The first fight was at the higher back of Mount Tatārah, *

Where forty thousand Mughals were scattered like chaff.

When their sisters and daughters fell into the bonds of the Afghāns,

With horses and camels, elephants and baggage, string after string.

The second battle was with Mir Husain in the Doābah, †

When his head was crushed, like that of a venemous snake.

After that again, was the affair at the fort of Nohs'hairah, ‡

When from the Mughals I extracted my own inebriation.

And then came Jaswant Singh and Shujaæat Khān,

Of whom, Ae-mal Khān plucked up the roots at Gandāb.

The sixth was over Mukarram Khān and Shamsher Khān,

Both of whom, at Khāpash, Ae-mal scattered to the winds.

These are the greatest triumphs that I hold in recollection;

But the lesser ones, in all directions, who shall compute?

Up to the present time, victory hath been always with us;

And for the future, upon God, is our dependence placed.

A year hath passed since Aurangzeb is encamped against us,

Disordered and perplexed in appearance, and wounded in heart.

It is now year after year, that his nobles fall in battle;

But his armies swept away, who shall number them!

The treasures of India have been spread out before us:

The red gold *muhurs* have been engulphed in the hills.

It would not have entered one's head in eighteen guesses,

That such events would e'er have happened in these parts.

Still Aurangzeb's malevolence hath not a whit diminished,

Though the curses of his father it before drew down. *

For this reason, also, no one can place dependence on him:

He is malignant and perfidious; a breaker of his word.

For this state of things, no other termination can be seen,

Than that the Mughals be annihilated, or the Afghāns undone.

If this, which is beheld, be the revolutions of destiny—

If in this be the will of the Almighty, the time is come.

Fate revolveth not in the same fashion at all times

Now 'tis propitious to the rose; now favourable to the thorn.

At a period so pregnant with honour and glory, as the present,

In what manner do these base and recreant Afghāns act? †

There is no deliverance in any thing, save the sword:

Afghāns, who nourish any other idea than this, are lost, indeed.

The Afghāns are far superior to the Mughals at the sword,

Were but the Afghāns, in intellect, a little discreet.

If the different tribes would but support each other,

Kings would have to bow down in prostration before them.

But whether it be concord or strife, or folly or wisdom,

The affairs of every one are in the hands of the Almighty.

Let us see what the Afrīdīs, Mohmands, and Shīnwāris will do;

For the Mughals are now lying encamped at Nangrahār. *

I alone, amongst the Afghāns, grieve for our honour and renown;

Whilst the Yūsufzīs, at their ease, are tilling their fields.

They who now act so dishonourably, and so shamelessly,

Will, hereafter, the upshot of their own acts perceive.

In my poor judgment, death is more preferable than life,

When existence can no longer, with honour, be enjoyed.

In this world, he will not always remain with life;

But the memory of KHUSHḤĀL will long, long endure!

It was the first of the Third Sister, † in the year of Ghafū ‡

That I, whilst at Barmawul, indited these lines.

II.

What wonderfully delicious wine is this,

Which the cupbearer, with welcome, presents!

The laughing of the bud in the parterre were impossible,
Did not the zephyr, every morning, over it pass.
Its counsel regarding the nightingale was this,
That the morn should the rosebud's garment rend. §
Appreciate thou the value of Philomel, O rose,
Although thou bloomest in this thy beauty now!
Since his cure dependeth upon the object of his heart,
Of the lover's disease, what do physicians know?
Save the beloved-one's beaming countenance, imagine not
That KHUSHḤĀL will be, with any other face, content.

III.

Spring hath returned: the narcissus in the garden wantoneth,
And the breeze of the morning, the spikenard disordereth.
For five short days, the rose of the parterre will bloom;
But on the sixth, it scattereth its existence to the winds.
The enamoured nightingale layeth its head at the rose's feet,
As the Brahman bendeth, in adoration, his idol before.
Acquire thou humility from the example of the cypress,
That with such loftiness, showeth this much lowliness.
The KARLĀRRNAEY * hath quaffed no other wine whatever—
The whole of this inebriety proceedeth from creation's cup. †

IV.

My beloved is offended: would there were any one who would conciliate her!

Arise quickly, O mediator! for my heart is grieved on her account.

He will be constantly plunging into the deep seas of injustice,

Who rendereth up his heart unto the heart-ravishers of these days.

What a vile world it is! what are its customs! what its ways!

It abandoneth, altogether, the starving, and giveth invitation to the cloyed!

Punished they cannot be; but would I could lay hands, as I wish, on them;

For 'tis those sable locks of thine, that are ever of hearts making theft.

The tyranny of thy dark tresses is by no means hidden from view—

The impassioned-one, who may be powerful, soon her tyranny displayeth.

Thou that givest thyself unto the tender passion, accept in love

The taunts and reproaches, that the world, upon lovers, ever cast.

Thy blood-thirsty locks have not made me, only, desolate;

And many more, like unto me, forlorn, will they, even yet, destroy.

Wouldst thou, this one so arrogant of her beauty see, draw near!

Alas! towards KHUSHḤĀL, her coquetry she openly displayeth.

V.

Wherefore doth Aurangzeb his throne and crown adorn?

For death will assail, and lay waste the both of them.

His evil name only will remain behind in the world;

Knowing, as he doth, whether he as Kasrā, or as Hujāj acteth. *

O'erwhelmed in grief, I know not of festival or feast,

Though the whole people of Dilhī make gladness and joy.

All the water went to the eyes, and the heart's fire blazed out—

Alas, how can any one, in such a state of mind as this exist!

They turn pale when they lay finger upon my pulse;

Then, by what means, can the physicians, my disorder cure?

Separation lacerateth my heart in the same manner,

As the falcon rendeth the partridge and the quail.

When two friends may be separated by a distant land,

How desirous God maketh them of a mere salutation!

My tears are produced through the emotions of the heart,

Like as fire expelleth the moisture from the roasting meat.

Alas, every arrow that is discharged from fatality's bow,

Destiny maketh poor KHUSHḤĀL'S heart the butt of!

VI.

Thou wast saying, "Grieve not any more; for I am thine, and thou art mine:"

Whether thou hast falsely or truly spoken, thou hast, indeed, given me life again.

What a lovely calamity thou art! a charmer, incomparable, art thou!

Would that there were not this defect, that thou hadst not such a cruel heart!

Should the whole universe, in every direction, be with the lovely filled;

Even then, it would be astonishing, if one were found beautiful like thee.

With so many victims slain, even yet thou showiest no pity or regret:

But what matter, though the executioner shed blood a hundred times over?

Since out of thy garden, or thy parterre, I beg for a rose from thee,
Shouldst thou but a straw on me bestow, yet I, as a rose, receive it.
As long as I may exist, I am, indeed, the captive of those ringlets,
In every hair of which, hundreds of hearts will ever be enthralled.
Whether old, or whether young, all are distracted about thee:
There is not a person in the town, that is not enamoured of thee.
The cypress-tree behold! it very soon ceaseth to be looked upon,
When thou, with this stature and figure, through the garden trippest.
The prospect of Heaven to come, is bliss to both monk and priest;
But KHUSHHĀL hath gained Paradise, at once, in meeting thee.

VII.

Again the minstrel's rebeck toucheth the heart profoundly;
For it discovereth new and fresh strains of melodious harmony.
Leave the monk in the monastery's nook! I will to the garden;
For the flowers of spring instruct me in righteousness' ways.
Beggars have much anxiety about filling their bellies;
And kings should be solicitous regarding dominion and realm.
If this be not the effect of my good fortune, what is it then,
That against the guardian she crieth out to this degree?
How much more will be the extent of the love of her constancy,
When, in injustice and inconstancy, such favour she bestoweth?
Within this city, the juice of the grape is thus so openly sold;

Because the censor, himself, favoureth the bibbers of wine.

From thy coldness to me, I grow both joyful and melancholy,

Like unto one that giveth thanks to, and yet complaineth of another.

If to love to look upon the pretty creatures be aught of sinfulness,

Then K͟HUS͟HḤĀL committeth iniquity, all his life long.

VIII.

When towards his father a son acteth perfidiously,

After what manner, to others, will he sincerity show?

See, what further perfidy must be within his heart,

When the hypocrite maketh avowal of his own misdeeds.

Neither will I pardon the enormities of the degenerate,

Nor will the Almighty forgive the fallen angel his sins.

All these minor hills are as nothing: desirous am I,

That my God, betwixt us, would place even Ḳāf * itself.

The conduct of his own son is best known to his father;

Then why will people commend the degenerate unto me?

Neither can any liar utter falsehoods like him,

Nor can any one equal him in cunning and deceit.

There are both a thousand varieties of vain lies in his heart,

And a thousand vaunts of morality upon his tongue.

That I cherished, and brought up such an undutiful son,

It was, alas! for this, that he should, against me, rise up!

Let me not, indeed, cast eyes upon him whilst I live;
And after death, let him not dare my grave to approach.
Sorrow and grief shall, whilst living, leave his heart,
If fate, unto K͟HUS͟HḤĀL, shall due justice grant.

IX.

Every sick person that is impatient with his physician,
Bringeth, if thou but consider, affliction upon himself.
The fish existeth in the river; but should it come out thereof,
Can it be comfortable, or at ease, upon the dry land?
Though the bat hideth himself from the light of the sun,
In what manner doth the sun sustain injury therefrom?
'Tis the nature of dogs to howl at the sight of the moon;
And thus, by their yelping, bring disgrace on themselves.
The dung-beetle is distressed by the flower's perfume;
Because its existence is sustained by offensiveness.
That the prophets are evil in the sight of the infidel,
Is, because whatever they do, is with the Devil's advice.
Unfortunate, indeed, is he, who acteth on his enemy's counsel:
Can an opponent and an enemy ever give good advice?
The heron, on the river's bank, is with thirst parched;
For every penurious creature followeth his own avaricious ways.
With the precepts of the Ḳur'ān, Fārūḳ is acquainted:

It pointeth not out the right path to Bū-Lḥab, or to Bū-Jhal. *

The purity of the Musalmān, O KHUSHḤĀL! is possible;

But no ablutions, no purifications, can make the Gabr * clean.

X.

Through sorrow at the poor-spiritedness of the Afghāns,

I have abandoned greatness, and taken meanness in hand.

Had this much even been gained in the matter, it were good—

Had I wreaked upon the recreant my full meed of revenge.

From the time when the jewel of my honour became broken,

I have not left, for a moment, my eyes free from tears.

That pearl came not into my hands, after all my trouble,

And, therefore, my boat I have drawn up on the sea-shore.

This waist of mine, that in resistance was a mountain,

Through chagrin and disappointment, unto the Mughal I bent.

But let good fortune once commence again to aid me,

That it may relieve me from the weight of affliction's load

This misery of mine is not to be compared to any other grief,

Although I may have experienced a thousand woes and sorrows.

The back of fortune, and. the world's, both are turned upon me;

Hence, through sorrow, I turned my face from all, the Mughal unto.

Were it in my power, or were it mine own free-will,

I would not, even two paces, towards them advance.

I am obliged to hearken to crooked words from the mouths of those,

Unto whom, in my lifetime, I never before a straight one gave.

The outcries of my own people, and of strangers, affect me,

Notwithstanding I used, even from a whisper, to screen myself.

I am now ashamed of those proud and boastful words,

That, before every one, were wont to issue from my lips.

A hundred reproaches and indignities are heaped upon me,

Who ever guarded myself from detraction and reproach.

'Tis for this reason the elephant streweth dust upon his head, *

That I made him acquainted with KHUSHḤĀL'S sorrows.

XI.

If, for once only, she will show her face from the veil,

She will take the diploma of beauty from the sun.

The tulip shall borrow bloom from her countenance;

The hyacinth will grow furious at the sight of her curls.

Wherefore Both the world accuse fortune thus falsely?

'Tis she, that with her eyes, hath desolated the world.

Either those orbs of hers are red from wine's effects,

Or some one hath roused her from sleep, unseasonably.

She quaffeth the blood of hearts in the place of wine;

Then again, taketh roasted hearts, as au incitement to more.

The special death of the slaughtered by the hand of the beloved,

Is that they may enter Paradise, without rendering account.

Let my heart be a compass, and let it never vary or turn

In any other direction, save the altar of thine eyebrows unto.

Do not be so overjoyed, O KHUSHHĀL! at all her vows;

For, from the bubble, no one hopeth for any constancy.

XII.

O zephyr of the morn! draw near unto the parterre;

For the flowers are overjoyed, in expectation of blooming.

What doth the hermit know, as to what thing love is?

Wherefore speakest thou to the owl, the garden concerning?

Though the monks perform their devotions five times a day,

I am ever prostrate, in devotion, unto the Giver of good.

As much as I behold thee, I do not become satiated,

Notwithstanding I gaze so intently upon thy face.

Again, indeed, place thou a scar on the anemone's heart,

When thou roamest in the garden, so joyous and gay.

Anger and kindness I perceive between thine eyebrows:

The tablet of thy forehead thou hast placed to be perused.

Sometimes, thou raisest strife; at others, showest kindness—

Simple hearted that I am, at such skill, I grow amazed.

If thou hast set thine heart upon my death, I too, say,

That thy tyranny hath brought me to death's door nigh.

XIII.

Draw near, and behold him now, with a clod beneath his head,
Who could not sleep upon a bed, without a pillow of feathers!
This, which they call the transient world, hath no existence, and is naught;
For this reason, O foolish man! 'tis hideous in the sight of the wise.
This world is a scabby sheep—then what good is there in keeping it?
The shepherd, when he findeth out its scabbiness, expelleth it from the flock.
Is this a tempest or hail-storm, that both standing corn and stacks also go?
Out upon such a corn-field as this, since an ear of corn can not be found!
With these eyes of mine, I have beheld the noble and massive structures of kings,
Who coveted the world's dominion, but left them, all at once, behind!
A hundred thousand squadrons assemble, and collect the treasures of the world;
Be as Sanjar * for a few generations, and then neither thou nor thy race remain.
Thy house is on the face of a flood, and this thy contemptible idea is still worse;
For no one would there his dwelling make, that it should be swept by the flood away.
Shouldst thou become a Shahdād * in the world, still calamity will remember thee;
And if here thou a Paradise preparest, of what profit is such an Aden † to thee?
He carried away along with him, this wealth ephemeral, O young man!
Who diffused it broadcast; but not they, that heaped it up for themselves.
I have beheld fortune's practices—its different usages and ways—
It clambereth unto thee with difficulty; but like a stone from a mountain, rolleth away!
If thou art foolish and imprudent, like unto Mir-bāz ‡ pursue it;

But if wise and prudent, like unto KHUSHHĀL, from it flee away!

XIV.

These dark waving curls, they are thine, thou dear one, so beautiful, so gay!

Black narcissuses are those eyes of thine, thou dear one, so beautiful, so gay!

When thou gavest me a kiss, I became intoxicated, beyond computation;

For like unto red wine are thy lips, thou dear one, so beautiful, so gay!

Now that I have with mine eyes gazed on this, thy lovely cheek,

I know that it is the tulip, thou dear one, so beautiful, so gay!

They, who murmur and complain unto others, of thy tyranny,

Are faithless and inconstant too, thou dear one, so beautiful, so gay!

Free of grief, how can he sleep—in tranquillity how shall he be,

Who is separated from thee? thou dear one, so beautiful, so gay!

He only will receive thy kisses, on whom thy affections may be,

Tho' many are enraptured with thee, thou dear one, so beautiful, so gay!

Thou wreakest injustice on me, then sayest, "This is not done by me"—

Then whose act is it, if not thine? thou dear one, so beautiful, so gay!

Thou sayest unto KHUSHHĀL, "There are others far prettier than I:"

Can there be one, than thee more lovely? thou dear one, so beautiful, so gay!

XV.

Wine's intoxication soon cometh, and as quickly disappeareth;

But the eternal inebriation leaveth not the inebriated one.

Tho', in the world, my name is become notorious for debauchery,

Still I will not abandon the ways of the bibbers of wine.

Though the king may cast him into prison, he will not grieve;

For the liberty of the free is from the beginning of time.

There is neither friendship nor relationship: all is deceit, I find,

Since I became acquainted with the ways and usages of mankind.

I am happy in hope of future joy, tho' now in sorrow plunged;

For the day ever followeth, in rotation, after the darkness of night.

The pearl of our yearnings lieth immersed in ocean's depths;

And after it, the divers plunge continually, into its dark abyss.

That fish, who may perceive danger from the sharp hook,

From the bottom to the shore, from prudence, will never look.

The thoughts of the lover's heart are like unto the deep, deep sea,

The billows of which, at times, rage in fury; at others, calmly sleep.

Affection for the beloved, from KHUSHHĀL'S heart, will never depart:

It is like unto the love of the idolater, for the idol of his worship.

XVI.

From out of the clear, azure flask,

O cupbearer! bring thou unto me

A full goblet of that potent wine,

The remedy for grief, the consoler in woe.

Speak not of the tributes of the world!

They cannot compare with one cup of wine:

Then, O censor, leave me and the wine, withal!

Tho' thereby my house should devastated be.

Become thou the beggar at the tavern's door,

If along with the crown, thou dominion seek:

The mart of the wine-bibbers is crowded,

From this extensive sale of wine.

Turning from the idol-temple to the monastery,

Is both an absurd and a useless act:

From the cupbearer, then take thou the glass;

For therein is much gladness and joy.

O cupbearer! let me ever behold thee—

Thou of the moon-like brow and sunny face!

Bring the crystal cup, to overflowing full,

And satisfy the yearnings of KHUSHḤĀL!

XVII.

Tho' the miser's house may contain the water of immortality;

Still, like unto the deadliest poison, is its effect on me.

Moses possessed nothing whatsoever, but one rod alone:

Ḳārūn had boundless wealth, and verily, calamity befell him. *

He who hath riches, with it hath vexation and misfortune mix'd up;

Hence the wise so act, that they may not their troubles increase.

The duration of the rose; the world's wealth; the mean man's friendship;

These three or four things are all inconstant and transitory.

He, who may neither possess modesty nor virtue, genius nor understanding,

Regard not his wealth, nor his beauty, nor his ancestral descent.

The wise man is in utter misery, whilst the fool reveleth in pleasure—

And well, indeed, may the world be amazed at such occurrences as these.

That he should continue happy all his life, and grief never assail him,

No one, into the world hath brought, a safe-conduct, such as this.

This is the way with fortune—some it maketh happy—some miserable;

And however clear now, the mirror will become cloudedhereafter.

Wherefore, then, trouble thyself! Be rejoiced at this, OKHUSHḤĀL!

That he, who hath neither riches nor wealth, hath neither pilgrimage to perform, nor taxes to pay.

XVIII.

Very many persons within my recollection,

Have come, and passed, like the wind away.

They, indeed, arrive and depart, in such a way,

That they appear to have no tarrying place at all.

It is an astonishing, and a vast workshop this,

That the Great Master hath organized, and set up.

Cast thine eyes upon the bubble in the stream!

What is it? and what its origin and its base?

Such art thou too, if thou canst understand:

An excellent example is demonstrated to thee.

Concerning thyself, thou knowest nothing:

Alas! alas! verily, thou knowest naught.

What are all thy grief and misery about?

And why becomest thou again overjoyed?

Since it is so very hard, O K͟HUS͟HḤĀL!

Is this thine heart, or is it but a lump of steel?

XIX.

Like unto the wind, every moment, life passeth away!

Let then every man have the remembrance of death ever before him!

Since the foundation of this life of his, is based upon the air,

Upon existence such as this, what reliance can be placed?

The dust of man is leavened with the water of mortality,

By the hand of Omnipotence kneaded, in the space of forty days. *

Both saints and prophets have, alike, gone down into the tomb—

Thou wouldst say, forsooth, that they had never existed at all.

If thou considerest it well, the term of life here is nothing:

No one hath attained in it the object of his desires and hopes.

If thou, indeed, seek life eternal, then I say unto thee,

War, for ever, with the infidels of the lusts of the flesh.

The prudent traveller, whose journey lieth before him,

Taketh provision with him, according to the length of the road.

Come, sever thine heart, O KHUSHḤĀL! from all extraneous things;

And in the hope of meeting Him, let it rejoice always!

XX.

The Almighty gave into my arms—and I am under obligation to the mediator *—

The fair-faced one, with the ruby lips, and the flowing sable tresses.

The beloved is kind and affectionate, and the consoler in every sorrow:

Should the guardian come, what will he do? neither grief nor concern have I.

Let them consume upon it, as a charm, to ward off evil from thy face;

For thy love is like unto fire, and thy lovers like unto wild rue † are.

These are not thy cheeks, nor are these thy dark flowing ringlets:

They're the fresh fibrils of the spikenard, that have fallen two roses upon.

I follow in her pursuit, in the hope that I may obtain, even one look;

But she casteth not her eyes behind; and, thus, along before me goeth.

If this much of thy affection is not good fortune, what is it then?

That when thou, upon KHUSHḤĀL, KHATTAK, smilest, the jealous weep.

XXI.

Unto the old man, who sigheth after youthfulness, say—

What is this? laughest thou at thy beard, old man?

Since in a year, it will have both youth and age,

Than the fate of man, that of the wild rue is better.

At times, he becometh so sated at table, that he cannot eat;

At others, he rolleth his eyes upon it, with greediness and voracity.

In their wishes, and in their words, and also in their proceedings,

The people of the world are doubtful and timid of each other.

With beard now grown white, why should I have fear of death;

When friends, in their prime, with beards black, have gone before me?

Him, under whose sway the whole of the earth's surface was,

Draw near, and behold now, in the surface of the earth!

This world's folks are like unto the moving sands, * if thou but consider;

For, in truth, they roll over, and upset each other, in the very same way.

With these eyes of mine, I have beheld the dread furnace of fate—

I KHUSHHĀL, myself, whom, like unto dried up verdure, it consumeth.

XXII.

Her sweet face took from me all thoughts of the wild white rose:

Her ringlets eradicated all consideration of the musk of China.

The curls of the pagan beauty became a cord about my neck: †

A thousand thanks, that she of my religion and faith divested me.

Although the folks offer up prayers for my patience and resignation,

Affection hath despoiled me of the "Amen," unto these supplications.

Save the lips of the beloved, I take no other name upon my tongue;

For love hath abstracted from me all other memory and recollection.

My heart, on that day became disgusted with my own life,

When the hard-hearted one took it, entirely, from me.

By what law, indeed, hath she deprived me of sleep and repose,

That I weep and lament, and sigh and bewail, all the night long?

Her two eyes are a falcon, and her waving locks are the king-feathers:

The falcon pounced on, and carried from me the pigeon of my heart.

At her coming, she used to bring with her comfort and consolation;

And by her departure, she would rob me of all tranquillity soever.

The flowers of the parterre hang down their heads, and this they say—

"The heart-ravisher hath appropriated to herself all admiration."

I was saying, I will consider, even yet, of some remedy for it;

When poor KHUSHHĀL, wholly withdrew his lacerated heart from me.

XXIII.

The skirt of fortune and prosperity cannot be seized by force!

Is the blind man without reproach, if he apply antimony to his eyes?

What is wealth, indeed? It is like unto a beautiful bride,

In an impotent-fellow's house, where her life is in torment.

Let it not be, that every bad rider should mount fortune's steed:

If it be ridden by any one, at least a good horseman let him be.

From a sorry, low-bred pony, another wretched one is produced;

'Tis from the high-bred horses of the course alone, that noble steeds come.

That into my dwelling, in the first place, such animals came,

My luck must have been bad, from the beginning of time.

These ponies are mere puppets—may confusion seize them!

They create disturbance and tumult in the stable continually.

Like unto a good and worthy son in his father's dwelling,

A treasure of silver and gold in his house is not to be compared.

O God! thou hast given me a numerous progeny, and I am thankful;

But let the fame of their goodness resound in every city and town!

They, who stir up enmity between brothers, are recreant and unworthy:

Would to heaven they had learnt good, or had learnt naught besides!

Give both thine ears and eyes unto the appeals of KHUSHHĀL;

Since Bahrām and Æābid * are, both of them, deaf and dumb!

XXIV.

It is the sweet spring time, and I am separated from my beloved!

Alas! alas! that thou passest away, O spring, without her!

Both the hills and the dales weep at the lover's state forlorn—

They are not from melted snow, those floods, that from the mountains flow.

It is the fire of wounded hearts, that hath enveloped the trees on the hills;

Hence, dense black smoke and flame arise, from the fir-tree and the plane.

Dost thou desire to become acquainted with the condition of the bereaved?

Behold then, that crane, which hath become separated from the flock!

It thus appeareth, that the world is a place of mourning and sorrow;

For the parrots have, with loud cries, green vestments donned. †

There are no other wailings besides—all are the wails of separation:

Draw near, if thou wouldst hear them from the rebeck's every string!

My disease lesseneth not—indeed, it increaseth every hour:

For God's sake, come speedily, O physician, that I may not die!

One, is death unto opponents—the other, is life unto beloved friends:

I swear, by heaven, that when lovers meet, both are brought about!

What though one still breathe, and is accounted among the living?

When the malady is yet without antidote, give up hopes of the sick.

Of mankind none remain—those that roam about are demons and devils;

Hence, they have no compassion for the agonies of the distressed.

Through love, alas! to this degree, wretched and miserable am I become,

That whether relations or strangers, they look not on KHUSHHĀL through shame.

XXV.

Although she quarreleth with me, by word of mouth—that dear one;

Yet in her heart, that dear one entertaineth much kindness for me.

When, with arms each other's necks around, she accompanieth me,

Verily, from my heart she removeth the rust-spot—that dear one.

There is no necessity for the sword—her coldness is sufficient,

If to compass my death should be the intent of that dear one.

Since she hath shown unto me the torch of her loveliness,

Upon it, another time, she will make me the moth—that dear one.

I am a poor beggar—she is a sovereign; hence it is becoming in her,

Even though she of my affection should feel ashamed—that dear one.

He, who may have turned Malang, * requireth but a carpet for prayer;

And in the end, too, a Malang will she make of me—that dear one.

With cheerful heart, she laugheth and smileth with every one besides;
But with me, indeed, she is mournful and sad—that dear one.
No gem-studded ornament hath she inserted in her nostril;
But with a single black clove she resteth satisfied—that dear one. †
Towards my opponents, her heart is gentle and soft as wax itself;
But towards K͟HUS͟HḤĀL, she hardeneth it like stone—that dear one.

XXVI.

Upon those lips of her's is there not a black hand-maid? ‡
Draw near! K͟hizr, § at the fountain of immortality behold!
The face of the beloved is rich, both in moles and in ringlets;
For in the house of the wealthy, every requirement will be found.
When their shade over-shadoweth me, I a king become;
For the shadow of thy dark curls is that of the Ḥumā itself. §§
Thy cheek is an enkindled flame—what then is thy braided hair?
It is like unto the dense black smoke, that from fire ascendeth.
The dust of those feet of thine, at the rate of amber thou vendest:
Who told thee that thou shouldst sell it at a price like this?
For how long wilt thou look another way, and appear unconscious,
When about me in every direction clamour and uproar arise?
It is through this loveliness that thou art beautiful like the rose,
If thou art, indeed, one of a father and a mother born.
He hath not the courage to take her name upon his tongue—.

The poor lover who feareth the censures and reproaches of the world.

I had given up wine, and had grown quite a penitent, indeed;

But the goblet of the cupbearer again put my contrition to flight.

He that placeth foot within her alley, bringeth destruction on himself;

Therefore, O unfortunate, into that vicinity do thou enter not!

Whether it were her coquetry, or her conceits, I could have borne them;

But towards me she manifesteth exceeding arrogance at all times.

The whole power of her mind hath she put forth against him;

And thereby hath deprived the poor lover of all energy and control.

When it may convey no significance, speaking is unprofitable;

But the Almighty willeth not that Khushḥāl's words be vain.

Since, on thy account, the black pupils of his eyes turned white,

Welcome unto me, O thou, of KHUSHḤĀL'S eyes, the light!

XXVII.

I am, indeed, a wine-bibber; then, wherefore, O monk! wranglest thou with me?

Men's destinies are from all eternity—would thou couldst like thyself make me!

Wisely thou counselest—a blessing, O monitor, be upon thy tongue!

But it were well, if by means of words, thou couldst the river's water disguise.

They, who possessed naught of sense or understanding, have gone to Heaven;

Whilst those, who prided themselves upon their wisdom, have gone to Hell.

Unto Abū-Jahl, * the precepts of Muḥammad were of no advantage soever;

For who can polish the mirror of him, whom God hath with rust corroded?

In loneliness and solitude seated, tell me, O monk! what thou gainest thereby?

Wherefore makest thou this wide and ample world, for thyself, so confined?

In every sect and religion, I, indeed, seek after the cause of the heart's sorrows;

But thou knowest, and thine own words know, the various tales thou tellest.

Draw near, thou minstrel! commence the song of the new year's day!

On rebeck, flute, and harp, strike up those thrilling strains of melody!

The flowers teem on all sides—there are tulips, narcissuses, and hyacinths too:

Thou attest unwisely, if thou purposest going in any other direction than to the parterre.

Some, taking with them much provision for the journey, set out to seek for her;

And others again, for her sake, bind the Santon's prayer-carpet round their loins.

O, that the scale of thy good deeds may be heavy at the judgment day!

For like wax shalt thou soften, towards the lover, his opponents' flinty hearts.

Though the whole of the armies of Dilhī have come to compass the death of K̲H̲US̲H̲ḤĀL;

Still, thou dost not consider thyself strong enough, and hangest back from shame.

XXVIII.

The world's affairs have all become turned upside down:

All those ways are not now, as they used to be seen by me.

Towards the father, the son showeth the actions of an enemy:

Towards the mother, the daughters are ready to act like rival wives.

In thine own house, there will not be two brothers together dwelling,

Who have not a thousand iniquities ready in their hearts.

The scavenger now feasteth on pulāo, * and rice, and sweetmeats;

And unclean things are become lawful, for Muḥammad's descendants.

The honoured and trusted of kings are now mere thieves become;

And in their royal courts, highway-robbers are grown trustworthy men.

The nightingales and the parrots fly about the wilds, astounded;

And crows and ravens caw and croak above the beds of flowers.

Babylonian steeds eke out an existence upon dry grass alone;

Whilst the tanner's asses receive a stipendiary allowance of provisions.

Fools, exempt from all care and anxiety, in tranquillity repose;

Whilst a hundred troubles and misfortunes, the prudent and the wise beset.

The meanest slave assumeth authority over his own proprietor;

And the slave-girls are more honourable than the mistress of the house.

Alas, O KHUSHHĀL! in the days of the Emperor Æālam-gīr, *

The house-born servants † have all a wretched and contemptible lot!

XXIX.

What numbers of boats in this river's depths have sunk and disappeared,

A single plank of which, even shouldst thou search, cannot be discovered!

Everywhere separation and absence have enkindled the flame of grief:

Like unto green wood thrown upon the fire, how long wilt thou weep?

Sorrow and joy—pain and pleasure—are, from the beginning, linked together;

And as much as one may have wept, so much even shall he rejoice again!

Many lofty minarets have I beheld, in their graceful symmetry standing;

But not a soul mentioned their names unto me, nor said unto whom they belonged.

The cares and troubles of the world are of a thousand varieties and forms;

And the summer skylarks trill and warble in a thousand different ways.

They are different, by far, from the cherished sentiments of my heart

The manifold rumours, that the folks bandy from one to the other.

This scroll is not the kind of thing, that it shall ever be brought to an end:

It is spread open, and examined into—it is read, and then rolled up again.

Thine own actions are of use to thee, both in this world and the next

Verily, the throat of every one is kept moist, by its own saliva.

The humblest fare, though barley-bread, unattended by care and trouble,

I will account more dainty than the viands, on the king's table outspread.

The ears of the reckless and imprudent are deaf—they cannot hear

The blunt, plain-spoken words from KHUSHḤĀL KHATTAK'Smouth.

XXX.

Every moment that a person may be thus in want of employment,

Than such, I hold him far better off, who is forced to labour for nothing. *

The sick and infirm, if they do not work, are to be excused;

But wherefore should not the hale man his living earn?

Even if thou mayest not have any employment of thine own;

Still, I say unto thee, sit not thus useless and unemployed.

Every amusement, by which care may be beguiled, is delight;

Whether it be chess, or backgammon, or the pleasures of the chase.

Every hour, and every moment, a man's state is different:

In one state unchangeable, is the Creator of the world alone.

Thy name, O KHUSHḤĀL, shall be remembered in the world;

For, in truth, thy employment is one great and mighty work!

XXXI.

Neither doth any one here seek to avail himself of my abilities and experience,

Nor are the capabilities of this country's people of any advantage unto me. †

We converse together in one tongue—we speak the Pus'hto language;

But we do not, in the least, understand what we to one another say.

The Suwātīs account themselves exceeding wise, whilst they are but fools;

And 'tis amongst such a set as these, that the Almighty my lot hath cast.

Now that I have beheld the Suwāt valley, I have this much discovered,

That there is no tribe more abject and contemptible than the Yūsufzīs.

Tyranny and self-conceit seem to be the innate nature of all;

And every man amongst them is covetous and ready to beg.

Although, in their dwellings, they have wealth and goods, they are hungry-eyed;

And their head-men, than the rest, are more villainous and infamous still.

'Tis said, that the water-melon deriveth its colour from the water-melon;

But their wise men and elders are more worthless than the people themselves.

The rights of the poor and helpless, they make out wrong and unjust,

If they can a single penny obtain by way of a present, or a bribe.

As to those I have seen myself—about others I am unable to speak

They are all either bullocks or skinners, without any exception soever. *

Peregrinations such as these, in all countries, are by no means useless;

Since all the secrets regarding them became known unto me.

Now that KHUSHḤĀL hath smelt the earth of Suwāt, and the Sama'h, *

He knoweth, that a single faithful man will not, in them, be found.

XXXII.

There is lamentation everywhere, from the hand of death!

In every place, in every habitation, from the hand of death!

'The form of man HE created for the sake of death itself;

And evil and misery, in this world, came from the hand of death!

The whole of the prophets and saints, that have ever existed,

Have all been hidden in the earth, by the hand of death!

Surely, and without doubt, in the end shall be brought

Ruin and desolation on these fair abodes, by the hand of death!

Come! do thou, too, occupy thyself in laying by viaticum for thy journey;

For whole caravans have been dispatched, by the hand of death!

O KHUSHḤĀL! though in body thou shouldst a Shāh Julian be, †

Even then, thou wouldst depart in sorrow, from the hand of death!

XXXIII.

Whilom, indeed, I was always wise; and wise, even yet, am I!

I was ever mad and beside myself—mad, even yet, am I!

There is association, not separation: from Him, disjunction is unreal:

With Him, with whom I was a dweller, a dweller, even yet, am I!

Since I have entered into the world, I have come to know myself:

I was a treasury of mysteries; and of such, a treasury, even yet, am I!

In the world, the mention of my goodness is made, far and near:

Amongst the folks I was a fiction; and a fiction, even yet, am I!

When the veil of His face was drawn aside, unto me a torch appeared;

At that moment I was a moth thereon—a moth, even yet, am I!

The arrows of His eyelashes, they are the misfortune of my life:

I was a target for them an age; and their target, even yet, am I!

When He made me a friend of Himself, He turned me from all others away:

I then was a stranger unto the world; and a stranger, even yet, am I!

That ocean which is circumambient, boundless, unfathomable,

Of that ocean I was the pearl; and its pearl, even yet, am I!

In the same manner, with mine own beloved, without agent or delegate,

As I, KHUSHHĀL, used in amity to be, in amity, even yet, am I!

XXXIV.

Amongst the whole village, my beloved is that person,

Who, throughout the whole tribe, is celebrated—that person.

Though, in resemblance and in qualities, she may human seem;

But, in truth, from head to foot, she is like a fairy—that person.

'Tis for this reason that I am as a nightingale towards her,

That, in loveliness, she is like unto a bower of roses—that person.

Notwithstanding she may reproach me, or become angry with me;

Yet still, from her mouth, she is a scatterer of sweets—that person.

Whether her curly ringlets, her top-knot, or her side locks;

She is the fragrant musk of Tātāry entirely—that person.

Let it not happen that I miss her in a crowd, but in case I should,

Know, that she is fawn-eyed and rosy-cheeked—that person.

In place of a veil, I will present her my head as an offering,

Should she nourish the desire to possess it—that person.

When I seek to kiss her, she censureth and rebuketh me—

She is severe and tyrannical beyond measure—that person.

When arrayed, from head to foot, in gold-embroidered garments,

From head to foot she is a golden picture—that person.

Wherefore, O partridge! art thou so proud of thy gait;

For her step is far more graceful than thine—that person!

Since her form and disposition perfectly harmonize together,

Unto the heart of KHUSHHĀL she is precious—that person.

XXXV.

There will be none of the world's vanities and ambitions within the tomb:

Thine own good deeds will go with thee, and naught else besides!

Without the parrot, the cage is useless—be convinced of this!

And the soul is like unto the parrot—the body like unto its cage.

Be careful, that it may not be, altogether, lost unto thee;

For, like unto a pearl of great price, is this breath of thine.

Whoso casteth this pearl, so precious, unprofitably away,

He is not a whit better than the beasts of the field.

Pass near the graves of the chiefs, and the nobles of the land!

Behold, out of their dust, thorns and brambles have sprung up!

Whatever hath happened, cannot be changed; wherefore, then

Dost thou manifest such apprehension, and such dread?

'Tis thy lot, from the world to bear, at most, but a shroud away;

And that, too, will be but eight or nine yards, or may be ten.

All these things, my dear! will remain behind thee;

Whether pretty maidens, noble steeds, or robes of finest satin.

Be ready, O KHUSHḤĀL! for the time of departure is come

In every direction may be heard the sound of the warning bell! *

XXXVI.

The Turānīs are all turbulent, quarrelsome, and oppressive;

Liars, perjurers, and concoctors of calumny and slander.

The Iranīs * are of a friendly disposition—they are true and faithful:

They have urbanity, and breeding—are respectable and deserving.

The Afghāns are malevolent, and ruthless, and contentious;

But give them for their modesty and valour due praise.

Whether Balūch or Hazārah, both are dirty, and abominable:

They have neither religion nor faith—may shame attend them!

Whether Hindūstānī or Sindhī, may their faces be blackened;

For they have neither modesty nor shame; neither bread nor meat!

The Ka<u>sh</u>mīrīs, whether male or female—may they all be undone!

They have none of the chattels of humanity amongst them.

Behold! they are not of the human race—what are they?

May perdition swallow them—both Uzbak and Kazalbā<u>sh</u>!

The La<u>gh</u>mānīs, Banga<u>s'h</u>īs, Suwātīs, Tirāhīs—all of them,

Are dancers and fiddlers—and who will be friends with such?

Unto him, all matters are manifest, regarding other folks' ways;

Then render unto <u>KH</u>U<u>SH</u>ḤĀL'S shrewdness, its due meed of praise. †

XXXVII.

I am well acquainted with Aurangzeb's justice, and equity—

His orthodoxy in matters of faith—his self-denial and fasts;

His own brothers, time after time, cruelly put to the sword—

His father overcome in battle, and into prison thrown!

Tho' a person dash his head against the ground a thousand times,

Or by his fastings, should bring his navel and spine together;

Until coupled with the desire of acting with virtue and goodness,

His adorations, and devotions, are all impositions and lies.

The way of whose tongue is one, and the path of his heart another,

Let his very vitals be mangled, and lacerated by the knife!

Externally, the serpent is handsome, and symmetrically formed;

But internally, is with uncleanness and with venom filled.

The deeds of men will be many, and their words will be few;

But the acts of recreants are few, and their boastings many.

Since the arm of KHUSHḤĀL cannot reach the tyrant here,

In the day of doom, may the Almighty have no mercy on him!

XXXVIII.

I am intoxicated with that countenance, which hath sleepy, languid eyes:

By them, I become so cut and gashed, thou wouldst say, those eyes sharp swords contain.

My beloved, in loveliness and grace, is incomparable, and without equal:

But, than her whole person, more splendid, and more radiant are her eyes.

I have seen the fine eyes of very many fair ones, in my lifetime;

But only one, here and there, hath lashes full and long like thine.

Tho' the prelate and the priest may admire them a hundred times,

Can the Ḥourī * have brighter eyes, than those dark ones of thine?

Those marplots are sitting together, talking about the poor lover;

Consequently, he keepeth his eyes, to this degree, averted from thy face.

Wheresoever thou art, there, and there only, will my sight be directed

Wherever the heron may be, there the falcon directeth his eyes.

There is not, in the wide world—tho' I am constantly in search—

One such fair charmer, that may, to day, possess bewitching eyes.

She looketh upon no one—to what degree will the pride of her beauty go?

See how long this wayward creature will look so proudly from her eyes.

'Tis well for them, who are happy in the society of the beloved of their hearts;

For every hour, on the face of their dear ones, they charm their eyes.

Draw near, if thou wouldst behold KHUSHḤĀL in sorrow and grief—

Day and night, from thee severed, his eyes with tears o'erflow!

XXXIX.

A man is he, who is courageous, and whom success attendeth—

Who is gentle and affable, unto all people, as long as life lasteth.

His face, his real face—his word, his word—his promise, his promise:

With no falsehood in him, no deception, not witless and lewd.

His words few, but his deeds many, and in silence performed—

With mouth closed, but bosom laid open like the bud of the rose.

When humility may be necessary, or when stateliness be required,

To be in loftiness, like the heavens—in humbleness, like the dust.

In dignity, like the cypress—in generosity and bounty, like the vine—

Its branches, on all sides, under the weight of its clusters bending.

Like unto a fresh and fragrant full-blown rose in the parterre,

Around which the sweet nightingales raise their plaintive songs.

I am quite amazed, since he speaketh in this manner,

As from whence did KHUSHḤĀL all this mental genius bring.

XL.

In this parterre, a single leaf of thine there will not be, O rose!

Shouldst thou become acquainted with autumn's dire inclemency.
Account as great good fortune, these thy few days in the garden,
That the nightingales, for thy sake, beat their breasts and bewail.
Nothing whatever of the glory and dignity of that garden will remain,
When the plaintive melody of the nightingale is hushed within it.
Upon that wine-flask, which the cupbearer hath with him,
The eyes turn not towards, since it is devoid of any wine.
Behold the passage of this bridge, by the people of the world!
See! some fall, whilst some outstrip others, and cross before them.
It will never be effaced from its memory, as long as it liveth,
If the partridge may ever have felt the talons of the hawk.
The decrees by fate ordained, cannot be changed by any means,
Tho', over thyself, thou shouldst read the four *kuls*, *unceasingly.
Lovers, who unto love devote themselves, will never grieve;
Nor for the backbitings of marplots, and tale-bearers, will they care.
What shall I, a poor darwesh † do? neither hand nor might have I,
Otherwise, indeed, I would have exhausted the whole upon the world.
Such a dear one I possess—from this, thou mayest of her loveliness judge,
When the fragrance of musk is nothing to that of her ringlets.
How can he possibly lie on his bed, free from sorrow and care,
Who may be aware of the dread earthquakes and tornados of fate?
In the assumed coldness of the beloved, there is a pleasure withal;

But miserable KHUSHHĀL, alas! from her real indifference, dieth.

XLI.

Should any one speak about intellect and ability, certainly, I possess them;

But since good fortune assisteth me not, unto whom shall I mention such things?

In this world, the gift of fidelity and sincerity is alchemy itself; ‡

Wherefore, then, should I be covetous to obtain it from any one?

The fruit of constancy and faith, is not to be found in the world's garden

I search for it, bootlessly, and unavailingly, upon every tree.

That rain which falleth upon the waters, and mixeth with them,

How shall I such rain account, amongst other genial showers?

My foolishness hath become predominant over my sense and prudence—

Unprofitably, I cast back my pearls into the depths of ocean again.

By means of fate, it will neither decrease, nor will it increase—

I do not consume that daily-bread which belongeth not to me.

Whatever may remain redundant, out of my daily sustenance,

Like unto a thing given in trust, I preserve for the use of others.

What place, in the present time, is free from deceit, and from imposture?

O tell me where! that there I may flee, and escape from them.

If there had been any safety in flight, from destiny I had been free;

But, alas! where shall I direct my steps, to be safe from its decrees?

Cruel fortune stoneth me with the stone of calamity and perfidy;

Whilst I, silly that I am, carry a shield of glass before my face.

When, from its advent, I obtained neither happiness nor joy,

Wherefore should I make my heart sad, by severance therefrom?

They were wont to say that patience is the sign of success;

Therefore, I KHUSHHĀL, with resignation gird up my heart.

XLII.

Notwithstanding thou art unto me a sovereign, and I a beggar;

Still turn not from me thy face, for I am distracted and distressed.

I, who bear the brand of thy thraldom and enslavement,

Do not consider any one equal with myself; for I am a king.

The door of my heart I have closed unto all extraneous things—

Associating with the world, I am filled with anxiety for thee.

If any one is wretched about thee, I am that wretched being:

If any one is the dust of the sole of thy foot, that dust am I.

Sometimes, I write upon paper the words of thy mystery—

At others, through grief for thee, I tell, unto my pen, my state.

The admirers of thy pretty face, are beyond computation;

But amongst the whole of them, I am without compare.

Exclude me not from being accounted among the dogs at thy door,

Although I may be debarred from all benefits, and favours beside.

Shouldst thou love and kindness bestow, of them I am unworthy—

If thou treat me with harshness and severity, I merit them.

Unto KHUSHHĀL, thou wast saying, "Of what use art thou?"

If I am of use, or if I am of no use; still, still I am thine!

XLIII.

Gentle breeze of the morn! shouldst thou pass over Khairābād, *

Or should thy course lead thee by Sarā'e, on the banks of the Sind; †

Hail them, again and again, with my greetings and salutations;

And with them, many, many expressions of my regard and love!

Cry out unto the swift Abā-Sind with sonorous voice;

But unto the Landdaey, mildly and whisperingly say *—

"Perhaps, I may drink, once more, a cup of thy waters;

For, whilom, I was not on Ganges' nor on Jamna's banks."

Of the climate of Hind † should I complain, how long shall I cry out?

Whilst the vileness of its water is far more horrid still.

Shouldst thou drink water from a rivulet, it racketh the vitals;

And that of the wells, too, is not free from danger and peril.

Since therein, from hill streams, the cool element is not to be had,

Defend us from Hind, tho' it should teem with all the world's luxuries besides.

Surely, no one will continue in utter helplessness in this world—

The mercy of the Merciful will be shown unto the forlorn, at last!

Of the restoration of the wounded, hope may be entertained,

When the sore, of its purulence, shall become somewhat free.

Once more, O God! delight, by uniting me unto her again,

That heart, which now, from her separated, is rent in twain.

The wise murmur not, neither do they ever demur,

At any stroke of misfortune, that emanateth from the All-wise.

In Hind, O KHUSHḤĀL! thou wilt not remain for aye;

For the sinner, even, at last, will escape from the fire of Hell!

XLIV.

I never will carry my face unto the mirror again, *

Nor will I again anoint mine eyes with antimony!

Never more will I dye red my white hands with ḥinnā, †

Nor smoothe out, with the comb, my long hair any more!

I will not arrange the little ringlets, in clusters round my face,

Nor will I redden my lips with the betel-leaf ‡ again!

For whom shall I deck out and ornament my person,

When my beloved friend is not present the same to behold?

My whole frame turneth into red flames and dense smoke,

When, in my heart, I think of the secrets of our love.

Though life is sweeter than aught else in the world besides,

What shall I do with it? 'tis bitter now, from my love severed.

May he be HAPPY, that dear friend, wherever he may be!

Let him for his own happiness care—I alone will mourn! §

XLV.

I am intoxicated! I am a worshipper of wine! I indulge! I indulge!

Give ear, O censor! dost hear me? I drink wine! I drink wine!

All other wine soever, I have given up to the world to drink of;

But her lip is a wine that I will not resign—for it I die! I die!

I shall not become satiated therefrom; for my thirst is unquenchable,

Although, such overflowing cups I should quaff for ever! for ever!

I, indeed, who on such a path as this, still journey on my way,

Used not always to be in safety; for it is the path of love! love!

What askest thou me?—"What was thy state in separation?"

Well—I knew nothing else, save that my heart was burning! burning!

People say unto me, "Verily thy colour is become sallow—thou art in love!"

I do not deny it: truly, my friends, I am in love! indeed, I am!

With the lover it is customary, that in love he should brook censure;

For this reason, I, KHUSHḤĀL, undergo it—I suffer it, and endure!

XLVI.

I become quite astonished with the people of the world,

To see what these dogs do, for the sake of the flesh's lusts.

Such acts and proceedings are developed, and perpetrated by them,

As the Devil would never have thought of, and never have uttered.

The Ḳur'ān they always place before them, and from it they read;

But none of their doings will be in conformity with the tenets thereof.

What road shall I follow in pursuit of them? where shall I seek?

For, like unto Alchemy itself, the wise have become scarce indeed.

Good men are like rubies and garnets—they can rarely be found;

But like unto any common stones, the worthless are not a few.

Do they belong to the afrīt, * the demon, or the goblin race?

For, among the lineage of Adam, the Afghāns I cannot account.

Notwithstanding thou mayest give one the best of counsel and advice;

Still, even the counsel of his father is not acceptable to his heart.

The whole of the deeds of the Pattāns † are better than those of the Mughals;

But they have no unity amongst them, and a great pity it is.

The fame of Bahlol, and of Sher Shāh too, resoundeth in my ears—

Afghān Emperors of India, who swayed its sceptre effectively and well. ‡

For six or seven generations, did they govern so wisely,

That all their people were filled with admiration of them.

Either those Afghāns were different, or these have greatly changed;

Or otherwise, at present, such is the Almighty's decree.

If the Afghāns shall acquire the gift of concord and unity,

Old KHUSHḤĀL shall, a second time, grow young therefrom.

XLVII.

Separation turneth sweet existence bitter unto man—

It layeth the very vitals upon fierce, devouring flames!

Whatever strength and energy the heart in the breast may possess,

Separation, out of these eyes, expelleth them, every now and again.

Than such existence as this, annihilation is preferable by far,

When one's days and nights all pass away, in misery and woe.

He faileth not to hit—he woundeth me to the very heart's core;

For the archer of grief hath bent the knee, to take aim at me.

The book of my heart is on the subject of constancy and love—

It was torn up; but no one acquired the meaning thereof.

If the gauze, which the moon rendeth, * can be again repaired,

Then the restoration of my poor heart, may also be effected.

Would to heaven such a person would appear—I am quite willing—

As would bring back my truant heart from the path of the beloved!

In separation, if there were no hope of meeting once more,

For the bewildered lover, there would be no possibility of existence.

When thou placest thy foot on that path, thy head payeth the forfeit;

Yet on such a dangerous road as this, I continually wend my way.

One succeedeth unto another's place; for such is the way of the world—

And I, KHUSHHĀL, also, am the successor of poor Majnūn. *

XLVIII.

The carnality of my heart is an Afrīdī, † who, for religion, careth not—

Its good thoughts are but few; but unto wickedness it is exceedingly prone.

Like unto Akhūnd Darwezah, ‡ I point out godliness and piety to it;

But the flesh teacheth it impiety and infidelity, like unto Pīr Ros'hān. §

Two-and-sixty years, by computation, my own age hath now reached;

And my black hair hath turned silvery, but my heart not the least white.

There are not, in the red carnelian caskets, those white pearls now; §§

Neither do those narcissuses remain, nor those white roses of the parterre. **

With my head on the soft pillow laid, I sleep without sorrow or care;

Whilst those who shared it with me, are now in the cold grave laid!

Very many boats have sunk in the Indus of mortality and death;

And with them engulphed therein, were many companions and friends!

What! is it the veil of wretchedness that hath fallen my sight before,

That with mine eyes I cannot perceive the truth, though 'tis manifest to me?

With body in such agony, and so many physicians in the world, I die

Malediction on such conduct as this, that I seek not my own cure!

'Tis past—'tis gone! his place is Hell, unless God have mercy on him;

For along with KHUSHHĀL associated, are both the Devil and the flesh!

XLIX.

How handsome soever thou art, thou art not Canaan's Joseph!

However wise thou art, with Lokmān * thou canst never compare!

Notwithstanding thy pomp and state, and that thou art the ruler of the land,

Remember well, in thy heart, what a magnificent king was Sulīmān. †

How many lovely-faced ones—how many sages and princes have there been?

As they came, so they departed—in the world, do even their names remain?

A good name will remain behind—naught else soever will survive:

The wicked for evil are remembered—the good, for their virtues, in the memory live.

Shouldst thou hear of Hujāj, * thou wilt also hear the name of Noshīrwān †—

For justice, the unbeliever is venerated—for tyranny, the believer is cursed.

If thou desire to practise goodness, now is the time, whilst of the living accounted—

There will be neither advantage nor profit, shouldst thou regret its neglect, in the grave.

The infidel is that man, who constantly followeth after the flesh's lusts—

The true-believer is he, who is ever anxious about his religion and his faith.

There is not the least doubt in this, that all will fall victims unto death;

But in this there is uncertainty, as to who will obtain a graveyard to lie in.

Happy, truly happy shall he be, who may die with piety's blessings attending—

A grave in honour he obtaineth, and over him the blessed book is read.

The season of youth hath passed—now, O KHUSHḤĀL, old age hath come!

Then leave thou all other things, and the equipments of the grave prepare!

L.

Were thine heart a little compassionate, how good it would be!

Were a little of thy love bestowed upon me,, how kind it would be!

I, who through grief for thee, weep and lament at thy threshold—

Were thine ear inclined to my complainings, how meet it would be!

Whoso blame, and cry out against me for my love for thee—

Were they aware of thy beauty's perfection, how proper it would be!

They who now boast, before the world, of their austerity and self-control—

Were they to refrain from looking at thee, how seemly it would be!

After death, should my grave, in some such place be situated,

Where the path of the beautiful may ever lie, how delightful it would be!

In thy alley, many greyhounds and other dogs are lying about—
Were I, too, accounted amongst them, how fortunate it would be!
My grief for thee, cannot he quenched in this short existence—
Were the life of KHUSHHĀL to be very, very long, how fitting it would be!

LI.

Both fair and rosy, too, are the Adam Khel Afrīdī maids;
Indeed, amongst them, all sorts of pretty lasses there are—
With large eyes, long drooping lashes, and arched eyebrows—
Honey lips, rosy cheeks, and moon-like faces, too, have they.
Small mouths, like unto rose-buds, teeth regular and white—
Their heads round, and covered with dark curls, of amber redolent.
Their bodies soft and sleek, and like an egg, so smooth and glossy—
Their feet diminutive, their heels round, their hips prominent.
Thin stomached, broad chested, and small waisted
In stature, straight, like the letter *alif;* * and of complexion fair.
Although my peregrinations may, like the falcon's, be among the hills;
Still, many pretty plump partridges my quarry I have made.
Young and untaught, or old and trained, the falcon seeketh his prey;
But more scientific, and more unerring, is the old bird's swoop.
It is either the water of the Landdaey river, or of the Bārah stream, †
That tasteth sweeter, and more delicious, than sherbet in my mouth.
The hills in the Mātarī Pass ‡ shoot straight up into the sky;

And one's corpulence soon diminisheth, climbing and ascending them.

Along with the Adam Khels into the Ti-rāh country I came;

And having dismissed them to Khwarrah, with regret I returned.

Love's affairs, O KHUSHḤĀL! are fraught with fire to excess;

For shouldst thou conceal the flame, the smoke thou still wilt see.

LII.

Say not unto me—"Why swearest thou by me?"

If I swear not by thee, by whom shall I swear?

Thou, indeed, art the very light of mine eyes;

This, by those black eyes of thine, I swear!

Thy countenance is the day—thy curls the night;—

By the morn I swear! and by the eve I swear!

In this world, thou art my life and my soul,

And naught else besides; unto thee, my life, I swear!

Thou art, in truth, the all-engrossing idea of my mind,

Every hour—every moment—by my God, I swear!

The dust of thy feet is an ointment for the eyes—

By this very dust beneath thy feet, I swear!

My heart ever yearneth towards thee, exceedingly—

By this very yearning of mine, unto thee I swear!

When thou laughest, they are nothing in comparison—

Both rubies and pearls, * by thy laugh I swear!

Truly, I am thy lover, and thine, thine only:

And this, I, KHUSHHĀL, by thy sweet face, swear!

LIII.

By the laughter of the happy and the gay, I vow!

And by the lamentations of the woe-begone, I vow!

By the inebriation of the intoxicated with wine;

And by the piety and abstinence of the monk, I vow!

By the hundred transports of meeting and association,

And by the thousand miseries of separation, I vow!

By the beautiful and fragrant roses of the spring,

And by the sweet melodies of the nightingales, I vow!

Compared to which the graceful cypress is as nothing,

By that tall stature, and form symmetrical, I vow!

That are tinged with the antimony of expression,

By those dark narcissus-like eyes, I vow!

That which is more slender, even, than a hair,

By that delicately slight waist of thine, I vow!

On account of which, lovers pine away and die,

By that beauty, and by that elegance, I vow!

By that which cometh from the direction of the beloved—

By the balmy breath of the morning breeze, I vow!

Who is the bearer of the message for an interview,

By the footsteps of that bearer of glad tidings, I vow!

In the which there is not the least insincerity,

By the truthfulness of the true and sincere, I vow!

With the whole of these many oaths and protestations,

A hundred thousand times again and again, I vow

That I love thee far more dearly than life itself;

And this, by thyself, I, KHUSHḤĀL, KHATTAK, vow!

LIV.

The Afghāns have gone mad about posts and dignities;

But God preserve me, from such plagues and troubles!

Unto whom belongeth the gift of discretion: to the swordsman?

Just the same as one learneth the Ḳur'ān, in the schools?

Not one amongst them is gifted with the art of prudence;

For, with the dispositions of all of them, I am well acquainted.

The Afghāns have one very great failing, if thou but notice—

That they, with the titles and dignities of the Mughals, coquet.

Shame and reputation, fame and honour, are of no account;

But, certainly, they talk enough about offices, rank, and gold.

Look not towards the Mughals with the eyes of cupidity;

Even, if in the habit of doing so, from any other cause!

The trusty Khattakī sword is buckled round my waist;

But not the custom of servitude, in village and in town.

The dark night of Aurangzeb's prison, I hold in remembrance, *

When all the night long, "O God! O God!" continually, I cried.

If the Afghāns would but oppose the Mughals with the sword,

Every Khattak, by the bridle-rein, should lead a Mughal away.

Amongst the Khattaks, O KHUSHHĀL! no council of honour existeth;

Hence, I cannot conceive from what lineage they have sprung.

LV.

A white beard is a mark of respectability among men;

But the falling out of the teeth is a discredit and reproach.

When a man's teeth are in their place, though the beard be white,

There is no old age in that; far from it, there is youthfulness.

Let not the old man trouble himself concerning old age,

If his eyesight be good, and free from all signs of failing.

What is the sight of a sweetheart, unto an old man?

Really and truly, it is mummy * for the wounds of the heart.

Would the monk ever relinquish love entirely? No, no!

Unto it, he cannot attain; hence his devotion and piety.

Although the age of KHUSHHĀL hath gone beyond seventy years;

Yet, in his heart, are still, love and affection for the fair.

LVI.

When thou severest thyself from cupidity with regard to every one, it is sovereignty:

If thou understandest silence, it is equal to the eloquence of Saḥbān. †

Mention not a word, regarding Ḥātim's liberality and munificence; ‡
For, even in so Going, there are, indeed, indications of venality.
How many different kinds do the attributes of friendship embrace?
Lip-friendship—loaf-friendship—and friendship from the soul.
Upon the altar of sincere friends, make all things an oblation;
Indeed, for this alone, is the transitory world of any use.
In the troubles and trials of the world, there is much gain;
But in the gain of the world's wealth, there are misery and woe.
They, who treat both friend and foe, with gentleness and humanity,
The lives of those men are, indeed, admirably and worthily passed.
Whatsoever my dwelling contained, I entirely relinquished—
Such is the extent of my hospitality, my own friends toward.
The priest readeth, again and again, out of thousands of books;
But if the true faith be his study, the letter *alif* * is enough.
Even for the ignorant, O K͟HUS͟HḤĀL! there is mercy
Their ignorance and stupidity, are a sufficient excuse for them!

LVII.

Altho' happiness was a delicious food; lo, 'tis all passed away!
Though lordly power was an elegant garment; lo, 'tis all passed away!
Altho' there were the ties of wife and child, this is their state now:
Altho' there were life and abiding amongst mankind; lo, 'tis all passed away!
Altho' I possessed both rank and dignity, chieftainship, and command

Altho' lands and possessions were mine; lo, they all have passed away!

Altho' in my houses were carpets and divans, embellishments and ornaments—

Altho' my couch, too, was perfumed with *œaṭr;* † lo, all have passed away!

When I used to return home from the chase, in pride and gaiety,

My saddle-straps were ever red with the blood of the game; but, lo, 'tis passed away!

Kinsmen and strangers—the good and the bad, from all directions, came:

In my audience-hall were bustle and clamour; but, lo, all is passed away!

Scattered and dispersed, the family of Akhorr Khel * struck camp, and departed:

At this noise, my heart-strings broke; but, lo, 'tis all passed away!

Unto him, 'tis now the day of mourning—of sackcloth and of ashes;

For Sarā'e, † that was the home of KHUSHḤĀL, is now all passed away!

LVIII.

The sword that is sharpened, without doubt, is for smiting; is it not?

The locks that are curled, certes, are for one's own lover; are they not?

Wherefore sayest thou unto me, "Cast not thine eyes upon the fair!"

The eyes that have been given one, doubtless are for seeing; are they not?

Let the monk fast and pray; but I will the flowing goblet seize:

Every man is created to fulfil, each his own part; is he not?

Thou wast saying, that the kissing of thy lips is like unto an elixir—

I stand in need of such: 'tis for the wounds of the heart; is it not?

Thou drinkest my very heart's blood; but it is for none else besides—

My heart was formed for thee, thou barbarous one! was it not?

Why weepest and complainest thou about the dark curls of the beloved?
Thy going before those black snakes, * is of thine own accord; is it not?
They will themselves appear like unto mere weeds in comparison to it—
Then, the tulip and the rose thou wilt bring before thy face; wilt thou not?
There is wine, O KHUSHHĀL! there are harp and flute; therefore, with thy beloved,
With thy tablets in thy hand, unto the garden thou wilt go; wilt thou not?

LIX.

Every misfortune that befell me, throughout the whole period of my life,
When examined carefully, I found it was all the work of my tongue.
That, which in a single hour, turneth prosperity unto desolation,
When well looked into, I found it was precipitancy in affairs.
With these eyes of mine, I have beheld the friendship of every one;
And, truly, he who was my friend proved a source of misfortune unto me.
He would never experience any perfidy or duplicity, at any time,
If a man's own intentions were conformable unto honesty and truth.
Fortune showeth not severity towards the submissive and resigned—
Those, who are impatient and unsteady, the persecutions of destiny pursue.
Within this garden, very many roses have passed before mine eyes;
But at the side of every rose, I perceived there was a thorn also.
The heart, that nourished the hope of constancy from the unfaithful,
Was unto itself, indeed, its own tyrant, and its own oppressor too.
Since it healeth not at all, although ointment is applied unto it,

What sort of grief-wound was there the heart of KHUSHHĀL, upon?

LX.

Whoso acquireth wealth, spendeth it, and bestoweth it, a man is he:

Whoso hath a sword in his possession, the lord of the sword is he.

A mine of rubies, of garnets, and of other gems, what is it after all?

That, from which bounty and beneficence are obtained, *is* a mine.

Whatsoever thou eatest for the belly's sake alone, is thrown away;

But what is eaten, in sociability and companionship, *is* the fare.

Whether it is the power of wealth, of lands, or of authority, what then?

If unto any one their power becometh useful, that is power indeed.

Throughout the whole night and day—throughout both month and year,

The time that passeth in the remembrance of the Almighty, is time truly.

Though people run before thee, and others follow after, what is that?

When in the individual person there is dignity, that dignity is real.

Call none else besides degenerate and undone, O KHUSHHĀL!

Whose word and promise are broken, undone and degenerate is he!

LXI.

The call of the mu'azzin * is not to be heard throughout Tī-rāh, †

Unless thou listen unto the crowing of the cock, at the dawn of day.

As to the Wurakzīs, they are, altogether, from orthodoxy astray;

And the Afrīdīs, ‡ than those erring ones, are more heretical still.

They neither say prayers over the dead, nor ministers have they;

Nor alms, nor offerings, nor the fear of God within their hearts.

Excellent is he, who is steadfast in the laws and precepts of the Prophet;

But wicked is he, who is unsteady and wavering in their observance.

The affairs of the world are all of them transitory and fleeting:

O If there is anything eternal, verily, 'tis the name of the Most High.

Whoso is wholly sunk in the cares and concerns of the world,

As for that son, remiss and reckless, alas! alas! we can only say.

By means of water, impurity is from the person cleansed;

But by contrition and repentance alone, is sin washed away.

The believers in Ṣūfi mystics, * and the unbelievers are all one;

For they both account, as iniquity, the laws and precepts of Muḥammad.

Now and then, upon an occasion, this much they ejaculate

Some few among them—that, "There is, than God, none other God."

Whoso at all times commit sin, and no repentance show,

Refuge and protection, from such a people, is what KHUSHḤĀLasketh.

LXII.

Everywhere, throughout the world, I am become dishonoured and humiliated

House by house, my dissoluteness, and my profligacy, are manifest grown.

That which I kept closely covered up, concealed within my sleeve, †

The people of the world have come, the spectacle of that goblet to behold.

This is no heart at all, that now entertaineth kindness towards me;

But that adamantine stone, towards me, path somewhat softer grown.

That which was the capital stock of life, I renounced entirely;

And the country of happiness and felicity, became farmed to me.

Wherefore, now, should I regret or complain? for I triumphed,

When the marplot became a fugitive, from the door of the beloved.

I appreciate his worth, and I will make myself a sacrifice unto him,

Who, in grief and sorrow, became the sustainer of the helpless, and forlorn.

Unto sleeping fortune many times I cried out with a loud voice;

But it awakened from its slumber, only, upon the last soft, gentle call.

Separation from them is death itself—and man soon breatheth his last;

But the society of the heart's idols, hath a second existence become.

Though he putteth his heart upon its guard, yet it will not be prudent;

Hence, KHUSHḤĀLis accounted now, among the crazy, and the mad.

LXIII.

Be content with thine own lot, and do not always envy the fortune of others!

Shouldst thou secure both these things, may happiness and affluence be thine!

The links of existence are bound together by a single flimsy thread alone:

Leave the world's sorrows: why mourn for others? Weep for thy thyself!

Whether thine own kith and kin, or strangers, draw thy pen thro' all:

It is the age of iniquity and depravity; so be not vain of brother, or of son.

In whatever direction I wend my way, I perceive such acts from them—

The attainment of their wishes is on to-day, and gone is all concern for to-morrow.

Behold! what blasting wind is it, that hath blown over all the world?

The heart waxeth not kind to any one; and the whole world is deceitful grown!

I was saying that the hamlet is peopled, but, lo! when I came near unto it,

Mere rubbish is lying about—it was an utterly desolate and deserted abode.

In whatever direction thou goest, pass them by with "God preserve us!"

They have a hundred evils in their hearts, a hundred-bead rosary round their necks.

Much traffic hath been effected, and a hundred demands with avidity made;

But the time of evening prayer is come, therefore now let this mart be closed.

Thou art always saying, O KHUSHHĀL! "Upon the world I will turn my back;"

But as yet, indeed, this world is still standing face to face with thee.

LXIV.

Whether it is the wise man, or the ignorant—the honest man, or the robber,

I do not see any one a true colleague united with me in my task.

A sincere friend in distress, I cannot discover throughout the land;

For people merely give the empty consolation of their tongues.

Like unto the ants, directed towards the grain are the steps

Of those who favour me, with their coming, and their going.

Did not these ants entertain the hope of obtaining a store,

They would never make any journey in that direction, at all.

Abandon not thine own stricken mountain-land, O KHUSHHĀL!

Though blood is, at every footstep, and in every direction shed.

LXV.

Let the mouth of the liar, forsooth, be filled with dust;

But kiss the man's mouth, that uttereth truthful words!

Every deed that a man doeth shall not be concealed:
Did any one tell thee to kindle a fire, and make no smoke?

If thou knowest that there is a reckoning in the next world,
Then mind to scrutinize well thine own acts in this also.

The fountain of thy mouth is both colocynth and honey;
Therefore, see thou pour out thy sweetness every one upon.

When the affairs of religion, and of the world come before thee;
Before worldly matters, first those of thy religion discharge.

In order that the fragrance of the musk-pod be disseminated,
Show unto me those dark tresses and sable ringlets of thine.

'Tis the season of spring! O cupbearer, bring, bring the wine!
And add the delicious dessert of thy lips thereunto.

Do not, to-day, O Zealot! impede the drinking of pure wine;
When the spring shall have passed away, then prohibit it.

Since it is not free, for a moment, from the fire of love,
Hast thou, O God! the lover's breast a chafing-dish made?

In the era of thy sweet countenance, I am Jahāngīr Shāh—
Sit near unto me: practise the caresses of Nūr Maḥāl! *

These dark eyes of thine are, in themselves, black calamities;
Who, then, told thee to make them still more so with koḥl? †

Shouldst thou, O KHUSHḤĀL! profess sanctity a thousand times,

When a pretty creature cometh near thee, to kiss her take care!

LXVI.

Thy society is like unto the sea, and I, a fish therein;

But, separated from thee, I lament and bewail always.

Weeping, I would ask her to let me her fair cheek press;

But, laughing, she would ask, "What doth this man say?

She asked, too, "Who art thou, that wanderest in my street?"

To which, "Thy dog am I;"—thus to her a ready reply I gave.

I grieve in various ways, and my body hath a reed become:

Separation hath brought me to the plaintive pipe's condition. ‡.

Alas! alas! that this spring-time of youth is past!

Ah! that this spring continued in the world for aye!

The rose, the hyacinth, the wild rose, the tulip, and the buds—

Thou didst bring with thee, on thy coming, the whole spring.

When I press her unto my bosom, she looketh towards me,

Like a young gazelle inebriated with the milk of its dam.

When I die, I shall never see these sweet friends any more;

Then let me, O God, remain in this world for ever!

I grieve, indeed, for thy honour alone, not for myself:

Thou shouldst see how I would act, had I not this solicitude.

Thus severed from thee, in the fire I burn and consume,

Like unto the dry fuel, that one casteth into the flames.

Upon the beauty of the fays many encomiums are lavished;
But I see not any fairy with so lovely a face as thine.
There is no epithet that can express thy charming ways:
Would that, to thy lover, thou didst a little tenderness show!
Is there an anvil in thy breast, or a kind, benevolent heart,
That, for the sighs of KHUSHḤĀL, thou showest no sympathy?

LXVII.

Upon the difficult path of love, there is exceeding peril:
Every footstep I take thereon, my life in danger I place.
Shouldst thou my bosom rend asunder, thou wilt perceive,
That, thro' grief for thee, my whole heart is turned to blood.
The genial rain of thy kindness falleth not upon me,
That the seed of thy love, planted in my heart, might germinate.
Thy treasured secret, even unto my tongue, I will not impart;
For the secret, that hath reached the tongue, is ever a fireside tale.
I am ignorant with regard to love, as to what thing it is;
But this much I hear, that from beauty its effect proceedeth.
But who is he, that, unto the love ineffable, hath attained?
Tho' in this matter, indeed, every one boasteth of success.
It was when thou and I were not, that love was born:
'Tis not that this influence hath been originated by thee and me.
Hide, O KHUSHḤĀL, from the world, the woes of love!

But how can I conceal that, which it knoweth full well?

LXVIII.

I was not, at first, aware, that thou art so utterly inconstant—

Thou makest a hundred vows a day, and still art heedless of them all.

The world raiseth an outcry against me, who have given my heart to thee;

But ’tis not aware what a lovely, bewitching creature thou art.

And thou, too, that sagest unto me, "Look not upon the fair"—

Who will give ear unto such deadly words as those thou utterest?

A single hair of the head of one's beloved is more precious than the Ḥūrī's *—

What use is it, then, O priest! to laud the virgins of Paradise, unto me?

Not every crow and kite, but the nightingale appreciateth the rose's value;

Then ask not, O fool! what sort of person hath thus enamoured me.

These are not black eyes, that have carried away my yearning heart

Thou, O God!—All-wise, All-seeing—knowest they are calamities greater still.

That is not a mole upon thy chin, nor are those dark dishevelled tresses:

They are, if thou canst comprehend this saying, a mystery divine.

Whether the censures of the world, or people's worst upbraidings;

All these, I willingly accept, if thou art but reconciled to me.

I will light no lamp in my dwelling to-night, that they may not suspect

These neighbours of the Sama’h *—that thou art a guest of mine.

I was saying, I would tell thee my heart's sorrows, when thou earnest;

But what griefs shall I mention, when thou, the grief-dispeller, art near?

Since thou tossest unto the wind the musk-pods of thy fragrant tresses,

K͟HUS͟HḤĀL, full well knoweth, that thou art a deer of K͟haṭā̤. †

LXIX.

'Tis grief and sorrow—joy and gladness, that affect so deeply;

But like as they are excessive, even so they pass away.

The source of this link cannot be found by any one:

The vicissitudes of fortune assume such manifold forms.

So many things will happen—so many incidents befall,

As may never have entered the thoughts of thine heart.

In absence, there is sorrow on account of the beloved,

That, continually, encircleth and besetteth the afflicted heart.

But whatsoever hath vanished from the eyesight away,

That, too, at last, becometh forgotten by the heart.

Let them that ridicule the words of K͟HUS͟HḤĀL, beware!

Perhaps they may themselves full soon like him become.

LXX.

Whoso like unto the dust, may not be prostrate at the threshold,

For them, there will be no approach unto heaven and to bliss.

The nightingale that bewaileth when he approacheth the rose,

Thus saith:—"Alas, some day the parterre will cease to be!"

The rent in my heart will, by no means, unite again,

Till it shall be sewn together, with the thread of thy locks.

The name of thy tresses I will ne'er take upon my tongue again;

For the prudent snake-charmer hath naught with black snakes to do.

Be not inferior unto the Hindū female, for the honour of thy beloved;

For the blazing funeral pyre will have no terrors for her. *

Every moment, that I behold the object of my love, is a jubilee to me:

I shall then be without a festival, when my beloved may not be.

Upon what part of me wilt thou place a plaster, O physician!

When the wound of the eyelashes of the beloved may not be seen?

The name of love is unlawful upon the lips of him,

Whose whole frame may not be suffering about his beloved.

O KHUSHḤĀL! let there be no estrangement between thy love and thee;

For the world's short hour will not be immutable always.

LXXI.

When the tresses become dishevelled about her fair, white face,

The bright day becometh shrouded in evening's sombre shade.

If this, which is seen, be the beauty of her countenance,

Very many more, like unto me, will grow distracted for her.

Those are not tears pendant from her long eyelashes;

They are all bright gems and pearls, that are being bored.

With new tints and dyes,.fresh fragrance, and green young leaves,

An astonishingly rare flower is blooming, the parterre within.

Should he, who is wont to repose upon her tresses, be aware

Of my tears and sighs, he would in sleep never close his eye.

The words of KHUSHHĀL'S mouth are not idle and meaningless—

They all are spoken from a certain emotion of the heart.

LXXII.

If the damsels of Kashmīr are famed for their beauty,

Or those of Chīn, or Mā-chīn, * or Tartary, noted likewise;

Yet the sweet Afghān maidens, that mine eyes have beheld,

Put all the others to shame, by their conduct and ways.

As to their comeliness, this, once for all, is the fact of the matter,

That they are, in lineage, of the tribe and posterity of Yaækūb. *

Of the fragrance of musk, or of rosewater, they have no need—

They are, as the ottar of the perfumer, by prayer five times a day.

Whether jewels for forehead or for neck, or any other trinkets,

All these are contemptible, with their dark locks compared.

Whether veils of gold brocade, or whether silken mantles,

All are a sacrifice unto the snow-white kerchief of theirs.

The beauty of their minds excelleth their personal charms—

Than the external form, their hearts are far sweeter still.

From first to last, their occupation is in seclusion and privacy;

Not seen in the markets, with garments open, and persons exposed. †

They cannot look one full in the face, through modesty—

They are unused to abuse, and the discipline of the shoe. ‡

KHUSHHĀL hath mentioned, more or less, somewhat of the matter;

But much remaineth, that may be suitable, or unsuitable to the case.

LXXIII.

If the Afghān people are of the human race,

In disposition and ways they are very Hindūs. §

They are possessed of neither skill, nor intellect;

But are happy in ignorance, and in strife.

Neither do they obey the words of their fathers;

Nor do they unto the teacher's instruction give ear.

When there may be one worthy man amongst them,

They are the destroyers of his head and life.

They ever lie in wait, one to injure the other;

Hence they are, always, by calamity, remembered.

They neither possess worth, nor do others esteem them,

Though they are more numerous than locusts or than ants.

First I, then others, as many as there may be—

We all of us require aid, and a helping hand.

Whether it is valour, or whether liberality,

They have cast, through dissension, the both away.

But still, O KHUSHHĀL! thank God for this,

That they are not slaves, but free-born men.

LXXIV.

Vain is his affectation respecting the end of his turban; *
For in the time of his manhood his condition is changed.
The rank of all will not be on a parity together—
The burden of the ass is but a grain on the elephant's back.
Whilst some have not a single drop of wine in their cups,
The goblets of others are running over with the purest wine.
May this delightful garden for ever fresh and green continue;
For every year do lovely and fragrant flowers bloom therein.
The just value of the tree is known from its fruit's sweetness—
A man's worth is discovered by his good and virtuous acts.
Let no one, indeed, be blamed and rebuked unjustly—
The enemy of the wicked is their own wicked deeds alone.
Though they should transport one to Heaven, and bear another unto Hell,
I cannot perceive in the matter aught save their own acts.
Would to Heaven it might continue always, for thy sake!
Since thou art at odds with every one, for the sake of the world.
That son who may not inherit the virtues of his father and grandfather,
Must have been born in an unlucky and unfortunate year.
And thou, that boastest concerning the battle-field of the brave—
What valour, what fortitude, hast thou ever brought to the field?
Doth the gnat ever attain unto the high rank of the falcon,
Even though he is furnished, both with feathers and with wings?

Though all the world may agree to disparage, and speak ill of him,

Poor KHUSHHĀL is KHUSHHĀL * in his own merits and integrity.

LXXV.

Like as I my dear one love, there will not be another so loving:

Like as I am disconsolate for her, there will be none other so wretched.

She herself killeth me, indeed, and then again she mourneth over me

How good a friend! how great her love! such be my death and elegy!

A perfect garden is her lovely face, containing flowers of every hue:

Enjoy spring's pleasant time; for garden such as this, none other will there be!

Behold the tulip—that heart-seared flower—in blood ensanguined! *

No martyr, from time's beginning, e'er donned such winding-sheet!

Look upon those her sable locks, and upon both those lovely cheeks!

Within the world's parterre are no such spikenards, no such lilies found. †

Shouldst thou a mantle from the rose-leaves make, even they would irritate:

Like unto this delicate body of thine, no one such another possesseth.

Such as that, which both day and night, I behold, my dwelling within,

Poor Majnūn, during life's whole course, will never have looked upon.

If such the law, or such her custom be, the Hindū female's right is constancy,

That sitteth down upon her lover's pyre: what other would such burning bear? ‡

That some one, in sorrow, might wring her hands, and weep and wail for thee,

Such is not death, but life itself, if such thy death might be.

The bliss of Iram * I enjoyed, the precincts of thy courts within,

Delighted with fortune and fate, that such a home to KHUSHHĀLgave.

In Persian, thou must know, such strains will not be heard,

As those that KHUSHHĀL, KHATTAK, reciteth, in the Pus'hto tongue.

LXXVI.

It is the navigator, that guideth the ship upon the ocean;

But it is the Almighty, that preserveth her, or sinketh her therein.

Empire and dominion, upon fortune and destiny depend

'Tis the Ḥumā of happy omen, that casteth its shadow o'er one's head. †

Verily, if any one should stand in need of aught from another,

Though the sovereign of the universe, he is but a beggar still.

Who told thee not to unloose the knots of difficulty thereby?

For thought and deliberation are the unloosers of all men's troubles,

'Tis either the sound of the women's joy-songs, at the child's birth;

Or 'tis the dirge, and the wails, from the sword's fatal field!

He will be under no uneasiness about missing the right way,

Who, as the companion of his journey, may have a trusty guide.

'Tis the reed, wholly dried up, breast-scarred, and void within,

That giveth utterance to separation's plaintive wails.

It behoveth to look to the virtues and qualities of the beloved,

'Though her beauty be most ravishing, in manifold ways.

Thou, O nightingale! laudest her with a thousand songs;

But the rose herself, is self-praising of her own loveliness.

Whether gardens, or whether wilds, or any other place soever—

Where the heart hath become K͟HUS͟HḤĀL, * that is the happy spot!

LXXVII.

Since those dark eyes of thine are such enchanters,

My boastings of devotion and piety are wholly unjust.

With these eyes I have beheld such Afg͟hān maidens,

That he is in error, who laudeth the damsels of K͟haṭạy.

Verily, those hearts must be hard like the stones of the desert,

That may look upon thy face, and feel not love for thee.

Notwithstanding folks praise the fairies so exceedingly,

With thy grace and beauty, by whom are they compared?

As to the Ḥūrīs of Paradise, that the preachers remind us of,

In this world, such have I seen, with these eyes of mine.

Either I will obtain possession of those tresses for myself,

Or I'll stake my life upon them; and these my two vows are.

Speak not unto K͟HUS͟HḤĀL of honour and reputation;

For they, who are in love, care not for name or fame.

LXXVIII.

The vicious are vicious, while yet in the womb of their mothers;

And vile and vicious are they, when their mothers bring them forth.

In this world, they live and subsist in wickedness and iniquity;

And unto the next, they must, wretched and miserable, go.

When they do any laudable action, they are unhappy thereat;

But are overjoyed at what is reprehensible, whatever its degree.

They pursue the path which the lusts of the flesh point out to them;

Indeed, their following is after the devil, in every act and deed.

Should they at any time take a footstep in the right road,

Immediately, at the next step, they are sorry for it again.

The books of heaven, and the books of earth, they read and learn;

But their acts are as remote therefrom, as the heavens from earth.

Internally, their hearts are imbued with scepticism and distrust

Externally, they are followers of Islām, by the words of their mouths.

Nothing good or kind, is discoverable in their conversation:

Their creed is empty words—their promise to be evaded, or unblushingly denied.

Though, in devotion and adoration, they may equal Balæām, *

Even then, through giving ear unto carnality, they are infidels at last.

The humble servant of that man, I KHUSHḤĀL, KHATTAK, am,

The ways of whose heart are in conformity with his words.

LXXIX.

However tortuously the snake moveth about,

It proceedeth straight enough unto its hole.

Awaken from the sleep of thoughtlessness;

For pleasant existence is every moment passing away!

Relentless death will not pass any man over—

Time by time, all creation will pass away!

The traveller, knowingly, throweth away his life,

Who ventureth into total darkness without a guide.

He misseth his footsteps, and staggereth in his gait,

Who, convicted of crime, before the Ḳāzī proceedeth.

He rendereth the fire of Hell harmless, altogether,

From whose eyes the tears fall, at the dawn of day.

That existence, like as the wind, passeth away,

Which, more or less, passeth in misery and woe.

If resignation be shown unto the Divine decrees,

Verily, sorrow and grief will vanish from the heart.

Since thou hast flung, uselessly, the musk away,

What rigour bringest thou, the camphor upon? *

He, who hath neither wealth nor possessions to care for,

Goeth about, everywhere, cheerful, and free from care.

Abandon not, O KHUSHHĀL! His footmarks,

Though thy head, like that of the pen, should go. *

LXXX.

Certainly this man is, thro' polish and good breeding, a human being;

For he, who is not possessed of these, is no better than the beast of the field.

They are not men, who may not inherit either faithfulness or constancy;

Otherwise the dog, in these matters, is far more estimable than they.

The just and conscientious are, unto me, as the flowers of Paradise's parterre;

But the false and tyrannical are, unto me, as the fuel of the fire of Hell.

When the dog groweth familiar with any one, and obtaineth something to eat,

At him, he will never bark nor growl again, as long as his life may last.

He, who is with justice and equity endowed, need have no fear of Hell;

And justice, in my sight, is far more important than even piety itself.

From good nature and qualities, the estimation of a man's worth is formed;

For, by disposition, a man is either a devil, or an angel—a fiend, or a fay.

Flee speedily from him, who may possess neither learning nor attainments;

For the man, without knowledge and information, is but a straw.

When he cannot be restrained by thy counsels, nor be guided by thy advice,

Fetters are required to control him, even though he a lion may be.

What, indeed, is either vice or virtue—right or wrong, atheists unto?

According to the creed they follow, the dog's whelp is an innocent lamb.

In the sunshine of prosperity, the sincerity of friends cannot be tested;

But they are thy friends, who help thee, in adversity, thy load to sustain.

Every ascetic, who without a spiritual guide, assumeth a life of austerity,

In the estimation of KHUSHḤĀL, KHAṬṬAK, is but an empty husk.

LXXXI.

What is it, but a sound and healthy body,

Which, more than empire and sovereignty, is preferred?

Altho' the world's wealth is an excellent thing,

Glory and renown are, than riches, more precious still.

What are more inestimable than the most perfect thing?

The one, is purity—the other, is sincerity of heart.

What is it that disenthralleth a man from sorrow?

Yea, what is it?—it is contentedness of mind.

Shouldst thou boast thyself of thy godliness,

That godliness, thereby, is rendered bootless and vain.

What is that, which hath a value beyond compute?

Yea, what is it?—it is deliberation in all our affairs.

That, which as a favour and obligation is conferred,

As generosity or liberality, is it ever accounted?

What is that, which, in this world, is a Hell indeed?

Verily, it is the society and acquaintance of a fool.

Then, O KHUSHHĀL! guard thou well thy mind;

For if there be aught good, 'tis a mind upright.

LXXXII.

Such an amount of misery is there in my family this day,

That the world is amazed and confounded, at the sight of our troubles.

A degenerate son soweth thorns in the path of his own father;

But the deserving son is a rose-garden, that bloometh all life long.

An incapable, worthless son, maketh a very Hell-upon-earth therein;

But a worthy son is, truly, a Paradise in his father's dwelling.

A good child becometh a refulgent lamp in. the house of its parent;

But a graceless, misbegotten one is murky darkness within his abode.

In maturity, his nature becometh that of a trap and a beast of prey;

Therefore, the good conduct of a child is the greater, the younger it may be.

The vicious son destroyeth the name and reputation of father and grandfather,

Though the banner of their greatness and renown be up-reared on high.

The virtuous son is wholly occupied in concern for name and fame;

But the good-for-nothing son maketh the belly the object of his regard.

Indeed, since dogs of such description have been born unto him,

I have my doubts, whether KHUSHḤĀL is a human being at all.

LXXXIII.

Either let it be a sovereign upon his throne,

Or let it be the poor darwesh of a monastery!

Many there are, who are in the right path—

Would there were a few, like myself, astray!

I am ready, at all times, the work to commence—

Would that my friends were also as ready to begin!

He, whose actions are unbecoming a man,

A man cannot be, but a crazy old crone.

By computation, I have thirty sons, no less

Would that I could a good word for some of them say!

Were there any steps taken for assembling troops—

Every hill and dale with them to profusion teem.

The black and the white * are useless in any affair—

Either let all be white, or let all black be.

It is, alas! the gloomy night of woe and sorrow—

Would that the morn of joy and delight would dawn!

Unjust towards KHUSHḤĀL they would not be,

Were people with the state of the case acquainted. *

LXXXIV.

Verily, the Afghāns are deficient in sense and understanding—

They are the tail-cut curs of the butchers' slaughter-house.

They have played away dominion, for the gold of the Mughals;

And they lust after the offices, that the Mughals can give.

Though the camel, with its lading, hath entered their dwelling,

They are first taken up with stealing the bell from its neck.

Out upon him, who first the name of Sarrah-ban † bore!

And malediction upon the whole of them, that after follow!

The recreant occupy themselves in baseness and dishonour;

But every breath of the noble is devoted to the cause of renown.

They commence from Ḳandahār, and reach unto Damghār; ‡

And all are worthless and good for nothing, who dwell between.

LXXXV.

I went and turned anchorite—such is my case, such my situation—

My sole worldly wealth this broken bowl within my hand, and a coverlet of rags.

Behold the unfortunate! see what manner of meretricious acts they commit!

They all desire prosperity; but prosperity is evanescent, and continueth not!

I will become a sacrifice unto him, who hath made the world his sacrifice;

But let him be an oblation unto me, who hath become an oblation unto gold.

There is nothing whatever in it—there is a great bustle in an empty shop:

When I duly considered the matter, I found it all mere fancy—a phantom—a dream.

One is being laid in the cold grave, whilst another, at home, sitteth unconcerned;

Then there are three days of mourning; and on the fourth, the case is changed.

With hands placed to my ears, I flee from it, that I may escape therefrom;

But others grow wretched after it—O God, what a dreadful plague it is!

What hast thou to do with others? show resolution for thine own deliverance;

For thou, O KHUSHḤĀL! art entangled therein—alas! what a net of calamity it is!

LXXXVI.

O rose! who art the true cause of the garden's loveliness,

Why condescendest thou to join, in laughter, with thorns and weeds?

How cometh it, that thou art not conscious of thine own dignity?

For thou art the one and only beauteous object in this parterre.

The songs of the nightingales will not always be made for thee;

For thou, O lovely rose! art notorious for thy lack of constancy.

Delight, then, the senses of the nightingale with thine own fragrance,

For the few, short days, that thou freshly bloomest, the garden within.

Should I desire to mention, unto any one, thy injustice, 'tis unspeakable;

Yet with all this heavy amount of wrongs, thou art my life still.

But shouldst thou complain, unto any one, of the injustice of thy beloved,

May all love's calamities befall thee; for thou sayest what is false.

O KHUSHHĀL! thou that ascendest unto love and passion's giddy height

Consider well, in thy heart, upon whom thou hast thine affections placed.

LXXXVII.

When of the circumstances of the wise are the ignorant aware,

Who, through their own foolishness, are worthless and despicable too?

A star only twinkled in the eyes of the blear-eyed fellow;

Yet, he called out to the world, that it was the sun itself.

From those deep scars, that are branded upon my heart,

I am well aware, indeed, that it is thoroughly seasoned thereby.

Should one but restrain his eyes, there would be no misery:

It is the eyesight that hurleth the thunderbolts upon the heart.

Forbid, O God, that any one in the world should fall in love!

For it is like unto an invading army in the body's realm.

This poor, maddened heart of mine, began to laugh yestreen;

But see! to-day, it has commenced, once more, to weep again.

That I have drawn out the diver of thought from the depths of the ocean,

Come and behold; for the words of KHUSHHĀL are pearls, indeed!

LXXXVIII.

Of them, who always placed upon their heads the cap of vanity,
The black hair hath now become, like unto white wool, changed.
The running stream and life's career are both one and the same—
In this world, those joyous days and nights, return to us no more!
All love, save that of God, if thou perceivest, is, altogether,
As if one built a bridge of straws upon the surface of the stream.
With all this grace and beauty that I see possessed by thee,
Whether thou art of human mould, or a fay, I cannot say.
Without the wind's aid, I attain not to the object of my desire,
Notwithstanding I launch upon the waters the boat of my heart.
From the dusky snakes of thy tresses he entertaineth no dread,
Who, in his mouth, holdeth the snake-root of thy affection and love.
The heart of KHUSHḤĀL, in piety, was like unto a mountain;
But, all at once 'tis to a gossamer changed, through his love for thee.

LXXXIX.

Of the preciousness of youth what doubt can be entertained?
The period of old age is pregnant with infirmities and defects!
Every now and again, fresh wounds break out upon my heart;
And salt is spread and sprinkled upon my wounds always.
Should joy and gladness approach thee, be not overjoyed thereat;
For care and sorrow ever stare happiness in the face.
Murmur not at the tyranny, or the injustice of any one;

For it is fate that dealeth out misfortune upon us all.

Without some wise object, He hath not brought sorrow upon us;

For affliction is the test on the face of the dastard and the brave.

As much as happiness exceedeth, so much the more lavish is misery:

Fortunate is he, indeed, for whose belly sufficeth the dry crust.

Now that I am turned ascetic, for whom shall I gird on the sword?

It is well, forsooth, that I even bear a club my shoulder upon. •

Should any one make inquiry concerning wounded hearts,

There is K̲H̲USHḤĀL, K̲HAṬṬAK'S, by his own clan lacerated.

XC.

That one's blood should be upon one's own head, is, truly, some cause of concern;

Still, to think that I still live, whilst my friends are in the tomb, is irksome to me.

Since so many pleasant and familiar faces are buried beneath this earth,

When I shall join them in the grave, it will be a very paradise to me.

Is old age come upon me? am I imbecile grown? or is there aught else?

For that doth not succeed which I set about; and yet people and country are the same.

Tho' I speak unto folks ever so kindly, they take in bad part what I say unto them

'Tis either the good fortune of the Mug̲hals, or my intellect hath deficient become.

No! 'tis not the good fortune of the Mug̲hals, nor am I in intellect wanting

'Tis, entirely, through old age, that my affairs are all disordered and confused.

The Mug̲hals whom I now set eyes upon, are not such as were wont to be:

The day of their swords is past and gone, and but the pen remaineth unto them.

They gain over the Afghāns by gold; and by fraud and deception entangle them: *

Upon me these things have no effect; for the favour of God is still upon me.

I am neither a fly nor a crow, that I should hover over rottenness and filth:

The hawk or the falcon am I, that must my heart, with my own quarry, delight.

Were there but others like unto me in this affair, I should rejoice indeed;

But since there are none like me, with distress and grief I am o'erwhelm'd.

Both Ae-māl Khān and Dar-yā Khān have passed away, in honour and in fame; *

And, through bereavement from them, these my sighs, and this mourning proceed.

XCI.

The faithlessness of the world hath become manifest unto me;

Therefore, through the word 'friendship,' I have drawn my pen.

Like as when fire reacheth brushwood, and it ceaseth to be;

So with absence's pangs—they last, only, for a few short days.

Than the sun's light, that of true knowledge is still more bright:

Forbid, that any one should emerge from such effulgence as this!

See what an admirable form, from a single drop proceedeth!

Truly, the works of the Almighty are worthy of Himself!

Thou, O nightingale! wouldst, erewhile, have given the rose thy heart,

If this mart of its beauty were to continue to flourish always.

There will not be, henceforth, repose like this for me again,

Since I have become aware, O solitude, of thy preciousness!

They, who by their own efforts, seek, the world's prosperity to gain,

The wisdom of such people is as nothing in my sight.

From whom shall I seek to obtain a such-like panacea,

That hath been purposely prepared, for the cure of my pains?

Since the calamity of separation is ever linked along with it,

Wherefore is the beauty of the beloved so lauded and extolled?

Since the gem is grown of less value than the kaurī shell *—

There can be no jeweller, clear-sighted enough to distinguish them.

Seeing, that wherever there may be beauty, there the heart is,

To what degree shall KHUSHḤĀL'S self-denial and abnegation praise?

XCII.

It is false that aught of evil or misfortune proceedeth from the stars—

All good and evil—weal and woe—emanate from the Almighty's decrees.

If their colour be their excellence, whence is their fragrance?

For flowers of paper are similar unto the flowers themselves.

Fortune is like unto a child, in its disposition and its ways;

For when the child giveth one any thing, it soon regretteth it again.

When the world's prosperity turneth its face from the ignorant,

At their words, and their proceedings, the wise become amazed.

But when the wise man may not possess aught of its wealth,

In the world's eyes, he is the same as a blockhead, or a fool.

When possessed of power and influence, my words were as pearls;

But now, I am satisfied if they be, even as corals, received.

Let us see what events will, hereafter, show their face;

Though, in the meantime, the world will prate a deal thereon.

As much as the love of wealth exceedeth, so much misery it bringeth;

For they, who accumulate much of it, grow miserable indeed.

I am that same KHUSHḤĀL, but me they value not now;

For 'tis of the Afghāns, that all these my complainings are.

XCIII.

Wherever thou reclinest, that place a parterre of flowers becometh

When thou in the mead roamest, the breast of the tulip is scarred.

When the sable locks about thy fair face, the zephyr disheveleth,

The fragrance of musk and amber is diffused in every brain.

Since, in thy tresses, my heart is lost, show thou thy face to me;

For in night's gloom, lost things are, with lighted lamp, sought for.

Equal to that deliciousness, which I have, from thy lips, imbibed;

Term me a liar if such, as luscious, be in the wine-cup found.

Bear, O zephyr unto the nightingale, this message of mine—

"The rose's fragrance or its trace, in this parterre, will, doubtless, be."

For one moment, at least, sit thou with KHUSHḤĀL in tranquillity,

That his heart may, from its heavy sorrows, some slight solace find!

XCIV.

From the lustre of the internal, the exterior is clear and bright;

But by intercourse with the base, there are a hundred ills.

Like the name of alchemy and of the phœnix, that we hear about,

Than both of these, sincerity and fidelity are more rarely found.

From the lips of the despicable thou hearest a thousand things;

For when will they rest satisfied with a single harangue?

Do ṇot allow thyself to be deceived by friends of the present day—

Before thy face, they are for thee; but behind thee, back to back.

Do thou, O KHUSHḤĀL! call in that great physician's aid,

In the refulgence of whose face there 's perfect cure for thee!

XCV.

Account him a good man, who, in heart, is innocent and pure;

For modesty and uprightness are manifest in him always.

He, who may not possess these few qualịties, is not a man;

And whatever he wisheth let him do; for he is absolved from all.

They who contend with the world, for the sake of worldly goods,

Are like unto dogs, fighting and snarling, a mass of carrion upon.

If a wise man be, in appearance unsightly, what mattereth it

What though a homely scabbard hath been for a good blade made?

In these matters, no one else hath any business or concern whatever;

For 'tis the money-changer, that, distinguisheth the pure from the alloy.

The jeweller will himself make them show their respective qualities,

Though, in colour, the agate may be more pellucid than the ruby itself.

I wander everywhere in search of friendship, and find it not:

In what direction do they dwell, that know aught of faithfulness?

He will not be acquainted with the art of weaving velvet,

Although the maker of mats is, also, among weavers accounted.

Love hath not proceeded either from what is true, or what is futile;

But manifold are the pilgrimages made to the idol of its shrine.

Those charming ones have grown so numerous, that I fear them now

I, KHUSHHĀL, that of my piety and godliness have boasted so much.

XCVI.

All woman-kind are of intellect deficient;

And the voluntary causes of all life's ills.

Thou mayst be straight and even with them;

But they are crooked and wayward with thee.

Do them a thousand benefits and services;

Yet, at a single word, their hearts sulky grow.

They become poison unto thee, and kill thee—

They, whom thou deemest a healing balm.

They have no fidelity in their composition:

They are, naturally, unto perfidiousness prone.

Created, indeed, in the figure of mankind;

But, in reality, with no humanity in them.

They make thee out culpable, on a slight offence;

But they cannot be wrong, however great their sins.

The more crossness borne, the more petulant they:

The more whims brooked, the more capricious they grow.

In all things, they are fickle, and changeable:

Tame in tongue, * but untameable in heart.

They are beautiful in person, from head to foot;

But are like unto the wily serpent within.

Say no more about them, O KHUSHHĀL!

It would be better had they never.existed!

XCVII.

I am of those eyes of thine enamoured—look thou upon me!

I am the Hindū slave of thy locks; but dispose not of me!

With this form, and these charms, that thou possessest,

It would be, indeed, wonderful, were any other born like thee.

In grace and loveliness, there is no one equal unto thee—

This is the pity, that thou art, wholly, pitiless and unkind.

Though I die of grief for thee, still thou turnest away from me:

What! is the love of thine heart turned so dark for me?

I will never abandon thy door, nor thy dwelling-place,

Though thou mayest, without fire, cruelly, me consume.

Shouldst thou inflict a thousand cruelties on me, imagine not,

That the love of my heart will, towards thee, ever be changed.

I am well off, sunk down contemptible, in the dust at thy door;

But not so elsewhere, though I should upon a throne recline.

XCVIII.

The mercy of the Almighty be upon Akorraey, * that selected Sarā'e † for his home!

Since I have on the subject reflected, if thou believe me, 'tis, of all others, the spot.

Its dark mountain-range of Hoddaey, ‡ runneth directly into the Tī-rāh country,

And the Nīl-āb and Landdaey have, wonderfully, laid their heads at its feet. §

The great high road of Hindūstān and Khurāsān, is made along their banks;

And by Attak lieth its ford, which both kings and beggars hold in dread.

Every blessing of the earth, that can be called to mind, cometh to us thereby;

And, as the country is rainy, who shall tell how beautiful is its spring?

Whether it be the district of Suwāt, or Ashnagar, or whether Pes'hāwar,

They have recourse unto it; and its abundance goeth forth to them all.

There is game around, in every direction—sport for falcon, hawk, or hound:

Hail! hail! Kālah-parrnī! * what heart-ravishing sport dost thou contain!

The youth of Sarā'e are healthy and stout; active and agile, in every thing:

Merry-eyed; white and red; and tall in stature are they, the eye unto.

Whether it be son, or grand-son; whether family, or whether tribe,

May the protection of the Almighty be extended to all who dwell therein!

Fate, alas! hath taken him from it—can the arm of any one reach fate?

KHUSHḤĀL, hath not been severed from Sarā'e of his own accord—ah no! †

Footnotes

150:* These are the Afrīdī chiefs, who aided Khushḥāl in his wars with Aurangzeb.

150:† The name of a Pass leading from Peshāwar to Jalālābād.

150:‡ A small State, held by independent Afghān tribes, NẈ. of Peshāwar.

150:§ He had gone into the Yūsufzī country, to endeavour to persuade that tribe to assist the confederates.

150:§§ See note at page 139.

151:* The lofty mountain to the right of the Khaibar Pass, looking from Peshāwar, and giving name to another Pass, leading to Jalālābād.

151:† A *parganah* or division of the Peshāwar district, lying, as its name implies, between two rivers, the Landdaey and the Kabūl.

151:‡ A town of the Peshāwar district, on the northern bank of the Kabūl river.

152:* Aurangzeb dethroned his father Shāh Jahān, whom he confined in prison until his death, which took place seven years after.

152:† The Yūsufzīs who would not aid.

153:* A small district of Afghānistān, of which Jalālābād, famous for its defence by Sir Robert Sale, is the chief town.

153:† The fifth month of the Afghān year, so called.

153:‡ According to the *Abjad* system of the Arabs and other Muḥammadans, of computing numbers by letters, the word غفو(ghafū) is equivalent to the year H. 1086 (A.D. 1675.)

153:§ Cause the bud to open its leaves.

154:* One of the three great divisions into which the whole Afghān nation is divided, and in which the Khattak tribe is included.

154:† See the Introductory Chapter, page xix., on the word "ALASTO."

155:* Kasrā, or Cyrus, King of Persia, is the model of a just king; and Hujāj bin Yūsuf, Governor of Khurāsān, under the Khalīfah, Æabd-ul-Malik, the conception of a perfect tyrant.

158:* The fabulous mountain, the boundary of the world, and surrounding the horizon on all sides.

159:* Bū-Lḥab and Bū-Jhal, the former the uncle, and the latter the cousin of Muḥammad, were his greatest enemies and opposers in the propagation of his new faith. Æumar, the second Khalīfah after Muḥammad, is called Fārūḳ, The Distinguisher.

160:* Gabr is the name given to Fire-worshippers, or Pārsīs.

161:* The elephant is in the habit of sprinkling himself with dust, to drive insects away; but here it is to indicate sorrow.

163:* Ṣulṭān Muezz-ud-dīn Sanjar was the son of Malik Shāh, sixth monarch of the race of Seljūk, and for upwards of twenty years Governor of Khurāsān. His life is remarkable for the vicissitudes he suffered, having once been confined for four years in an iron cage, by the Guzzian tribe of Turkomāns, but subsequently escaped. He died the 25th of Rubbīah-ul-awal, A.H. 552, after a reign of forty-one years, paramount sovereign of Persia, and in the 73rd of his age. With him the grandeur of the race of Seljuk terminated. He has been equally praised for his piety and modesty of disposition, and for his benevolence, and the love of his people; for his respect for, and his encouragement of learning and learned men; and for his zeal and exertions to promote the advancement of his religion.

164:* For an account of Shahdād and his garden of Iram, see note at page 81.

164:† Ibid.

164:‡ Mir-bāz Khān, a connexion of Khushḥāl's; who was a worshipper of the wealth of the Mughals.

167:* Ḳārūn, son of Yeshar, the uncle of Moses, and identical with Korah of the Scriptures, who, at the complaint of Moses, against whom he had brought a false accusation, was swallowed by the earth, at the command of the Almighty.

168:* Referring to the Muḥammadan account of the creation, for which see Sale's edition of the ḲUR'ĀN.

169:* A person who acts as go-between of the parents in cases of marriage or betrothal.

169:† The rue-plant was anciently regarded as an infallible antidote against poison, pestilence, and the devil. It is much used in exorcisms, and has been extravagantly eulogized and extolled by all writers, from Hippocrates to Bœrhaave. By the Afghāns, the herb and its seeds are used as fumigations, to ward off the evil-eye.

171:* See note at page 15.

171:† A belt, or cord more particularly, worn round the middle by the Eastern Christians and Jews, and also by the Persian Magi. It was introduced A.D. 859, by the Khalīfāh Mutawakkil, to distinguish them from Muḥammadans.

172:* This appears to refer to some of the poet's wives, who bore him disobedient sons.

173:* Two undutiful sons of the poet, particularly Bahrām.

173:† The species of parrot here referred to we should term paroquet in this country. Green is the mourning colour in Muḥammadan countries.

175:* A kind of Darwesh or devotee, who goes about almost naked.

175:† It is usual with young females to wear a clove in the nostril, to keep open the orifice pierced for the insertion of the nose jewel, on marriage.

175:‡ A black mole.

175:§ See note at page 48.

175:§§ See note at page 137.

177:* Lit. "The father of ignorance," an uncle of Muḥammad's. See also note at page 159.

178:* A kind of dish made from flesh and rice, to which are added raisins and almonds, etc.

179:* Aurangzeb, son of the Emperor Shāh Jahān.

179:† Literally, house-born slaves; but here the term applies to the trusty chiefs and followers of Shāh Jahān, who was dethroned by Aurangzeb.

181:*

"A want of occupation is not rest;

A mind quite vacant, is a mind distress'd."—COWPER.

181:† Written on the poet's return from Suwāt, where he had gone to endeavour to induce the Yūsufzīs to join the confederacy against Aurangzeb.

182:* A skinner or tanner is looked upon with great contempt by the Afghāns.

183:* Sama'h signifies a plain in the Afghān language, and is the name given to that tract of country, lying between the Kabūl river, near its junction with the Indus, and the mountains bounding Suwāt on the south.

183:† Referring to the unhappy end of the Emperor Shāh Jahān, dethroned and imprisoned by Aurangzeb his son.

186:* See note at page 74.

187:* Under the two names of Irān and Turān, from whence the people are termed Irānī and Turānī, Eastern authors comprehend all the higher Asia, except China and India. Irān, which is the Eastern name for the Persian Empire, includes all that immense tract of country, lying between the Oxus or Bākhtrus on the north, the Arabian sea on the south, and the Tigris on the west. The region beyond the Oxus is Turān or Scythia, or Turkomānia. In some instances, Irānī and Turānī include all mankind, in the same manner as Greek and Barbarian—Jew and Gentile—Arab and Ajam.

187:† All the different tribes here mentioned are not Afghāns, but are either located in Afghānistān or border on the Afghān country. The Panjābīs and Sikhs not being mentioned, would indicate that in Khushḥāl's days they were not recognised as separate people, but included amongst Hindūstānīs.

189:* A black-eyed virgin of the Muḥammadan Paradise.

191:* Reading over the *sūra* or chapter of the Ḳur'ān, entitled " *kul huwa-l-lah*," by way of benediction, and to preserve one's self from evil and misfortune.

191:† A religious mendicant or devotee.

191:‡ That is to say, an impossible thing.

193:* An old fortress and village on the west bank of the Indus, facing Attak.

193:† The town of Sarā'e, belonging to the Khattak tribe of Afghāns, lies amongst the hills to the west of Attak, and not far from the west bank of the Sind or Indus. It is one of the chief towns of the tribe, and was the birthplace of the poet, and most of his ancestors are here buried; but Khushḥāl himself was buried at a different place. See notice preceding his poems.

194:* Abā-Sind, signifying "the father of rivers," is the Afghān name for the Indus. The Landdaey-Sind, or "little river," is that known as the river of Kabūl, after its junction with the Suwāt (the ancient Suastus), until it joins the Indus a little above Attak.

194:† Hind, or Hindūstān.

195:* This poem was written by one of Khushḥāl's wives, the mother of Ashraf, himself a poet, who died in exile in Southern India. It would almost appear to be a reply to the poem preceding, which was written by Khushḥāl, whilst in exile in India.

195:† The leaves of a tree (*Lawsonia inermis*) from which a bright orange red colour is extracted, and with which the Muḥammadan people of Asia dye the hands and feet on festive occasions.

195:‡ Used to give a bright red colour to the lips; but the bark of the walnut-tree seems to be the favourite substance for the purpose among the Afghān females now-a-days.

195:§ The play on the words in these two last lines are nearly lost in translation; for instead of inserting her own name, the writer uses her husband's, which signifies 'happy.' To have inserted her own name would have been considered indelicate.

197:* Afrīt—one of the most fierce and cruel of the genii, or demons, of Oriental tales.

197:† Pattāns, another name for the Afghāns.

197:‡ The Afghān Emperors of India, of the Lūdī tribe, were Sulṭāns Bahlol, Sikandar, and Ibrahīm, who reigned from A.D.1450 to 1526, when Bābar conquered Hindūstān. His son, Humāyūn, was again dethroned by Sher Shāh, an Afghān of the tribe of Sūr, in A.D. 1540. To him succeeded Salīm Shāh, his son, whose son, Muḥammad Shāh, was dethroned by Humāyūn, the previous Emperor, and father of Akbar, in 1556.

198:* A kind of cloth or gauze, which is said to be rent by exposure to the moonlight; and, hence, is represented by Oriental poets as enamoured of the moon.

199:* See note at page 29.

199:† A tribe of Afghāns, dwelling in the hills to the west and south of Peshāwar, who are about the most uncivilized of the Afghāns.

199:‡ The celebrated saint of the Afghāns, and great antagonist of Pīr Roshān, the founder of the Roshānīān sect of schismatics. He changed the name of Pīr Roshān, signifying, "Saint of Light," into Pīr Tārīk, or "Saint of Darkness."

199:§ Bāyazīd Ansārī, who took the name of Pīr Roshān, as above stated. For further accounts of this man, see page 51.

199:§§ The red carnelian caskets refer to the gums, and the pearls are the teeth in them.

199:** The eye is compared to the narcissus, and white roses to a clear complexion.

200:* Æsop.

200:† Solomon.

201:* Hujāj, the Governor of Khurāsān under the Khalīfahs of the house of Omeyah, and a notorious tyrant.

201:† A Persian monarch, celebrated throughout the East for his justice and equity, hence he is known as "Noshīrwān the Just." It was during his reign that Muḥammad was born.

203:* The letter ا (*alif*), from its form, is adopted to denote straightness of stature.

203:† See Poem XCVIII., third note.

203:‡ The name of a pass or defile, leading into the Tī-rāh country, held by the Afrīdī tribe of Afghāns.

204:* The rubies signify the lips, and the pearls the teeth.

206:* See page 142.

207:* Mummy—the substance with which Egyptian mummies are preserved, a medicine held in great estimation in Oriental countries for wounds and fractures.

207:† A celebrated Arabian poet, famous for his eloquence.

207:‡ The name of an Arab, celebrated throughout the East for his liberality and munificence.

208:* The letter ا (*alif*) is an emblem of the Almighty—the One and Only.

208:† Attar of roses.

209:* The family of the Khattak tribe in which the chieftainship was, and still is hereditary.

209:† See note at page 193.

210:* The long curls of the hair of the Afghān females, often reaching below the waist, are compared to black snakes. See note at page 136.

212:* A crier, who summons the Faithful to prayer, by proclamation from the minaret of a mosque.

212:† The name of a small district to the west of Peshāwar, and south of the Khaibar Pass.

212:‡ Two of the three independent tribes of the Khaibarīs, altogether about 120,000 souls, who hold the Khaibar Pass. They are the most uncouth and uncivilized of the Afghān tribes.

213:* See Introductory Remarks, for an account of the Ṣūfis and their tenets.

213:† Long and wide sleeves are worn in the East.

215:* This was written during his wars with the Mughals.

217:* Jahangir Shāh, signifying "the world-conquering king," is the title assumed by the fourth Mughal Emperor of India, and son of Akbar. Nūr Maḥāl, "the light of the ḥaram," is the name of his favourite queen.

217:† Antimony, used in Oriental countries to increase the blackness of the eyes, by applying it to the lids. See "LANE'S MODERN EGYPTIANS."

217:‡ The reed or pipe is an emblem of slightness and weakness, and the utterer of plaintive sounds.

219:* The black-eyed virgins of the Muḥammadan Paradise.

220:* See first note at p. 183.

220:† Khatā or Khatay, the northern part of China, or Chinese Tārtary, famous for its musk and pretty damsels.

221:* The Hindū women boldly and fearlessly mount the funeral pyre of their deceased husbands, for what they consider honour's sake.

222:* China and Chinese Tartary, famous for beautiful women.

223:* The patriarch Jacob.

223:† Referring to the scanty garments of the women of India.

223:‡ Indian husbands chastise their wives with a shoe for very trivial matters.

223:§ In a contemptuous sense, as sold unto gold and infidelity.

224:* There is a good deal of foppery manifested in the East regarding the tail or termination of the turban, which hangs behind.

225:* The poet's name signifies 'happy;' hence the play upon the word here, which would lose by translation.

226:* This would appear to refer to the dark red tulip.

226:† The hyacinth or spikenard is compared to the dark locks, and the lily or jasmine to the fairness of the face of the beloved one.

226:‡ See note at page 221.

227:* An earthly paradise, a fabulous garden in Arabia.

227:† See note at page 137.

228:* As before stated, the name of the poet signifies 'happy;' hence, "where the heart has become happy," is the meaning above.

229:* "Balæām (Balaam), son of Beor, who, being requested by his nation to curse Moses and the children of Israel, refused at first, saying, "How can I curse those whom the angels protect?" But afterwards he was prevailed upon by gifts; and he had no sooner done what they wished, than he began to put out his tongue like a dog, and it hung down upon his breast."—Al Beidāwī, Jalāl-ud-dīn, Al Zamakhshārī.

230:* Musk here signifies 'youth,' when the hair is of the colour of musk; and camphor, 'old age,' when the hair turns silvery.

231:* Referring to the nib of a pen.

234:* The faithless and insincere.

235:* This poem appears to have reference to the coldness of the poet's confederates in the war with the Mughals, and to the trouble Khushḥāl had with his sons.

235:† The name of the ancestor of one of the great divisions of the Afghāns, including some of the western tribes, and also the Yūsufzīs of the north-eastern parts of Afghānistān, who refused assistance to Khushḥāl and his confederates, in their wars with Aurangzeb.

235:‡ Damghār is the name of a small town in Suwāt.

239:* Ascetics and darweshes carry a club or staff.

240:* The Emperor Aurangzeb, finding that Khushḥāl and his brother confederates could not be subdued with the sword, tried gold and diplomacy, to which the most of them succumbed. See page 144.

241:* See Khushḥāl, Poem I., 'An Ode to Spring,' stanza 17.

242:* Cypræa moneta.

246:* Not always, at least, as far as the tongues of most Englishwomen go.

247:* Akorraey is the name of Khushḥāl's great-grandfather, who conquered from the Wurakzī tribe, the country now held by the Khattaks. There is a town also named after this chief, between Attak and Peshāwar.

247:† See note at page 193.

247:‡ The high mountain facing Attak, and a little lower down than the village of Khairābād on the same side, which rises up directly from the Indus, is mount

Hoddaey, which gives its name to the whole range, reaching as far as Tī-rāh, a district lying about south-east from Pes'hāwar. The Bārā river rises in Tī-rāh, which is beyond the Khaibar Pass, and is inhabited by Afghāns of the Afrīdī and Tī-rāh tribes.

247:§ The Nīl-āb, or Blue-water, is one of the names of the Indus, which washes the base of Hoddaey. A few miles further up is the Landdaey, in Pushto signifying the Less or Little, a name given to the river of Kabūl, which joins the Indus a few miles above Attak, a town on the east bank of the Indus, on the high-road between India and Khurāsān.

248:* Kālah-parrnī is the name of an extensive forest in the Khattak country, once famous for its game.

248:† This poem was written during the poet's exile in India; and Sarā'e was his place of birth.

ASHRAF KHĀN, KHATTAK.

ASHRAF KHĀN, eldest son of Khushhāl Khān, the subject of the preceding notice, was born in the year H. 1044 (A.D. 1634); and when the war, which had been carried on by his father and other Afghān chieftains, against the Mughal Emperor, died out, Khushhāl, wholly disgusted with the world, resigned the chieftainship of the Khattak tribe in favour of Ashraf, A.H.1093 (A.D. 1681.) The circumstances, which brought these matters about, having been related at length in the notice preceding Khushhāl's poems, need not be repeated here.

Ashraf endeavoured for some time to carry on the government of his clan, and also to perform his duties towards the Mughal Government, by aiding the Pes'hāwar authorities in the administration of the affairs of that province; but he was opposed and thwarted in all his endeavours by his brother Bahrām, the same who endeavoured to take the life of his father, who styles him "Bahrām the Degenerate," and "The Malignant;" and by whose machinations, Ashraf was, at last, betrayed into the hands of Aurangzeb, in the year H. 1095 (A.D.1683). The affairs of the Dakhan having called for the presence of that monarch, who continued in that part of India for several years, the Khattak chief was taken along with him, as a state prisoner; and was subsequently sent to the strong fortress of Bijāpūr, situated in what is, at present, termed the Southern Mahārata country, where he continued to languish in exile for the remainder of his life. He died in the year H. 1105 (A.D. 1693), and in the 60th year of his age.

Ashraf used, occasionally, to devote some of his leisure time to poetry, before he assumed the government of his clan, incited, doubtless, by the example of his brave old father, and his brothers Æabd-ul-Ḳādir and Ṣadr Khān, who were also gifted with the " *cacoëthes scribendi.*" During his exile he wrote a great number of poems, and collected the whole, as they now stand, in the form of a Dīwān, or Alphabetical Collection. According to the usual custom among Eastern poets, Ashraf assumed the name of "The Severed" or "Exiled;" and many of his poems, written in the most pathetic style, plainly tell where, and under what circumstances, they were composed. The original Dīwān, or Collection, arranged and written by himself, at Bijāpūr, is still in the possession of his descendants, and from it the following poems were extracted; indeed, I am not aware that any other copy of his poems exists. Ashraf is regarded by the Afghāns as a good poet; but his effusions are, without reason apparently, considered difficult and abstruse.

When Afẓal Khān, his son, became firmly established in the chieftainship, he caused the remains of his father to be removed from Bijāpūr to Sarā'e—where the Khattak chiefs have been usually interred—a distance of some fifteen hundred miles.

THE POEMS OF ASHRAF KHĀN, KHATTAK.

I.

THE promise of the kiss, the beloved ever putteth off for to-morrow;

Then how can my heart place confidence in a pledge like this?

Whoso is vain enough to depend upon the affairs of the future,

The wise and sagacious will laugh that foolish man to scorn.

My friend is not acquainted with the deceitfulness of the world;

Yet still she deceiveth, having, in her heart, naught of truthfulness.

Do not presume to this degree, upon the loveliness of the face:

Behold the autumn! doth it ever, to the rose, any bloom impart?

Thou, who through arrogance, attest thus falsely towards me;

Time will pay back unto thee the requital of these deeds of thine.

In the land of association, the appliances of pleasure will be many;

But the troops of bereavement, full speedily, lay it waste.

Never cast thou thine eyes upon the rose, O nightingale!

For separation will make those fresh wounds of thine still worse.

But is the nightingale wont, through advice, the rose to forswear?

No! 'tis the blast of autumn only that separateth them by force!

Full many have departed in sorrow, with the hope of to-morrow;

Then who will place any reliance on life's fidelity to-day?

Thou, who in the hope of existence therefrom, restest in tranquillity

Doth the empyrean ever any opportunity for continuance allow?

To-day, I perceive the crisis of a contingency on the world impending;

But the future may make apparent unto it some other event. *

THE SEVERED had never beheld Bijāpūr, even in his dreams; †

But, at last, that presenteth itself, which his destiny decreed!

II.

When, in the shape of a shield, the hair on the forehead is plaited ‡

The roses wreathed therein, impart the intrinsic virtues of the sun.

The live-coal-like ruby in her nose jewel § is fire itself;

And the red bulāḳ, §§ like unto a spark of fire, is placed by its side.

The chamkala'ī * on her forehead is hence red with her lover's blood,

That every jewel therein, for piercing, is like a lancet disposed.

Her eyebrows are a bent bow; her eyelashes, arrows adjusted:

The ornaments of beauty are sometimes a sword; at others, a dagger made.

The devotee of a hundred years is, with one of her glances undone,

When she decketh out her beauteous person, and goeth forth.

When she disposeth her flowing tresses in curls about her face,

To the Ethiop army she accordeth permission, devastation to make.

Her dark eyes she maketh still more black, by the antimony;

And every eyelash she will make moist in her lover's blood.

Soft and tender tales she telleth, but they are all dissimulation:

She casteth her enchantments round the heart, by pretexts and pleas.

For her lover, Tartarus and Elysium are ready provided;

Since the sweet Paradise of conjunction, separation turneth to Hell.

The shadow of love is, undoubtedly, the philosopher's stone;

Since upon whomever it may be rubbed, his body is turned to gold.

The punishment is death, in the creed of passion's votaries,

For him, who entereth love's path, and feareth its struggles and strife.

Never let him, at any time, gaze upon the face of the beloved,

Who may be partial unto life, and for his head may fear.

Like unto the inroads the heart-ravishers make my heart upon—

When do the Khaibarīs such upon the Mughals' heads ever make?

THE SEPARATED will not, thro' injustice, turn his back to the beloved;

Though she should make his body red with blood all over!

III.

With the scar of sorrow, he will his own heart afflict,

If, on the world's affairs, any one should reliance place.

Do not grow vain of its favour; for all is deception:

Do not imagine, that, in reality, it benevolence showeth.

When it did not act faithfully with those that have gone,

Whoever seeketh constancy from it to-day, erreth greatly.

The foundation of all its acts is on injustice based:

From the age hope not for good faith; for it knoweth it not.

Do not pride thyself on the friendship of that friend,

Who, in the same breath, in a thousand other places smileth.

I place not an hour's reliance on the permanence of life:

He is a fool who nourisheth great hopes of immutability.

All those splendid edifices, that thou, in the world, beholdest,

Cruel destiny, at last, will them to a naked desert turn.

THE SEPARATED, in the Dakhan, would not have a moment stayed;

But when doth fate ever fulfil our wishes and requests!

IV.

What shall I say unto any one regarding the anguish of separation?

Since it hath not even left within me the power to complain!

Since every injury she heapeth upon me is right and lawful;

At least, let the proud one stand once with face towards me.

The gold bracelets upon her wrists make an amazing display:

Fit Let them never become broken from the disasters of fate!

For my case, O physician! thou ever showest commiseration—

Thou sayest, "by antidotes, thou wilt be from thy afflictions relieved."

The diseases of the body thou knowest, without doubt;

But when is the agony of the heart laid bare unto thee?

Khattak that I am, with exile I am never content;

But affection for my friend hath from my kin severed me.

The grief of THE SEPARATED shall be changed into gladness,

If any one, from the tavern, shall bring wine unto me.

V.

Like as absence from the beloved hath made day dark to me,

Let there never be, unto any one, such a dark and lurid day!

Do not be overjoyed, O marplot! on account of my disjunction;

For at last, dark and overcast like this, shall be thy day!

Though constancy may grant to no one the opportunity of association,

The night of separation, at last, shall become the unclouded day!

The spring-time of youth was, than the flowers more pleasant;

But, alas! it was not so very lasting, the constancy of that day!

Draw near, O friend, and honour me with a sight of thee!

For the Almighty hath not in the world created an unchanging day!

Thou that ever puttest off, for to-morrow, the promise of meeting,

Consider what phase may be assumed by to-morrow's day!

The day of delight and pleasure hath passed, as the wind, away—

For how long shall malice on me be vented by trouble's day!

TTruly, it will be, at last, like the wind that hath passed away,

This, that I now behold—separation's long, dreary day!

The grief and joy of fortune's changes shall not last for aye:

Verily, O SEPARATED! it shall reach its end, this oppression's day!

VI.

Account as wind or as dust, the world's pains and pleasures:

The free man is not disquieted, by either its troubles or its cares.

Their coming, and their going, are more speedy than the dawn; *

For I have, myself, experienced the heat and the cold of time.

Show thou no hankering for the fare on the board of fortune;

For there is not a morsel thereon, free from bitterness and woe.

In a moment it produceth forms and figures of manifold fashions—

As a mere throw of the dice account the revolutions of fate.

Whoso may plume himself on a lucky turn of good fortune,

It dealeth him a painful wound, at the moment of exulting thereon.

If, with the eye of understanding, its sorrows and joys be viewed,

The permanence of their duration is, than that of the flower no more.

Turn thy back, O SEPARATED! unto evil; thy face towards good,

That, on the Great Day of Assembly, * thou mayest not, with fear, be pale.

VII.

In love for thee, O never let my heart grow cold

Like thine, that in perpetrating injustice, never groweth cold!

When will any one a true and sincere lover style me,

If my heart, in grief for thee, unto constancy turn cold?

No! my heart shall never wax cold unto faithfulness;

Nor, in this world, will thy nature, unto tyranny grow cold.

Nal, with all his wrongs, did not his back on Daman turn; †

Then how can any one's heart now, unto thee turn cold?

What clamour did the unscathed raise on him always;

Yet the love of Majnūn for his Laylā grew not cold.

Advisers would, unto him, good counsel ever give?

But no admonitions made Wāmik, unto Æaẓrā cold!

Neither did the world show constancy unto the departed;

Nor have the souls of the covetous, unto the world grown cold.

My burnt-up heart hath become as fresh at a sight of thee,

As the seed of sweet basil maketh the heat-stricken cold.

The hope of my meeting hath cooled the fever of absence;

And the perspiration of recovery always maketh the feverish cold.

Even at thy death, THE SEPARATED will not thy love renounce;

And forsworn is he, if, in life, his heart unto thee turn cold!

VIII.

O thou, who pridest thyself on the plenitude of the world's wealth!

How is it that the condition of thy forefathers restraineth thee not?

Their obvious existence, than that of the flowers hath been less;

Place then no reliance upon the mere phantasies of the world.

What is it to thee, though the face of the earth be broad?

But three yards, in its bosom, is all thy portion thereof.

Since, beneath the earth's surface, thy abode is appointed,

Fruitlessly, upon it, thou buildest thy mansions and thy courts.

Gaiety and enjoyment are intended for the callous and unconscious;

But sorrow and concern are, wholly, the portion of the enlightened.

The votaries of the world are all tyrants and oppressors;

From any one of them, of faithfulness, I have never yet heard.

They evince not a particle of shame, even in humanity's name:

They worry and rend each other, like unto ravenous beasts.

Outwardly, they may practise the appearance of friendship;

But the heart of every man is filled with opposition and strife.

Those deceptions that the world's sons now-a-day practise,

Even the fox would not be guilty of such wiles and deceits.

Weep not, though thou shouldst experience adversity's frowns!

For the evils and afflictions of this transient world shall not endure.

With the true and sincere, O SEPARATED! love and affection are good;

But with the deceitful, friendship advantageth not the least.

IX.

Since I am ever hopeful of meeting thee, either to day or to-morrow,

Uselessly, in this insane idea, passeth my sweet life away.

With cries and supplications, I seek it to-day, but find it not;
For the soldiery of separation destroy the period of my joy.
The tree of prosperity yielded not to me the fruit of my desires:
In wails and lamentations, unjustly, my body I wearied make.
In the beginning, when the tree of affection was created,
Its innate properties brought forth absence's bitter fruit.
I was wont, unconsciously, to eat of the fruit of separation,
When, in the garden, I planted affection's tender sprout.
In disjunction, O friends! I perceive no fault whatever:
The heart, this misfortune permitteth, when acquainted therewith.
With the sword of separation, He cleaveth asunder, at last,
The heart of him, whom He, of a lovely face, enamoured maketh.
The game of absence, He at that time made so absorbing,
When, in the world, He thus the mart of affection thronged.
THE SEPARATED mentioned not, unto a soul, the secret of love;
But, in the alley of his beloved, the world humiliated him.

X.

When He, of His omnipotence, first the pen produced,
The destiny of every one, He then with its tongue * wrote down.
To-day, at every respiration, that allotment arriveth—
To the share of some, He joy assigned; to the lot of others, grief.
By strife and contention now, he cannot great become,

Who, from all eternity, was entered in an inferior degree.
Thro' the hatred of the envious, never can become crooked—
The lot of him, which, in the beginning, He made straight.
When doth death seize the skirt of any one, out of season?
Yet they will not tarry a moment, whose time is fulfilled.
The will of destiny ejected him from the abode of bliss;
And then it charged unfortunate Adam with the sin.
At the wounds of fortune, O SEPARATED! do not sigh;
For God hath, for the stricken, prepared a wondrous salve!

XI.

Whoever dwelleth in this abode of calamity and affliction,
For every one, there is trouble, each according to his case.
I seek after a place of safety, but I am unable to find one;
The world, to this degree, is so full of misery and woe:
Though fortune may, a thousand joys, on thee bestow,
With one affliction, it trampleth them all in the dust.
Neither is its most propitious time worthy of rejoicing;
Nor is its most portentous hour for lamentation befitting.
Be not cast down at its sorrows, for they do not continue;
And with its pleasures also, do not thou grow overjoyed.
If fortune grant unto thee an interview with a pretty one,
With the sting of separation, it speedily pierceth thy heart.

Prosperity never entereth within the precincts of one's abode,
Until misery and adversity its companions it maketh.
Good fortune, by its own words, saith, "I am not lasting,"
If thou shouldst but reverse the letters of that word. *
The pigeon of vitality, it bringeth quickly down from its flight,
When the falcon of destiny spreadeth its pillions to the wind.
It draweth, without pretext, the dragon from the cave:
From the river it extracteth the fish, weak and paralyzed.
There is no cause for arrogance in life's immutability;
For it passeth by like the wind, both month and year.
Like a fool, O SEPARATED! do not thou its slave become;
For the world's joys and sorrows are a phantom and a dream!

XII.

Whoever have fattened on the fleeting wealth of the world,
The worms of the earth, at last, have become glutted with them!
The world's great ones too, whose history the books relate,
One after the other have fallen, slaughtered by the knife of death!
Their wealth, lands, and mansions, they have transmitted to others:
Body by body, they have fallen asleep in the house of the tomb!
Of the empty adulations of the world, they were amazingly vain;
But they were overcome with regret, when the time of departure came.
Seeing that the world showed no constancy to the departed,

How are those who remain, so ardent, to-day, in its pursuit?

The world is a faithless bride, that destroyeth her husband;

Hence the wise, for this reason, are to her friendship so cold.

The flowers, that every season bloomed in the garden so sweetly,

Have likewise, in the autumn, thus been scattered to the winds.

O thou, of vain pleasures so proud! for thy departure prepare!

Thy cotemporaries have grown weary in looking out for thee!

Behold these graves! say, what wilt thou with gardens do?

Look upon thy dear friends! observe what they have become!

Bend thy looks upon them—comely youths, and youthful brides!

Separate from each other, in their graves they have withered away!

By virtuous actions, O SEPARATED! Heaven is attainable;

Then never follow in the way of those who have gone astray.

XIII.

For the soul's journey, the white steed became saddled in the heart,

When upon my chin grew white the hair of youthful days.

When the spring-time of youth unto the body bade adieu,

The black hair waxed silvery in the autumn of old age.

Since the miseries of absence have not reduced them to ashes;

What! have these bones of my body, all, into iron turned?

Either my good fortune, fallen asleep, giveth me no aid,

Or the rulers of the present age have stony-hearted grown.

Whereas the heads thereof make no impression on their bodies,

On their armour must have broken the arrows of my sighs.

Sorrow, to this degree, causeth the blood from mine eyes to flow,

That the garments of my body have become tinged therefrom.

Behold the state of my eyeballs, by separation caused!

They have assumed the appearance of red roses within the parterre!

Though in the heart it may not have fallen, woe's seed sprouteth,

When, by the plough of disjunction, its ground-plot may be turned.

Would, O SEPARATED! that absence were, in the world, unknown;

For from its inroads have become desolate the people thereof!

XIV.

Of the pangs of separation I became deserving that day,

When, weeping and sobbing, from my love I was severed.

At that time, for my life, in tears of blood I mourned,

When, turning my back upon Attak, I weeping began.

How shall I now pine after the rocks and shrubs of my country?

For, having made my parting salutation, I bade them farewell.

Embedded in my heart, from Roh * an arrow I brought away—

I failed to bid adieu to my bower, or its sacrifice to become. †

With much toil, in the world I had a garden laid out;

And, as yet, I had not smelt a flower, when from it I was torn.

The blue heavens laughed from delight until they grew red,

When facing Hoddaey's mountain ‡ I turned from it away.

There is no magician in the Dakhan that can charm me;

For I am a prisoner become, in a dragon's cavern profound.

The assignment of union was hung on the horns of the deer, *

When I crossed to the other bank of Narbada's swift stream. †

The riches of association were a hoard that I gloated over;

But in absence's wars, I have to a mere thread and fibre changed.

How shall I, to-day, complain of bereavement unto any one?

I, myself, made a purchase of sorrow, when I a lover became.

The vast dust of separation hath hidden happiness from me—

I am utterly weary grown at the noise of summoning it back.

I, KHATTAK, call unto my beloved, but she is not forthcoming:

Mortified and despairing thereat, I have become wedded unto woe!

XV.

Come, my love! let us, in one home, our abode take up;

And from our minds dismiss all long and lingering hope!

Hand in hand we will saunter about; for such is fortunate:

It is not advisable that to-day's inclinations we for to-morrow defer.

From all eternity, revolving fortune is cruel and unjust:

It is a fallacy if we, to-day, nourish a hope of its constancy.

We were many friends, like unto a flock, gathered together,

When the wolf of separation, by violence, tore us from each other away.

Our dear, dear friends have from the world departed:

How long then shall we exist in this sublunary sphere?

How can any one the hope of joy and happiness entertain?

For He brought us into this abode, grief and misery to endure!

Living, O friend! THE SEPARATED would not have left thee;

But 'tis the king's tyranny that hath, by force, parted us! *

XVI.

The wise, for this reason, unto the world's affairs will be cold;

That all its griefs are like the blast, and like the dust its joys.

Do not, O Darwesh! false account my sorrow and my sighs;

For, at that time, the eyes will weep, when the heart may aching be.

The head of courage will not bow for the sake of throne and crown;

When the man, of spirit free, may know what the world's gifts are.

That man, who may traffic in perfidiousness, and in iniquity,

Will be pale and ghastly, when he entereth the assembly of the just.

In the estimation of the wise, even worse than the ox they are,

Who may be constantly overwhelmed in gluttony's cares.

The revolving heavens are a mill, and man the grain therein:

He is no sooner in the world, than he will into meal be ground.

It is out of the question altogether, that in Pus'hto any other bard,

Shall, like THE SEPARATED, so unrivalled, in the art poetic be.

XVII.

Completely false and lying are they all, from first to last,
Who are gathered around the table of the transient world!
The universe is like unto the shop of the sweetmeat-seller:
Account its resorters nothing else but the flies that they are!
The degree of affection, that the flies in that quarter bestow,
Is according to the quality of the sweets therein contained.
Place no reliance soever upon the mere display of their sincerity:
Falsely, they deception practise: they are their own weal's friends!
In the day of prosperity, of constancy, they ever make boast;
But when a slight disaster occurreth, they all take to flight.
The heart's eyes, for its own objects, show sycophancy to the tongue;
Then do not pride thyself on their oaths; for all are knaves.
Should they become aware of a good friend's affliction,
Their tongues cry, "Dear! dear!" but they exult in their hearts.
Hope not, in this world, to find a friend, sincere and true;
For the sons of the present day are hypocrites and rogues.
There is neither love, nor affection, nor friendship in them:
By some craft they acquire; for they are all the loaf's slaves.
The world's interests and profits are their object, and these they pursue:
They are neither stedfast on faith's path, nor infidels are they.
Like as they plot against the very heart's blood of one another,
In hatching each other's ruin are wolves ever thus occupied?

As yet, the day of doom hath not been viewed by human eye;

But its operations * I, to-day, perceive; since all are for themselves.

Never yet have I found, in any one, either fidelity or truth;

Whether it be in brethren or kinsmen, in relations or friends!

Since I, THE SEPARATED, became acquainted with its secrets,

I find the world hath countless women, and but few, few men!

Footnotes

252:* The poet here appears to refer to some chance of release from captivity.

252:† Bijāpūr, the name of the fortress in which he was confined.

252:‡ This refers to a custom prevalent amongst all the Afghān tribes in the days of the poet, and still observed by the Ghalzīs and other tribes of Central Afghānistān, of plaiting the front hair of young girls, from about eight years of age until the day of marriage, in a round plait about the size of a small saucer, which is allowed to hang down in front, and often reaches to the tip of the nose, but not covering the eyes, thus acting the part of a mask. On the marriage-day it is opened and plaited in the ordinary way. A picture containing a girl wearing the hair in this manner will be found in CAPTAIN L. W. HART'S work of "SKETCHES OF AFGHAN COSTUME," lithographed by HAGHE.

252:§ An ornament worn by women in the left nostril.

252:§§ A ring of gold worn in the cartilage of the nose.

253:* An ornament for the forehead. These names are Indian, not Afghān; but Afghāns bordering on the Panjāb and India have borrowed these terms and ornaments from the people of those parts.

256:* The coming and departure of day is very rapid in the East, there being but little twilight.

257:* The resurrection.

257:† The names Nal and Daman, Wāmik and Æaẓrā, Majnūn and Laylā, are those of lovers, celebrated in Eastern poetry.

259:* The nib of the pen.

261:* This very pretty idea of the poet's is a play upon the Arabic word اقبال *ik-bāl*, signifying, 'good fortune,' which, if read backwards, becomes لابقا *lā-bakā*, meaning, 'without stability or permanence.'

263:* Roh is the name applied to the Afghān countries generally; hence the name of Rohilahs, by which the Afghāns are sometimes distinguished.

263:† See third note at page 139.

263:‡ See third note at page 247.

264:* Referring to the custom of Eastern governments, of granting assignments on persons or revenues of villages, for payment of money. An assignment on a deer's horns is a proverb, with reference to any impracticable, or very difficult matter next to impossible, it being first necessary to catch your deer.

264:† A river of Central India.

265:* Referring to his captivity in India.

267:* All ties will then be broken; for all will be so much occupied with their own affairs and interests, that they will pay no attention to others, however dear they may have been in this world.

ÆABD-UL-ḲĀDIR KHĀN, KHATTAK.

ÆABD-UL-ḲĀDIR KHĀN, son of Khushḥāl Khān, Khattak, and brother of Ashraf, the subject of the preceding notice, was born in the year E. 1063 (A.D. 1652), and is the most eloquent writer and poet of all Khushḥāl's sons, several of whom were poets of no mean ability. Although his father had little reason to be very partial towards his sons generally, on account of their very unnatural conduct, and unfaithfulness towards himself, on too many occasions; yet, upon the whole, Æabd-ul-Ḳādir appears to have been a favourite, and to have shared considerably in his father's affection.

Æabd-ul-Ḳādir was as good at the sword as at the pen; and in the battle with the Mughal troops at Kottah, a place in the vicinity of the Pes'hāwar district, the victory of the confederate Afghāns was chiefly owing to the skill displayed by the poet on that occasion; and it was he also who led the assault against that fortress, which, after three hours of severe fighting, he captured. He afterwards distinguished himself; in like manner, in the war of Bangas'h, during which operations he was wounded; and the successes gained in the war were celebrated in his name.

When his father abdicated the chieftainship of the tribe (as related in the notice of Khushḥāl and his writings), and the sons were each struggling to supplant each other, and grasp the vacant authority, Æabd-ul-Ḳādir did not hold back. He tried very hard to gain the chieftainship, but fortune was unpropitious; and Ashraf, who, as the eldest son, had certainly the best right, was chosen by his father and the tribe to succeed him. When Ashraf was betrayed into the hands of the Mughals, and sent by Aurangzeb into the Dakhan as state prisoner, "Bahrām the Malignant," the brother, who had betrayed him, seized the chieftainship; but, subsequently, Afẓal Khān, the son of Ashraf, became chief of the clan.

To pay obedience to this nephew appears to have been extremely difficult and bitter for Æabd-ul-Ḳādir, who wished to hold the authority himself; and although the whole of his brothers, then living, sided with him in his ambitious designs, it was of no avail; for the tribe were unanimous in favour of Ashraf's son Afẓal, in whom was the hereditary right, as previously stated. The upshot, however, was, that Afẓal, the nephew, saw no other practicable solution of the difficulty, according to the custom of those days, than to get rid of all rivals; and, accordingly, Æabd-ul-Ḳādir, together with ten of his brothers, and a number of their sons, were put to death, at the village of Zamān Garraey, in one day, and buried in one grave; thus escaping the sorrows and troubles of chieftainship.

The poems of Æabd-ul-Ḳādir, which are deeply imbued with Ṣūfi mysticism, are thought very highly of by the Afghāns; and his language is extremely polished. His chief works, now known, are a Dīwān or Collection of Odes, from which the following poems are taken; a translation of Molawī Jāmī's celebrated poem of Yūsuf and Zulīkhā, from the Persian, which is rendered by the translator into the most difficult style of Eastern poetry, and is considered the most perfect of its kind in the Afghān language; the affecting love tale of Adam and Durkhāna'ī—which three or four other authors have written on, both in verse and prose—together with translations of Shaikh Saædī's Gulistān and Bostān, from the Persian

He is said, by his descendants of the present day, to have been the author of about sixty different works; but with the exception of a small volume on enigmas, charades, and verses of mysterious meaning, even the names of them are now unknown.

Specimens of his Odes in the original Pus'hto, together with a portion of Yūsuf and Zulīkhā, and the first part of the Gulistān, will be found in the "GULSHAN-I-ROH," or Selections in the Afghān Language, published by me last year.

THE POEMS OF ÆABD-UL-ĶĀDIR KHĀN,KHATTAK.

I.

ARISE, O cupbearer! bring the goblet; for see, the leaves burst forth!

They give, unto the parterre, the happy tidings of the coming of spring.

In thy wine there is the intoxication of uniformity and sincerity,

That changeth my intellect's black and white to one uniform tinge.

Like unto ice, shall the heart of the tale-bearer melt away altogether,

If the beloved, unto me, will show her countenance like the sun.

The black-eyed ones have not the fragrance of constancy within them;

On this point, regarding them, what hope shall any one indulge?

He, who may be existing on affection and love, never, never, dieth;

And the Almighty, too, is competent, my life, eternal to make.

With the whole heart she hath made away; but, even yet, behold

What enchantments, charms, deceits, and spells she employeth still!

What! hath ÆABD-UL-ĶĀDIR, this time, so benefited by her,

That he will place this much confidence in the beloved again?

II.

If I have my own friend chosen, with the censure attendant thereon;

The world's calumny and detraction I have accepted likewise.

The pangs of separation from her would not have been so great,

Had I, when enjoying her society, constantly lamented and wept.

Like unto the bee, I would have clasped the rose for ever to my breast,

Had I perceived in it the fragrance of constancy and faith.
They who, without asking, bestow, and mention not the obligation,
The generosity of them, above all others, have I ever preferred.
For this reason, the envious wandereth about from door to door,
Because I have driven him away from the threshold of my abode.
ÆABD-UL-ḲĀDIR, at that time, everlasting life acquired,
When, with the sword of her glances, she deprived me of life.

III.

Behold! the bee and the nightingale great folly commit,
Who, whilst the autumn is impending, give their love to the rose!
For how long shall this lamp in the garden continue to burn?
One day, the cold, boisterous blast of destiny shall extinguish it!
Totally changed to repulsiveness, in the morning becometh
The prettiness of the glow-worm, that, at night, giveth such effulgence and light.
The covert polytheist, equally with the open, appeareth unto them;
For when do the sanctified, to the whole or the parts, cast their eyes? *
The rose-bud openeth from the effect of the dew's moisture;
But the humidity of wine rendereth still harder the niggard's heart.
The spectators would declare the many beauties of her countenance;
But amazement calleth out to them the more silent to remain.
Thy pen, ÆABD-UL-ḲĀDIR! became, of musk, the diffuser;
Since thou greatly praisest the curls and ringlets of the fair.

IV.

Whether it be chieftainship, or lordliness, or a monarch's sway;

If thou perceivest, they are all fruitless trouble and anxiety.

Without the fair, both life and death, are one and the sane thing;

For the sake of the dear ones, alone, is existence of any usefulness.

By fate, the curls of the beloved must have been destined

For the derangement and disorder of my heart, from the beginning of time.

It is through inebriation, that the goblet hath fallen to the ground:

Account it not rage or anger, O cupbearer! 'tis but the levity of youth.

At the errors of the wise, indignation and reproach are levelled;

But the excuse of fools is their own ignorance and foolishness.

Thou wilt either give some one's dwelling to the flames, or shed his blood;

Seeing that thou hast donned garments of the Arghowān's red hue. †

The fire of love shall come forth from the earth over the graves

Of all, whose affection for their love, from the soul itself, proceedeth.

I will leave the walls of the cloister, and go out unto the tavern;

For therein is to be found safety from this, and the next world's ills.

The universe lieth under the seal of content and resignation:

Shouldst thou draw it on thy finger, it is Sulīmān's magic ring. *

The red tears that course each other down thy cheeks, OÆABD-UL-ḲĀDIR!

Are a sumptuous banquet of rubies for thine own dear friend.

V.

When I beheld the beloved with my rivals associated,
I would cry out and complain, coupled with piercing cries.
The mirror of the heart becometh bright through humility;
Hence, too, the meek and lowly are conjoined with the dust.
'Twas from the heart's anguish, that the nightingale bewailed,
Because he perceived the sharp thorn with the rose entwined.
But like unto a thorn, indeed, every flower my heart pierceth,
Whenever, without thee with me, I enter the parterre.
Through thy curls my heart hath become utterly deranged:
Let not then, O God, any Muslim be with Hind † connected!
Folly keepeth the fool ever occupied in delight and pleasure;
But prudence immerseth the wise in the river of care and woe.
Since, at last, departure therefrom is with great grief attended,
ÆABD-UL-ĶĀDIR will have naught to do with this place of spring.

VI.

Although it may be bitter, still swallow the wine of thy wrath:
Act not unjustly or tyrannically towards any one, upright man!
The falcon, that drinketh the blood of his quarry, dieth full soon:
Restrain thyself, then, my heart! from such ensanguined food.
There is no need of manacle, or fetter, or dungeon, to restrain them;
For the words of the wise are fettered in the prison of the mouth.
Every mild and gentle being, who clemency's armour weareth,

Is not pierced with the arrows of fortune's reverses and mishaps.

He who falleth from the heart's high rock is dashed to atoms:

Let not the Almighty, then, cast any one from such a rock as this!

Though men, in origin are one, yet their diversity is excessive;

Since one is equal to one, one to a hundred, one to a thousand others.

For a single *dinār* * a hundred pearls may be purchased;

And a single pearl is, likewise, for a hundred *dinārs* bought.

Whether monarch, or whether nobles, thou thyself shalt outvie them;

For thou, ÆABD-UL-ĶĀDIR! on any one, placest not thy hopes.

VII.

Why scornest thou me, O fair one! who so ill-favoured am?

'Tis destiny's doings that made me ungraceful; thee, lovely to behold!

Come once again, and upon the flowers cast thine eyes once more,

O zephyr of the morn! that thou mayest unclose the folded bud anew!

In thy absence, the rose would tear its own breast into a hundred shreds;

And the cypress, O charmer! from separation, would in tears dissolve.

Why, O rose! turnest thou thy face away from the lovelorn nightingale?

For even with these charms of thine, his wails have famous made thee.

When thou castest the fragrant *æūd* * into the fire, it yieldeth more perfume;

And I will constancy increase, if thou thy injustice shouldst augment.

Thou art the sun of beauty, and all these other beauteous ones are stars:

They will into nothingness vanish, if thou shouldst show thy face.

Thou always designatest ÆABD-UL-ḲĀDIR as hypocrite and deceiver;

But mayest thou, elsewhere, a more sincere lover find than he!

VIII.

Was it a pearl that was observed the nose jewel within,

Or was it a sparkling dew-drop upon the Arghowān's breast?

Musk-deer from far-off Khuṭan are both those eyes of thine,

That ever graze the spikenard and sweet basil upon.

I can discover naught on earth in comparison to thine eyebrows;

But I have found somewhat of similarity in the heaven's arch.

What connection is there between pearls and the teeth of the dear one?

Those are in the oyster's bosom—the teeth are in her mouth.

Because the poets were wont with thy lips to compare it,

The ruby became mortified, and fled back to the mine,

No one is capable of giving an explanation of their sweetness;

For the ambrosial nectar of Paradise is indigenous to thy lips.

When I look upon thy face, I am at the Almighty's works amazed,

Seeing that He preserveth thee safe and uninjured from its glow. *

I have well examined the display of the flowers of the universe;

But there is no flower like thee in any one of its parterres.

In gratitude, that He hath bestowed such curls upon thee,

By them, draw out those immersed in the well of thy chin! †

Those in thy presence, from modesty, know not what to say;

Whilst those absent, describe thee by metaphor and simile.
Close well, then, thine eyes, ÆABD-UL-ḲĀDIR! all things upon;
And then, within thyself, do thou the whole universe survey!

IX.

At last, he will depart from it, his heart with anguish seared;
Bootlessly, then, the gardener prideth himself on this parterre!
They who may have entered within the tavern of the world,
Shall all, in their turn, drink out of death's fatal cup!
He merely guardeth the portion of others, for they will take it;
Wherefore, then, is the rich man of his wealth so very vain?
He doth not revel, like the nightingale, among the roses;
But he sitteth perched, like a crow, a rotten carcass upon.
Sovereigns search about for it, but by beggars it is found;
Whether it be rest, or tranquillity; or peace, or repose.
The radiance of the lamp cannot be found within the tomb,
Except thou shouldst the lamp of sighs carry with thee there.
These are red tears thou seest, by unhappy Majnūn * shed;
For the tulip hath not bloomed, either in upland or in mead.
Set out, ÆABD-UL-ḲĀDIR! upon the path of inexistence;
Haply thou mayest find therein trace of the dear one's door!

X.

Whereas the oyster with a single drop of rain-water is satisfied, †

Its priceless pearls go out into every country, and every clime.

If thou seek after honour, be then with thy lot content!

Shouldst thou to eminence aspire, of what thou hast, liberally give!

The ties of the wealth of the world are the bonds of Hell;

Hence the free and noble placed it on the palms of their hands.

L have with mine own eyes well watched the world's people—

One amasseth wealth with great avarice; another wasteth it away.

Since life itself is not perpetual, what then advantageth it,

Though one, in magnificence, a Sulīmān, or an Aṣaf * be?

A man's superiority, in wisdom and knowledge consisteth;

The beast's, in grazing; and on hay, and on grass, growing fat.

If thou art magnanimous, pain not the hearts of others;

But make thine heart the target of the arrows of good and bad!

O ÆABD-UL-ḲĀDIR! have the fear of God ever before thee;

For unto them that fear, He hath said, "Fear thou not!" †

XI.

This exclamation from the nightingale at day-dawn reached my ear—

"O rose! thy merriment hath plunged me into sorrow and tears!"

Its languid effect is far more exquisite than its intoxication;

But the sleepy languor of thine eyes exceedeth that of wine.

The fair ones of the present day are worshippers of Mammon—

In their alley, without wealth's appliances, place not thy foot!

My love for the dear one increaseth from thy detractions;
Then, O traducer! as much as thy heart desireth disparage her!
From distressing thoughts and cares the mind becometh distracted;
But the heart acquireth comfort from reliance and resignation.
May the Almighty never leave those eyes from albugo free,
Which, when thy face may be visible, shall look upon a rose!
Thou art, when seated, the light of the whole assembly:
What matter, then, tho' the dawn of day the lamp extinguish?
When thou givest me wine, laugh heartily, O cupbearer!
Learn thou this from the merry gurgle of the flask of wine!
There is, doubtless, a difference in the sight of the beholders;
And if not so, the parts are by no means distinct from the whole. *
Metaphorically, this world is like unto eternity's bridge;
Then, O ÆABD-UL-ĶĀDIR, do thou over it swiftly pass!

XII.

In the world, there is no perfection without declination;
Then, on account of declination, mourn, O perfect man!
The dread of separation was as bitter as absence itself;
Hence from association I never any pleasure derived.
From thee, the sun luminous grew, and from it the moon:
Who then, with thy face shall the full moon compare?
At thy departure, my very soul even deserteth the body;

But do not thou for a moment leave me, O image of my love!
Since I did not die when separated from her; on meeting,
I am so ashamed that I am unable to look her in the face.
The same who hath inflicted the wound upon my heart,
Hath also applied the soft bandage thereunto.
Shouldst thou pass the alley of the beloved of my heart,
Deliver, O zephyr of the morning! this message unto her—
"Tho', without thee, I am not one moment from sorrow free;
Yet, ever joyful and gay, may the Almighty keep thee!"
With much sorrow, many loving ones have been torn away—
May God never send unto us the Ghowās year * again!
The fragrance of musk and amber emanateth from every word,
When ÆABD-UL-ĶĀDIR praiseth that black mole of thine.

XIII.

The flowers of spring have put forth their blossoms in garden and in mead:
On the house-tops there are flowers, in the lanes, and in the hedges too.
The stones, the bushes, the thorns, the weeds—all are by flowers hidden:
Of every blemish and defect the flowers have the concealers become.
Wherever the eyesight may be directed, all, all are flowers there—
Flowers in front, and flowers behind—flowers on every side.
No single spot whatever is of fragrant flowers left devoid—
Flowers in the market, flowers in the wilds, flowers in the hills.

The nightingale, to revel and disport, with a loud voice, crieth out;

For the spring passeth away, and every moment the flowers fade and decay!

The youths and maidens, in their gambols and revelry, place

Flowers in their hair, flowers in their bosoms, flowers in their turbans.

The entire person of the beloved is of fragrant flowers composed—

Her feet are flowers, her hands flowers, her sweet face flowers also.

Let the wine be rosy, the goblet rosy, the wine-flask rosy likewise!

The cupbearer a flower, the associates flowers, the scene all flowers too!

When she smelleth unto a flower, let great caution be observed,

Lest on her tender, delicate lips, the flower a wound should inflict.

Gentle and simple, they have filled with delight by their display—

The flowers have, on every one, a load of obligation conferred.

But though flowers may have bloomed of a thousand hues,

No flower hath been seen like unto the beloved one of my heart.

That they thus heartily laugh, with such gladness and such glee,

What! of autumn's near approach, are not the flowers aware?

Since in them may be seen the emblem of his own loved one;

ÆABD-UL-ĶĀDIR thus remembereth the flowers in his strains.

XIV.

The folks of the world give us their admonitions most unjustly;

For every man pleaseth himself according to his own mind.

What have others to do with us, forsooth, that they restrain us,

If, for the sake of the beloved, we sacrifice life and goods?

When love, like a mighty river, hath overflowed the heart,

Doth any one attempt a dam to raise on the face of the flood?

By the severance of all worldly concerns, sanctity is acquired;

But not by saddling oneself with worldly obligations and ties.

Involuntarily, and impulsively, the heart is given to the fair:

This matter is not brought about by counsel, or such like things.

The brutes chew the cud upon their food; but it behoveth man

To ruminate upon every word that issueth from his mouth.

As long, O ÆABD-UL-ḲĀDIR! as thy strains may be repeated,

From them flow so many varying, and delightful sweets.

XV.

If the surface of thy face be not soiled, be under no concern;

And the mirror of my heart, too, is not by rust affected.

Whosoever cometh near pitch, becometh defiled;

Then get thee away behind me, O thou so very white!

He, whose heart hath consumed in the flames of love,

What apprehension need he have of the fire of Hell?

She would make the dark night one of moonlight to her lover,

If the moon-faced one would draw aside the veil from her face.

From time to time, every thing hath gone out of my heart,

Save the remembrance of the fair, that will never depart.

'Tis from the wails of the nightingale it is thus so affected—

This rose-bud, that rendeth its garment into shreds.

All else is a mere vail, save the love of the Deity:

Then, O ÆABD-UL-ḲĀDIR, do thou no other love pursue!

XVI.

On ascending to the terrace-roof of wealth, show thou no arrogance;

But always have before thine eyes the fear of falling therefrom!

It hath raised up many, and dashed them again to the ground:

Fortune's wheel raiseth uppermost, that it may again cast down.

At the outset, acquire thou the wings of affection and love,

If of soaring in the heavens thou the intention nourish.

They whose hearts beauty's face may not with love inspire,

Their countenances are not worthy even to be looked upon!

I would say, I should go and consort with the dogs at her door;

But she would not, even then, one day, say to me " Come here!"

Since mine eyes became not blind, * from the absence of my love,

With all my heart I am now willing they should go out of my head.

Through contentment, and not through gold, is opulence acquired:

The whiteness of the heart is essential, not the whiteness of the hair.

Thou hast rendered it sweeter than Persian, ÆABD-UL-ḲĀDIR!

Although the Pus'hto language was so bitter before.

XVII.

Since the heart is torn from it, in the end, in anguish and woe,

Why do people set their hearts this fleeting world upon?

From this garden's roses, constancy's fragrance emanateth not:

Most unjustly do the nightingales hazard their hearts upon them.

Since the thought of the curls of the beloved is dishevelled and deranged,

Let my heart be disordered for ever! let it never be composed!

So hard, so pitiless, and so regardless, as is that heart of thine,

There will be none other like it, the whole universe within!

Wherever its ravisher may be, there will the heart be also;

For when do the heart-ravishers in their breasts retain their hearts?

Why hast Thou, O God! my heart filled with a giddy fair one's love?

That, though guiltless of any fault, every moment the heart afflicteth.

Proximity and remoteness—conjunction and separation—will be all one to him,

Whose heart hath a place acquired in immateriality's abode.

The flames of Hell I accept, with all my heart, a hundred times over;

But God forbid that in separation's fire the heart be consumed!

Eat! drink wine! raise the song! do all, ÆABD-UL-ḲĀDIR!

But this one thing—do not thou the heart of the Muslim afflict!

XVIII.

O cupbearer! unto me such a cup of forgetfulness give,

That on quaffing it I may oblivious and insensate become!

Reproached and reviled by the world, to the deserts and wilds I flee;

Like even unto Majnūn, I make the wilderness my home.

The fruit of its aims and desires, it shall then eat therefrom,

When the grain, in the earth, shall itself to extinction give.

Since it is filled with the conceptions of the faces of the fair,

The picture gallery of Mānī, * this mind of mine must be.

My heart becometh, through envy and jealousy, to pieces torn,

When her fingers draw the comb through her flowing hair.

For a minstrel, in the spring-time, I have no necessity;

The sweet melody of the nightingale is sufficient for me.

Nightly, in my dwelling, with this intent, I gather a party together,

That possibly, under this plea, the charmer might attend.

As an inducement, that he should risk his life to obtain it,

The diver desireth that the oyster-shell a pearl should contain.

A hundred times over, ÆABD-UL-ḲĀDIR would sacrifice it for her,

If, by parting with his head, he might his loved one obtain.

Footnotes

273:* See Introduction, page xi.

273:† See note at page 111.

274:* The magic ring of Solomon, which was supposed to reveal all things.

274:† India, the country of dark people, is compared to the dark curls of the beloved.

275:* The name of a gold coin current in Persia and Arabia, a ducat.

276:* The æūd, or wood aloes, celebrated for its fragrance.

277:* Alluding to the rosy colour of the cheeks.

277:† The dimple of the chin.

278:* See note at page 29.

278:† The pearl is supposed to be produced from a single drop of rain-water.

279:* The name of a great man, supposed to have been Solomon's prime minister.

279:† And God said unto him, "O Moses! draw near and fear not, for thou art safe."—AL ḲUR'ĀN.

280:* See Introductory Remarks, page xi.

281:* According to the *Abjad*, or an arrangement of the letters of the Arabic alphabet for numbers in chronograms, the letters *gh*, *w*, *ā*, and *s*, signify the year 1097 of the Hijrah (A.D. 1685), in which a terrible plague is said to have raged throughout Afghānistān and the adjacent countries.

284:* From excessive weeping.

286:* A celebrated Persian painter, who, about the middle of the third century of our era, gave out that he was the promised paraclete of our Lord; and soon established a numerous sect known as Mānīchæans. He fled into Tartary through fear of the Persian king Shāpūr (Sapor), where he amused himself by drawing a number of singular figures in a book called Ertāng; and, on his return, told his disciples that he had obtained it from the angels in Heaven, where he pretended to have been during his retreat.

AHMAD SHAH, ABDĀLĪ,

SHAH DURR-I-DURRĀN. *

AḤMAD SHĀH, the founder of the Durrānī monarchy, rose from the mere character of a partisan, to a distinguished command in the service of the Persian conqueror, Nādir Shāh. Of the family of the Saddozīs, and chief of the tribe of Abdālī, the most illustrious family of the Afghāns, he was, in his youth, imprisoned in a fortress, with his elder brother Zū-l-fiḳār Khān, by Husain Khān, governor of Kandahār for the Ghalzīs, which powerful tribe of Afghāns, after overrunning the whole of Persia, had, a few years previously, trodden the throne of the Ṣūfis in the dust, and conquered that mighty empire.

Aḥmad Shāh and his brother, whose tribe were at feud with the Ghalzīs, owed their freedom to Nādir Shāh, who in the year A.D. 1736-37, laid siege to Ḳandahār, which he captured. The brothers, with a powerful body of their clansmen, followed the fortunes of the conqueror, and greatly distinguished themselves in the war with the Turks; and were rewarded with the lands now held by the Durrānī tribe in the vicinity of Ḳandahār.

On the day subsequent to the murder of Nādir Shāh, (the particulars of which, as belonging to Persian history, need not be here detailed, although one among the causes of it has been attributed to his attachment to the Afghān troops in his service) a battle ensued between the Persians on the one side, and the Afghāns and Uzbaks on the other; but the event does not appear to have decided any thing. But after this affair, Aḥmad Shāh saw that no time was to be lost in looking to the safety of himself and clansmen, and he accordingly fought his way through the greater part of Khurāsān with a small force of between 2000 and 3000 horsemen, and repaired, by rapid marches, to Ḳandahār, which had now become the head-quarters of the Abdālī tribe, and chief city of southwestern Afghānistān. Here he intercepted an immense treasure, which had been sent from India for the use of Nādir Shāh, which Aḥmad appropriated, after compelling the Durrānīs, who had first seized upon it, to give it up.

In October of the same year, Aḥmad, then but twenty-three years old, assumed the title of Shāh or King of Afghānistān, and was crowned at Ḳandahār, with great pomp, the different chiefs of the various Afghān tribes, with but few exceptions, and the Kazalbāshes, Balūchīs, and Hazārahs, assisting; thus laying the foundation of the Durrānī monarchy. And although the warlike and independent people, who now became his subjects, had never been accustomed to a sovereign's yoke, save in being compelled to pay tribute to a foreign ruler; yet such were his energy and capacity for government, that he was successful in gaining the affection of his own tribe; and with the exception of the Ghalzīs, ever a most turbulent and unruly sept, he succeeded in instilling among the other Afghān tribes a spirit of attachment to their native monarch; and also in others, not Afghāns, but dwelling in Afghānistān. With the Balūch and Hazārah tribes, his neighbours, he formed an offensive and defensive alliance.

Having first brought the refractory Ghalzīs into subjection, Aḥmad Shāh began his conquests; and such was the uninterrupted tide of his success, that by the summer of 1751 he had conquered the whole of the countries, extending as far west as Nishāpūr in

Persian Khurāsān. In 1752 he conquered Kāshmīr, and obtained from the Mughal Emperor of Hindūstān, a cession of the whole of the tract of country as far, east as Sirhind, thus laying the foundation of a kingdom, which soon became formidable to surrounding nations.

Aḥmad Shāh had now leisure to turn his attention to internal affairs, and to the settlement of Afghānistān and the newly-acquired provinces. He thus passed the next four years in tranquillity, and appears to have had time to devote himself to literature. He used to hold, at stated periods, what is termed a Majlis-i-æulamā, or Assembly of the Learned, the early part of which was generally devoted to divinity and civil law—for Aḥmad Shāh himself was a Molawī *—and concluded with conversations on science and poetry. He wrote a Collection of Odes in Pus'hto, his own native tongue, tinged, as usual, with the mysticisms of the Ṣūfis, and from that work the following specimens have been taken. The work is scarce, particularly in eastern Afghānistān. He was also the author of several poems in the Persian language.

In the year 1756 Aḥmad Shāh had again to buckle on the sword, and advance into the Panjāb, which the Mughals about this time attempted to recover; but he quickly regained all that had been lost; drove them out of the Panjāb; and advanced straight upon Dilhī, which he entered after but a faint opposition. His troops having become sickly, from passing the whole of the hot season in India, warned Aḥmad Shāh to return, which he did soon after, having compelled the Mughal Emperor to bestow the Panjāb and Sindh upon his son Tīmūr, who had already been married to a Mughal princess. Aḥmad Shāh passed the next winter at Ḳandahār; but was obliged to set out soon after, for the purpose of quelling disturbances in Persia and Tūrkistān.

During the next year, matters had gone on badly in India; and Prince Tamar was unable to stem the tide of Mahāraṭa conquest, which had now rolled upon the Panjāb. The Mahāraṭas had taken Sirhind, and were advancing from the west, which put Prince Tīmūr under the necessity of retiring across the Indus with his troops. The Mahāraṭas, being now unopposed, pushed on as far as the Hydaspes or Jhīlum, and also detached a force to take possession of Multān.

These events happened in the summer of 1758; and Aḥmad Shāh was preparing to march into India, when he was detained by the rebellion of the Balūchīs; and although this matter was subsequently settled by negotiation, it was not until the winter of 1759 that he could cross the Indus and advance towards Hindūstān, the Mahāraṭas retreating before him towards Dilhī, with the intention of covering that city. After totally defeating them at Budlī, Aḥmad Shāh again captured Dilhī. He afterwards pursued his conquests in the Do-āb; but subsequently encamped at a place near Anūp-shahr, where, being joined by the Wazīr of Hindūstān, with the few available troops of the Mughal Emperor, he prepared for passing the monsoon, or rainy season, and for the final struggle with the Mahāraṭas, upon which the fate of India rested.

The strength of Aḥmad Shāh's army consisted of 41,800 horse, his own subjects, on whom he chiefly relied; 28,000 Rohilahs—Afghāns, who were descended from those tribes who had emigrated from Afghānistān at different periods, and settled in India

*—and about 10,000 Hindūstānī troops, under their own chiefs. He had also 700 *zambūraks*, or camel swivels, small pieces carrying balls of about a pound weight, and a few pieces of artillery.

The Mahārata army, under Wiswās Rāo, and Sheddasheo Rāo—

better known as the Bhow—consisted of about 70,000 horse, 15,000 infantry, trained after the European fashion, and 200 pieces of artillery, besides numberless *shuturnāls*, or zambūraks.

At length, on the 7th of January 1761, after facing each other for some months, the Mahāraṭas, who had been blockaded in their own intrenched camp at Pānīpatt, a few miles from Dilhī, were, from the extremities to which they were put, for want of food and forage, under the necessity of attacking the Durrānī army. The details of this great and important battle need not be enlarged on here: suffice it to say, that Aḥmad Shāh was completely successful. The Mahāraṭas were entirely defeated and put to flight; and Wiwās Rao, the heir-apparent of the Mahārata empire, and almost the whole of the army, perished in the flight or pursuit.

The crowning victory at Pānīpatt, which was fatal to the power of the Mahāraṭas, laid Hindūstān at the feet of Aḥmad Shāh; but he, seeing the difficulty of retaining so remote a dominion, adhered to the wise plan ha had, from the first, carved out, and contented himself with that portion of India that had formerly been ceded to him, bestowing the rest on such native chiefs as had aided him in the struggle.

In the spring of 1761, Aḥmad Shāh returned to Kabūl; and from that period, up to the spring of 1773, was actively employed against foreign and domestic foes; but at that time his health, which had been long declining, continued to get worse, and prevented his engaging in any foreign expeditions. His complaint was a cancer in the face, which had afflicted him first in 1764, and at last occasioned his death.; He died at Murghah, in Afghānistān, in the beginning of June 1773, in the fiftieth year of his age.

The countries under his dominion extended, at the time of his death, from the west of Khurāsān, to Sirhind on the Jumnā, and from the Oxus to the Indian Ocean, all either secured by treaty, or in actual possession.

The character of Aḥmad Shāh has been so admirably depicted by Mountstuart Elphinstone, * that I shall not hesitate to give it here in full.

"The character of Aḥmad Shāh appears to have been admirably suited to the situation in which he was placed. His enterprise and decision enabled him to profit by the confusion that followed the death of Nadir, and the prudence and moderation, which he acquired from his dealings with his own nation, were no less necessary to govern a warlike and independent people, than the bold and commanding turn of his own genius.

"His military courage and activity are spoken of with admiration, both by his own subjects, and the nations with whom he was engaged, either in wars or alliances. He seems to have been naturally disposed to mildness and clemency; and though it is impossible to acquire sovereign power, and perhaps, in Asia, to maintain it, without crimes; yet the memory of no Eastern Prince is stained with fewer acts of cruelty and injustice.

"In his personal character he seems to have been cheerful, affable, and good-natured. He maintained considerable dignity on state occasions, but at other times his manners were plain and familiar; and with the Durrānīs he kept up the same equal and popular demeanour which was usual with their Khāns or Chiefs before they assumed the title of King. He treated Moollahs and holy men with great respect, both from policy and inclination. He was himself a divine and an author, and was always ambitious of the character of a saint.

"His policy towards the different parts of his dominions was to rely principally on conciliation with the Afghāns and Balūchīs; with this difference between the nations, that he applied himself to the whole people in the first case, and only to the chief in the other. His possessions in Tūrkistān he kept under by force; but left the Tartar chiefs of the country unremoved, and used them with moderation. The Indian provinces were kept by force alone; and in Khurāsān he trusted to the attachment of some chiefs, took hostages from others, and was ready to carry his arms against any who disturbed his plans.

The handsome tomb of Aḥmad Shāh stands near the palace at Ḳandahār. It is held in great estimation by the Durrānīs, and is respected as a sanctuary, no one venturing to touch one who has taken refuge there. It is not uncommon for persons of even the highest rank, to give up the world, and spend their lives at the monarch's tomb; and certainly, if ever an Asiatic King deserved the gratitude of his country, it was Aḥmad Shāh, the "Pearl of the Durrānīs."

Aḥmad Shāh was the grandfather of the unfortunate Shāh-Shūjaæ-ul-Mulk, whom the British re-seated on the throne of the Durrānīs in 1839, which affair terminated so unfortunately for all concerned.

Footnotes

287:* Durr-i-Durrān signifies, "The Pearl of the Durrānīs," a name which the Abdālīs acquired from wearing pearls in their ears.

289:* A term equivalent to Doctor of Literature or Divinity.

290:* Also called Pat̲t̲āns in India; but the name, like that of Rohilah, is applicable to Afg̲h̲āns generally.

292:* "Account of the Kingdom of Caubul."

THE POEMS OF AḤMAD S̲H̲ĀH, ABDĀLĪ,

I.

To this degree is the heart affected by the love of Laylā,

That Majnūn, for aye, uttereth the praises of Laylā. *

He repeated no other lesson whatever, in this world,

Save that, on the black mole, and the ringlets of Laylā.

This, unto him, is sleep, from pain and anguish free,

That he be occupied, day and night, with thoughts of Laylā.

If, by the sword of anguish, he to death's agonies be brought,

He grieveth not, so that it be in the presence of Laylā.

Lovers, that cry out, "Laylā! Laylā!" and mourn and bewail—

Kill the body, and make it immortal, by the name of Laylā.

He desireth grief out of excessive woe, but findeth it not:

The lover is ever happy, in grief and sorrow for Laylā.

The whole of his love-pangs will, in a moment, disappear,

When the long sought interview is brought about with Laylā.

Draw near, AḤMAD S̲H̲ĀH! learn thou love from Majnūn!

For he is famous, in the world, for his love of Laylā.

II.

Lay thine hand very gently upon me, O physician!
Behold my condition, and take pity upon me, my beloved!
My heart, for this reason, is wholly filled with anguish,
That, thro' evil destiny, it beholdeth not its dear one near.
She is perfect and exquisite, in the excess of her beauty;
Hence my heart, distracted and disordered, raveth for her.
Tho' the dear one, by her mouth, many favours conferreth;
Still, every one receiveth the portion, by destiny decreed.
Notwithstanding, when I make many supplications unto her,
She saith unto me, "Grieve not, poor soul! I am thine!"
But next day, when I approach her, then, O my friend!
She saith, "Who is it I wherefore hath the rude fellow come?"
Tho' I would tear her from my heart, yet it will not be;
For she is, by nature, exceedingly generous, and noble withal.
The long sable locks hang her fair white face about—
She is gay and cheerful in disposition, and elegant in form.
Since God hath given unto the heart-ravisher the rose's beauty,
Wherefore should not the nightingale lover weep and bewail?
O AḤMAD SHĀH! the parrot-like soul weepeth and is sad:
It hath come again, O destiny! from the country of its love.

III.

May God annihilate thee, thou fly of human nature!

For no one mouth will have been left unpolluted by thy kiss!

Every wound, that may be thy place of alighting upon,

Will for ever be afflicted with the irritation of thine eggs.

Thou deafenest the ears of the whole world, with thy din;

Still thy mouth becometh not mute of its unpleasant buzz.

The whole world, through thee, hath into mere carrion turned;

Yet sorrowfully, and in spite, wringest thou still thine hands. *

O thoughtless man! follow not the nature of the fly!

These seeing eyes of thine from their ophthalmia cure!

Thou art the servant; then do thou the Almighty seek!

Existence, without God, consider utterly valueless and vain!

Take unto thee implicit faith; and scepticism's dark house,

Thereby shalt thou whiten with the whiteness of its lime.

Lowliness and humility are the height of perfection for thee:

The fiery nature of carnality, from pepper, take thou not!

Thine own original element thou wilt again obtain,

When the neck of thy pride thou shalt from the yoke set free.

Seize thou, O AḤMAD SHĀH! the good sword of courage;

And the Hindū temptations of the devil expel from thy breast!

IV.

Alas! alas! for the dreadful, rolling rock of bereavement;
That for aye committeth such ravages loving hearts upon!
It scattereth and separateth kind friends in all directions:
O my God! let the night of separation be always brief!
Since it thus, so ruthlessly, its arrows dischargeth,
The abode of the lover only an empty cavern remaineth.
For his poor heart there will be no relief save weeping;
He, like a widow sigheth, with raiment wet with tears.
His grief for the beloved rendeth the garment of reserve:
The torrent of his tears furroweth the channels of his eyes.
Wherefore should not the afflicted heart weep flesh and blood,
When the tears of bereavement form a lake therein?
Since separation giveth not to the lover so much respite,
The blood of his heart gusheth forth in streams from his eyes.
He will have no hope of finding relief in any direction:
His very frame becometh a load of anguish to bear.
If woe shall afflict, and press upon thee, O AḤMAD SHĀH!
In all sincerity and love, flee thou thy God unto?

V.

Would that the crows were not assembled in the nightingale's bower!
That loving friends were ever assembled in the parterre of flowers!
When the rose, without the presence of the beloved, may be looked upon,

The eyesight will merely encounter a bed of thorns and brambles.
The garden bloometh in beauty from the face of the beloved;
Then, without her, let not the heart unto the parterre incline!
Those clouds which may not contain the water of beneficence,
Forbid that such clouds should the face of the sky overcast!
When the snaky curls fall all dishevelled round her face,
Save mine own head, I see none other suitable penance to pay.
Since the dark mole upon her cheek is destroyed thereby,
Forbid that the rain of tears should ever her face suffuse!
The countenance of the beloved one is like unto the rose:
Let not autumn affect it: be it ever fresh in the parterre!
The blast of autumn, that scattereth the leaves of the rose—
Would to heaven that blast into the flames could be cast!
The anguish of separation consumeth AḤMAD S̲H̲ĀH'S heart:
O then once more unite him, the company of his friends unto!

VI.

O heart-ravisher! there will be none other in the world like unto thee:
Draw aside thy veil, or thy lover will of sorrow and grief expire!
With breast consumed by passion, I ever follow in search of thee;
But thy abode is neither on earth, nor in the heavens to be found.
I will wander throughout the world, as a Santon or a Darwes̲h̲;
Or I will saturate my garments with the flood of my tears.

O fragrant zephyr of the morn! news of her bring thou to me!
Make thou my heart to smile the parterre of flowers within!
When thus I weep and bewail, my object, in so doing, is this,
That my heart may a nightingale be in the rose-bower of thy face.
The heart, at the depredations of thy beauty, lamenteth,
Like as the nightingale's heart bewaileth when autumn arriveth.
In this world, the heart will not from spoliation be exempt;
Thou consumest hearts—a wondrous fire in thy nose jewel is.
The world's censures and reproaches he taketh not to heart:
The lover standeth in the plain, and raiseth his voice on high.
With all her tyranny and injustice, I would not abandon love,
Were I, AḤMAD S̱HĀH, with the powers of endurance prepared.

VII.

Alas! alas! for sweet life, that passeth thus away!
That, like unto a stream, floweth past, and is gone!
Wherefore, then, is the heart not aware of its departure,
When life, alas! passeth thus so swiftly away?
Why, O my heart! hast thou thus from grief become?
When existence, like the breeze, bloweth for ever away!
Tho' thou may'st erect mansions, in all symmetry and grace,
Filled with regret, alas! thou must leave them all behind!
Sorrow! sorrow! and for ever sorrow, O my heart!

That loving friends from each other are severed so soon!
Those dear ones are like unto spring's fragile flowers,
That in autumn's heats, alas! wither and fade away!
This separation is as hell, and absence its heated stones,
That fall, alas! the poor devoted lover's head upon.
It behoveth us here the world to renounce, for 'tis inconstant:
Alas! it possesseth neither good nor advantage to carry away.
Had meeting ne'er taken place, separation we had not known:
Alas! 'tis from meeting that the very heart's blood floweth.
If friendship be thy aim, with bereavement make friends;
For, alas! it cometh upon thee from thine own hands' deeds.
Friendship is like the rose; but its produce is the thorn:
The thorn becometh sharp, and, alas! to the quick it pierceth.
Why grievest thou, AḤMAD SHĀH! for 'tis a period of joy?
The drum of meeting soundeth: alas! union's hour is near.

VIII.

O would that there were not, in the world, the pangs of absence!
That the heart in this ocean of separation were not o'erwhelm'd!
Let not the heart of the beloved be of love and constancy divested,
Though the pains of bereavement may have the lover despoiled!
Wherefore may not the heart of the lover be lacerated,
When every moment it is stricken by separation's sharp sword?

Afflictions, like unto black snakes, twist and twine thereon,
When the flood of bereavement goeth straight unto his heart.
Whole bands from this world depart, one following the other;
For the ocean of separation hath laid the whole universe waste.
From this heat the very mountains will, like water, melt,
Should the fiery glow of bereavement unto them attain.
The cypress-like in stature have been laid low, AḤMAD SHĀH!
But let not thy body ever bend under absence's load.

IX.

Why weepest thou thus to-day again, O my heart?
Thou sighest and complainest ever, O my heart!
Like as the hart that loseth her fawn is distracted,
So thou showest thy alarm and inquietude, O my heart!
See also! thou acquirest not patience by exhortation:
Wailing and lamenting, thou rendest thy garment, O my heart!
Like as the Hindū widow advanceth impatiently to the pyre,
So thou turnest thy back to sweet existence, O my heart!
I do not comprehend all these complainings of thine:
What makest thee so soft and so sensitive, O my heart?
From the pangs of grief thou shalt then be again released,
When thou sacrificest thine own affections, O my heart!
Thou shalt take thy recreation in the court of the beloved,

If thou wilt resign thine own will and pleasure, O my heart!

The heart-ravishers are pert and capricious, and deceiving withal;

Then how long wilt thou sigh and weep for them, O my heart?

In the world the roses of spring are manifold in number,

If, like the nightingale, thou lamentest for them, O my heart!

The murky night will become unto thee the sunny day,

When, like the moth, thou sacrificest thyself, O my heart!

The rose-bud of desire thou shalt make to bloom thereby,

If thou make truth the rain-clouds of thy spring, O my heart!

The long night of autumn shall never be tardy in passing,

If thou on this path takest sincerity with thee, O my heart!

Thou shalt ever be gladdened with the sight of thy beloved,

When the dark mind thou the bright dawn makest, O my heart!

AḤMAD SHĀH, O world! remembereth no other prayer—

In beholding the dear one's face, employ me, O my heart!

X.

What an hour of bliss it was, when we, in retirement, each other's society enjoyed!

The beauty of thy face was a bed of roses, and my heart a nightingale disporting therein.

With the wine of union it was intoxicated: of the marplot it was free from dread:

Compared with the excessive torments of separation, to it was bliss, the meeting of to-day.

That was an hour of joy and felicity, when the Ḥumā * of union o'ershadow'd its head:

Why then should not the heart its yearnings show, when with sorrow it was constantly filled?

On whom the beloved her glance directed, the entire world was delightful unto him:

Union with the dear one is God's gift: not that it was brought about by other means.

Indeed, with but one look towards the charmer, even Paradise itself was forgotten by me:

My beloved was one without simile or resemblance, and her beauty the rose's excelled.

There are many cypresses within the grove; but in stature my friend all, all of them surpassed:

I enjoyed the contemplation of my dear one; for she than nectar was sweeter, by far, to me.

When I would her loveliness behold, how could sun or moon with it compare?

For hot, long shall AḤMAD SHĀH extol her, when all the world was occupied with her praise?

XI.

I cry unto Thee, O God! for I am of my sins and wickedness ashamed;

But hopeless of Thy mercy, no one hath ever, from Thy threshold departed.

Thy goodness and clemency are boundless; and I am of my evil acts ashamed:

'Tis hopeless that any good deeds of mine will avail; but Thy name I'll my refuge make.

When I my iniquities review, I say, O that I were but a mere blade of grass!

The lusts of the flesh and the Devil are so implanted within me, that, O God! I can nothing do.

Tho' I strive to the utmost, there's no escape for me out of the Devil's evil well:

If it be possible the heart from evil to guard, how shall the eyes be protected?

O AḤMAD! seek thou help from the Almighty, but not from pomp and grandeur's aid!

XII.

If I shall say anything of the beloved, what then shall I say?

Such is in my destiny, then of my fate, what shall I say?

Though the charmers are somewhat softened in heart,

Of fortune's crooked, wayward course, what shall I say?

I do not complain of the sable locks of the beloved;

But her eyes are blood-shedders: of the slaughtered, what shall I say?

I greatly longed to behold that sweet countenance of hers;

But it killeth the heart: of such a face, what shall I say?

They, who show no tenderness, are rivals unto themselves:

Thy beloved should be thy beloved: of a rival, what shall I say?

The morning's breeze, that causeth the rose to smile,

Is the zephyr itself; then of the morn, what shall I say?

The thorn which may be with the rose, is also the rose:

Since it belongeth to the rose, of the thorn, what shall I say?

The harsh words of the dear ones, tho' a load, are still acceptable:

Since lovers are under a load of obligations, of the load, what shall I say?

If the rose be the heart's bower, it is the lamp of the nightingale's heart:

Since it is the lamp of his heart, of the lamp, what shall I say?

The despoiled crieth out, and distracteth others' hearts too:

He remembereth the departed loved one: of the despoiled, what shall I say?

O AḤMAD SHĀH! tho' it be a stake, it is a bed of flowers also:

Since the stake of the beloved is a bower, of the stake, what shall I say?

Footnotes

294:* See note at page 29, and Introduction, page xx.

296:* This refers to flies rubbing their heads with both fore legs, which the author calls wringing their hands sorrowfully and in spite.

299:* See Horace, Ode 13th, Book II.:—

"Linquenda tellus, et domus, et platens

Uxor; neque, harum, quas colis, arborum

Te, præter invisas cupressos,

Ulla brevem dominum sequatur."

300:* Hell is said to be paved with stones, which thus make the infernal fire the more excessive by the transmission of heat.

302:* See note at page 37.

KĀZIM KHĀN, KHATTAK,

SURNAMED

SHAIDĀ.

KĀZIM KHĀN was the son of Muḥammad Afzāl Khān, chief of the Khattaks—and author of several extensive and valuable prose works in the Pus'hto language—who was son of the poet Ashraf Khān; and hence Kāzim was the great-grandson of Khushḥāl Khān, already noticed. He was born some time during the five years subsequent to H. 1135 (A.D. 1722). On the death of his father, the chieftainship fell to Asad-ullah Khān, Kāzim's elder brother, who, after a fashion too common in Eastern countries, considered it the safest and most prudent course to act with great severity towards his brothers and other near male relatives. Kāzim, who was quite a youth at the time, could not brook this tyrannical treatment, and therefore separated from him, and even abandoned the jāgīr, or grant of land, then in his possession. Asad-ullah, who appears to have been rather more favourably inclined to Kāzim Khān than to his other brothers, on becoming acquainted with the fact of his distrust, sent for Kāzim, and used every endeavour to soothe his fears and set his mind at ease; and, the more effectually to bring this about, he conferred upon him an additional grant of land, and betrothed him to a daughter of one of their uncles. However, the suspicions and fears of Kāzim—who doubtless had heard of the treatment the sons and grandsons of Khushḥāl had experienced at the hands of his own father—increased, at all this extreme kindness, to a greater degree than before; and he secretly fled from his home. Some say that he had an antipathy to his young cousin as a wife; and that, at the time, he requested his brother not to betroth her to him, as he did not like her. This Asad-ullah would not listen to; and, according to the Afghān custom, named her as the future wife of his younger brother. Be this, however, as it may, Kāzim took to a wandering life, and spent several years in Kashmīr, where he acquired considerable learning. He subsequently lived a long time at Sirhind, in Upper India, but afterwards proceeded to the Afghān principality of Rāmpūr, in that country, where he took up his residence; and there he passed the greater part of his life.

On several occasions his brother Asad-ullah sent many of his confidential friends to endeavour to induce him to return to his native country; but without effect. On one occasion the poet had gone as far as Ḥasan Abdāl, a town some few miles east of Attak, in the Panjāb, on a pleasure excursion, with some of his particular acquaintances, at which time a number of his relatives came to see him, from the Khattak country, beyond the Indus, and only two days' journey distant; but, notwithstanding all their entreaties, he would not return home, and went back to Rāmpūr again.

When the gift of poesy was bestowed upon him, he took the poetical surname of "Shaidā," signifying "The Devoted" or "Lovelorn;" for he had now turned devotee, and had become the disciple of the holy men of Sirhind; and, according to the mystic doctrines of the Ṣūfis, considered himself devoted to the love of the Divine. His poetry, like that of Mīrzā, is deeply tinged with the mysticisms of that sect.

The fame of Shaidā's poetry soon began to be noised abroad; and at length, Mī'ān Muḥammadī, son of Mī'ān Æabd-ullah of Sirhind, who belonged to the family of Shaidā's spiritual guide, •

expressed a wish to be furnished with a copy, on which the poet sent him the, at present, only known copy—which now lies before me—bearing the impression of his seal. These poems were alphabetically collected into this volume in the year H. 1181 (A.D. 1767), and, indeed, it is supposed to be the only copy that was ever made; for until shown to them by me, the descendants of his elder and other brothers, who dwell in the vicinity of Peshāwar, had never seen a copy of his poems, although so celebrated among them. This unique volume, which I procured at Lahore, is most beautifully written and illuminated, and contains a number of odes inserted on the margins of the pages.

Shaidā's poetry is highly polished, but deep and difficult; and approaches nearer to that of the Persians than of any other of the Afghān poets, whose simplicity is the chief charm of their writings. The poet also introduces a greater number of Persian and Arabic words.

Shaidā's first disappointment appears to have given him a distaste for matrimony; and he died unmarried, at Rāmpūr, where he had dwelt so long. Soon after his decease, his relatives came and removed his remains, and conveyed them to the poet's native country; and they found a resting-place at Sarā'e, where the Khattak chieftains, and their families, have, for centuries past, been interred.

Footnotes

306:* See Introduction, page xiii.

THE POEMS OF KĀZIM KHĀN, KHATTAK.

I.

WHAT pleasure shall the dead in heart take in beauty's display?

With Laylā's blandishments, what shall Majnūn's image do?

When, like unto the gazelle, they will not be familiar with any one,

What shall the effect of constancy with those bright eyes do?

The appliances of joy and pleasure were useless, unto the forsaken:

With the arrival of the morning's breeze, what shall the turban's chaplet do? *

Since, like unto the dawn of morning, his garment may be rent, †

How can one, as this so infamous, his condition conceal?

They never derive any share whatever of hands and feet,

What then shall the world of fishes with the ḥinnā's bright dye do? ‡

Folly and vanity have made thee lighter even than the bubble:

What shall the foaming of the ocean towards thy weight and power do?
Nourish not the hope, O Alexander! that it will to thee be constant:
Behold, what the vicissitudes of fortune shall unto Darius do!
By the violence of its ravages, the whole hath been to ruin brought,
Otherwise, in the desert, what doth the litter of its camel do?
Did he, like unto a falcon, soar in air, then it might avail;
But what shall the restraint of that net, now, unto SHAIDĀ do?

II.

Obtain for thy requirements the dun steed of the waves!
In the arena of the flood, practice the horsemanship of the waves!
The meek and humble, like the oyster, have the pearl acquired;
But naught of pearl's merchandise, beareth the caravan of the waves.
The lowly and humble are more powerful than the haughty and proud:
In the bonds of ocean, for ever confined, will be the rolling of the waves.
The obstinate and refractory are by the meek and humble subdued:
The ground-kisser unto the sea-shore is the tempest of the waves.
See, at what time they will swallow the dark earth altogether,
On the water's rolling throne seated, the kings of the waves.
Trouble not the inexperienced and incompetent with thy affairs:
For upon the target of the waters, become bent the arrows of the waves.
Woe and affliction are salutary to the mind of the heart-broken;
For firmly fixed, the flood upon, is the foundation of the waves.

They are the ups and downs of the world: O SHAIDĀ, behold them!

Rising and falling, without ceasing, is the world of the waves!

III.

Thou hast cast loose the dark tresses about that fair face of thine:

Thou hast, time after time, desolated the world's dwelling-places!

Thou hast not left one unscathed, the whole land within;

With the sword of amorous glances armed, whom now smitest thou?

Since from the sun of thy beauty, the veil hath been drawn aside,

The mart of love, the world within, thou wilt with bustle fill again.

Thou hast subdued the whole land with thy beauty and goodness:

Thy slaves thou wilt make all the fair ones of Hind. *

My phrenzy, O physician! will not in the least decrease:

Thine own rose thou wilt make even spring itself for me.

Since upon the target of the heart they so like straight ones strike,

How many wilt thou cause to groan from thine eyelashes' crooked darts?

Worthless himself, thou wilt draw demented SHAIDĀ to thy side again,

Shouldst thou even fill thy skirt with stones equal to a mountain in bulk.

IV.

Art thou come again in search of roses, thou seller of flowers!

That not a bird of the parterre ceaseth lamentation to make?

A bubble of the broad ocean is every one of its bells: *

The kar-wān † moveth along silently, this desert within.

In its desire to attain it, with its own blood it became tinged;

Yet still Both not the ruby reach unto the lobe of the ear?

Sometimes rising, sometimes falling, like the Pleiades they go:

How many inebriated ones have from thy banquet gone forth?

For thy sake, I would dye my garment of the colour of the rose;

Still, like unto perfume, it would from my bosom escape.

Draw near, and behold the black intoxication of her tresses,

That without the shoulder, ‡ cannot proceed a step on the road.

The heart of the vortex like unto a millstone might split;

Since fortune, towards SHAIDĀ, hath so unrelenting become!

V.

Everywhere the lords of love have become disgraced and dishonoured;

And neither tone nor harmony, absolutely, hath the rebeck of love.

Like as the dew, the mountain of Ḳāf it will displace also,

If the sun of love should rise over the head thereof.

What shall I say unto thee regarding this wave of calamity,

When equal to the firmament itself is the bubble of love?

That heart, which may for itself love's ermine acquire,

The vicissitudes of it are changed into peace and repose.

The thoughts of her, O SHAIDĀ! will never leave my heart;

For such a countenance I have beheld in the dream of love!

VI.

Again thou bringest thy dishevelled tresses thy face about:

Or the hyacinth, in the spring, disordereth its curled petals.

It must have been the insolence of the comb, and the wind's pertness;

For the locks of the dear one are not without cause deranged.

Look at them! what a wondrous moon-like circle are they!

The curls wreathed round the face of that gay, but imperious one.

To-day, from the arena, a new source of evil hath come;

Since thou hast brought the curls of dust upon thy face.

Like unto the comb, acquire a conception discerning;

For the ringlets of my rhymes a hair-like fineness have.

Although, from their exceeding length, they reach the ground,

Still, through coquetry, they place not their feet straight the path upon.

In what way shall SHAIDĀ become released from their noose,

When the curls, with a single hair, the lions of the forest bind?

VII.

In such manner, am I happy from the world apart,

That, like the forest's beasts, I am happy the desert within.

Rather than that I should behold the land of the sea-shore,

Like the billow, I am happy, wandering the waters upon.

When from the morsels thereon the hungry flies are driven,

With an invitation to that table, how can I happy be?

Since, like unto the sun's, its countenance is not warm,

I swear by thy head if, with the Ḥumā's shadow, * I am happy!

When, like unto the partridge, it confined me in a cage, †

Than such laughter, with lamentation, I am more happy by far.

Though, like unto a picture, it awakened not from its sleep,

In this state, O <u>SH</u>AIDĀ! with mine own lot, I am happy.

VIII.

Since, like the reed-pen, I have my head resigned,

I am now in search of these fair and charming ones.

This fire is from the glances of those bright eyes of thine,

Whereby I am burnt as black as those their dark lashes.

From the time when my heart became the home of these brunettes,

Behold me! I am, as it were, a new Hindūstān grown!

I vow by the hundred-times-rent vitals of the comb,

That I am more disordered even than the curls, in grief for thee!

From terror of the autumn, I am unable to look upon the rose:

I am shaking in this flower-garden, like the willow unto.

Though my flight is in the air; yet I was not released:

I am still of that graceful cypress the neck-enchained slave.

Like unto dust she carried me away, and showed no concern:

Of such a fiery steed as this, the attached skirt-holder am I.

With Indian requital, such acts she practiseth on me—

Me, <u>SH</u>AIDĀ! who in heart am a poor simple Af<u>gh</u>ān of Roh. *

IX.

Since from their complainings, its bells have not ceased,

The caravan must still be wandering this desert within.

What can beauty's splendour, with defective sight effect?

The mirror itself is amazed and astonished at the world.

From their eyes' wildness their intimacy cannot be gained:

The herd of gazelles, at the sight of the shepherd, taketh to flight.

What! hath Farhad † caused the covey of partridges to weep,

That from the mountains they come ‡ with eyes all inflamed?

I perceive the manner of her gait, like unto the zephyr:

She is again stepping gracefully, and is on slaughter bent.

From the time I became occupied in regarding the spring,

Naught was gained by me thereby, save sorrow and regret.

Many were the wailings from its rose-trees' every branch;

In sorrow and mourning for it, many were the garments rent. *

Like unto the waves, it riseth and falleth continually:

How then, from the world, canst thou aught of constancy hope?

Like unto the bubble, he wandereth in every direction, all forlorn;

Since SHAIDĀ from his home and friends a wanderer became! †

X.

Unto the trysting-place my charmer very slowly cometh;

And the verdant spring to the parterre very slowly cometh.

Now and then I perceive kindness beaming from her eyes:

Thou wouldst say that the languid ‡ ever very slowly cometh.

The dread of ill is a far greater slaughterer than ill itself:

The sanguinary one, to shed my blood very slowly cometh.

The partridge, for this reason, hath from laughing become purple,

That to make him her game, the graceful one very slowly cometh.

What! can separation, of his vigour, poor Farhad have deprived,

That the cries and wails from his mountain very slowly come? §

Under the weight of her majesty, the strength of Gulgūn §§ was lost;

Hence that Scythian ** of graceful mien very slowly cometh.

Give not utterance, O SHAIDĀ, without reflection, to a word;

For every parrot, to speaking well, very slowly cometh.

XI.

Although every drop of dew should be the seed of a rose,

The nightingales' hearts would not be satiated with beholding it.

When like unto that of the rose it hath not a face so lovely,

What shall one then do with the hyacinth's black locks?

About my dark destiny what shall I unto any one say?

For my forehead, like the sun's, is fit only to be branded. *

Is it the poor wayfarer hindered by night coming on,

Or my heart enthralled the noose of her tresses within? †

She hath made calamity's sword as sharp as fate itself:

With hands imbrued she goeth about, both night and day.

From the sea's cold-heartedness, the bubble bursteth and breaketh;

Hence it behoveth thee, O SHAIDĀ! to abandon all hope from thy kin.

XII.

The habitations of this world behold, and begone!

A nest like that of the Phœnix behold, and begone! ‡

The old in years, like little infants sport and play:

This very wonderful spectacle behold, and begone!

Should the sun, O Ḥumā! upon my brow ever rest,

Do thou, in that case, my independence behold, and begone!

With the torch of thine own mind, in this darkness,

Lightning-like, the road to follow behold, and begone! *

The fish have no share in the benefit of hands or feet;

But their swimming in the waters behold, and begone!

The wine-flask's one short hour in the convivial party,

With this full mouth laughing, † behold, and begone!

Every day it deceiveth SHAIDĀ with its friendship:

The friendship and constancy of fortune behold, and begone!

XIII.

Without a meeting I shall not recover: come and sit by me!

Make thyself acquainted with my state: come and sit by me!

Even the wild by nature have, at last, become tamed:

O thou gazelle, by nature wild! come and sit by me!
At the desire of the nightingale, thou, faithless rose!
After a year comest splendid again; then come and sit by me!
Like one dying, from other wounds, I ease obtain:
No napkin do I ask of thee; then come and sit by me!
With those arched eyebrows, and eyes at all times dark—
Thou evening and new moon of thy lover, come and sit by me!
That we may together recall the days when we knew not sorrow,
For one short hour, dear friend! come and sit by me!
The charms and beauty of thy beloved, in sweetest strains rehearse,
O SHAIDĀ! thou of imagination fine, come and sit by me!

XIV.

No sooner did spring acquainted become, with garden and with mead,
Than with eyes inflamed from weeping, it was separated again from them.
When the gate of the caravansary of the bud shall become unclosed,
The caravan of dyes and perfumes departeth, and morning's breeze setteth in.
The smoke of a world consumed, by the name of sky thou termest:
Of thy erroneous idea what shall I say? it is mere illusion and error.
That which even yet remaineth a source of amazement to the world—
Even Majnūn's name, hath come to behold the spectacle I am.
From thy well-directed aim, the arrow was pointed so truly,
That thou wert, neither of its flight, nor of its wounding aware.

It is beyond all possibility, O foolish one! to people it again;

For the prosperous city of S͟HAIDĀ'S heart that was, hath utterly desolate become!

XV.

Thou hast again unclosed those lips of thine to speak,

Or the parrot hath, for its dole of sugar, come again.

Unto the lot of the dark-hearted falleth not ecstasy's gem: *

Where is the lump of steel? the burnished mirror where?

Like as the pearl-oyster, open it at once to bestow,

When the indigent, at thy door, may his hand stretch forth.

The rose of thy cheek is, for thy tresses, all sufficient:

Neither for attar, nor for ambergris, hath it any need.

They, of open countenance, manifest no awe of the great;

For the mirror looketh even Alexander straight in the face.

All praise be unto the nakedness of that bare head,

Which hath neither under turban nor diadem bent!

From warmth, like unto quicksilver, she fleeth from me:

How, then, shall come to S͟HAIDĀ'S arms that impassioned one?

XVI.

Since I have turned my back home and family unto,

For other chattels or effects, what necessity have I?

That for ever smooth, and without wrinkle, thy forehead may be,

All these troubles make thou over unto the sovereign of C͟hīn. †

The blood of my own heart I am well pleased to drink;

For the fly never approacheth near unto this tray of mine.

It would not, with its consent, in the garden stay a moment:

'Tis well the thorn seized the rose's garment by the hem.

Do hearts then trip along in the direction of thy curls;

Or doth the caravan of Rūm * unto India wend its way?

How shall those eyes of thine a glance on the humble bestow,

When thine eyelashes, thro' arrogance, to the heavens are upturned?

In those worldly dwellings of thine, may all happiness be;

But wandering SHAIDĀ is going to the deserts and wilds!

XVII.

Thou art welcome again thou fresh festival of spring! †

Thou hast brought joy unto every wild, and every bed of flowers!

Like unto the bird within a cage, the lovelorn nightingale,

Even whilst yet within the egg, longeth on the wing to be.

The folks' garments have been dyed of such a saffron-like hue,

That every bird to the parterre, filled with laughter, hath come. ‡

Look at the rosy-bodied one in this garment arrayed,

Like unto the sun when he approacheth the time of his setting.

In the turban of every pilgrim a bouquet it will place,

When morning's dawn scattereth flowers into its own skirt.

The nightingale's heart towards the gaudy rose is inclined,

Or the flask hath approached the goblet, to pour out its wine. *

The rain of perspiration shall fall through shame therefrom,

When the lightning shall behold the gorgeous crop of flowers.

In the same manner as the rose, the beholders of this spring

Have not the least necessity for attar their garments upon.

The musician increaseth twofold wine's intoxicating strength,

When the bacchanals sit down the banquet to begin.

Why, O SHAIDĀ! termest thou it, the oyster of the deep profound?

When the pearl unto thy sweet strains its ear hath given.

XVIII.

What peace, in this world, doth the heart acquire,

Which ever quaketh and trembleth from dread of fortune's ills?

Thro' separation from the departed water, O thoughtless people!

Like the vortex, you have made strong your hearts, your breasts within.

Let not thy heart ever be unto this world's parterre given;

Since even the rose-bud, at last, left it heart-disordered behind.

Approach! behold the weeping of agony in tears of blood:

Like the wine-flask, my heart to shed blood I have brought.

The fissure therein, by the waters, was not filled up again;

And the whirlpool, like an anvil, hardened its heart unto pain.

Thou shalt, O SHAIDĀ! for flight, wings and feathers acquire,

If thou in the nest, like the egg, thine heart pure and spotless make.

XIX.

I possess none of the chattels of tranquillity, the encampment within;

Since I have a tent, like the bubble, upon the face of the deep.

If thou art not the owner of a single straw, grieve not thereat;

For then, the village-consuming fire will in thy Ḥaram * expire.

When thy face became bedewed with perspiration, by thy head I vow,

That therein the rose-scattering splendour of dew I beheld.

'When wert thou ever shrouded the veil of retirement within?

Thou art manifest in all the world, like a Phœnix unto.

Her eyes show not even as much regard towards me,

As the wild gazelle that looketh round ere it taketh to flight.

’Tis needless to apply any salve to my all-sufficient wound:

How can the recovery' of the slaughtered be brought about?

Morning and evening—day and night—with sable dress, and garment rent,

Like unto time itself, † in sorrow and mourning my existence is spent.

The beautiful lineaments of her face are most amazing:

In this writing there is no work soever for any one's pen.

His life perpetually from danger, how shall SHAIDĀ guard;

When the snaky curls are in total darkness shrouded ever?

XX.

When thy beauty, like the sun's, bursteth forth,

My garment, like the morning's, becometh rent.

In the society of thee, my bright-checked one!

My whole body, like the candle's, melteth away.

That person shall never die, whose head shall be

Struck off, like the candle's, by the sword of love.

Thy curly locks have drawn my heart towards thee:

The fish, by the hook, are always from the water drawn.

Call him not, hard-hearted one! a statue of the hall,

Who in dust and blood writheth in death's agony.

When, throughout the night, the rain of tears falleth, *

From its effects at last appeareth the dawn of day. †

He hath no strength to complain, who is by thy curls stricken;

Like unto one by a snake stung, he is speechless rendered.

The desert will rend its garment's skirt to tatters,

Should the trembling one from thy bonds escape.

Graceful words shall they write, their tablets upon,

Whose hearts, like the pen's, may crack and split.

On this account, SHAIDĀ cannot look upon a comb;

For the derangement of thy curly locks is seen therein.

XXI.

In the rolling of thine eyes the universe may have sunk,

Or its inhabitants may be submerged in the eddies of a flood.

Since they showed no mortification at thy lips and teeth;

Why should not the coral and pearl thus be in ocean engulphed?

I am a cotemporary of the water of those good blades,

Whose eyelashes may ever be in bloody tears submerged. *

Good men hold it far preferable to the perspiration of shame,

That they may be swallowed in Æummān's dark waves. †

What would the simpleton and dolt from Mānī ‡: acquire,

Though his pencil may be dipped in the rainbow's every hue?

Upon the raft of the bier unto the shore will approach,

The kings who may have sunk in the throne's troubles and cares.

O SHAIDĀ! no effort to escape maketh the master-mariner,

Whose eyes may be submerged the ocean of tears within.

XXII.

Since, like the sun, thou art the possessor of gold and silver,

Why art thou standing, every morning, at the door of others?

As with the candle, no one for my redemption endeavoureth;

And thou, like the snuffers, art a seeker after my head.

As doth shadow on the sun's setting, follow the eyes' dark shade,

If thou, for a pretty one, with sunny face, a candidate art!

By the slaughter of whom wilt thou, of roseate hue, thy garment dye,

That, to-day again, thy waist, like the rose-bud's, is girded?

Like unto mince-meat, wound after wound I receive;

Then, wherefore art thou of my state and my case unaware?

Thou didst depart like the bubble on the back of the flood

Than myself, O my home! a greater wanderer art thou!

Thou beautiful brunette! O thou of figure so graceful!

The straight and verdant pine, of whose grove art thou?

If in adversity thou bendest not thine head unto any one,

In the loftiness of thy spirit, like a dark beetling mountain art thou.

O SHAIDĀ! thou art that parrot with Indian disposition endowed,

That art with the confection of thine own words' roses content.

Footnotes

308:* A chaplet in the turban, when withered, cannot be revived.

308:† The break of day is termed the rending of the dark garment of night.

308:‡ See second note at page 195.

310:* Hindūstān.

311:* The necks of camels and other animals in a caravan of travellers are ornamented with bells.

311:† A caravan.

311:‡ The simile here refers to the long tresses resting upon the shoulder for support.

313:* See note at page 137.

313:† The bartavelle, a large bird of the partridge species, is kept on account of its sound, compared to laughter; as also is the common bird.

314:* See note at page 263.

314:† The name of a famous Persian statuary, the lover of Shīrīn, wife of Khusrau Parwez, king of Persia, and daughter of the Greek Emperor Maurice, who, to please his mistress, dug through an immense mountain. This is the subject of a poem by

Nizāmī, one of the most famous and the sweetest of Persian poets. See also note at page 87.

314:‡ The eyes of the Chikor, a species of partridge here referred to, are of a deep red colour, as also are its legs. See note on preceding page.

315:* The rent garments refer to the leaves the roses have shed.

315:† See memoir of the poet, at page 307.

315:‡ The glances of the sleepy, languid eyes of a mistress.

315:§ See note at page 129.

315:§§ The name of the steed of Shīrīn, the beloved of Farhad.

315:** See note (§) at page 129.

316:* The spots in the sun's disc are compared to brands; and it used to be the custom with the Afghān tribes to brand the forehead of a child born in an unfortunate or unlucky hour, to drive misfortune away.

316:† The heart is the wayfarer here, and night the dark hair of the beloved.

316:‡ Its nest is not to be found, neither a permanent home in this world.

317:* The lightning is supposed to obtain a glimpse of its own road from the light of its own flash.

317:† The gurgling of a full wine-flask is said to be its laughter.

319:* A state of ecstasy to which the Ṣūfis are supposed to attain when the world and all things worldly vanish. See Introductory Remarks, page xiii.

319:† The eastern name of China. Chīn in Persian also signifies a wrinkle, hence the play upon words.

320:* The people of Ram, or Asia Minor, are ruddy in complexion, and the heart is also red. The people of India are dark, so are the curls of the beloved. These are the metaphors used by the poet here.

320:† A festival observed by the ancient Persians and by the Hindūs, which season, among the latter people, is personified under the name of Basanta, who is said to attend on Kāma, the god of love. It is usual in the Panjāb and vicinity, on this day, for the Hindūs to dress in saffron-coloured garments, called also *basantī*, Krishna's favourite colour.

320:‡ Saffron, it is said, will cause a person to laugh to death.

321:* The nightingale sings on account of the rose which is *red;* and the metaphor here is, that, by its *gurgle*, the wine-flask is as though singing to pour forth the red wine.

322:* The most sacred part of a palace or dwelling, the seraglio, or woman's apartments.

322:† Time assumes the black dress of darkness in the evening, and its garment is rent at the dawn of day.

323:* The night of sorrow.

323:† The morn of relief or joy.

324:* The curved shape of the scimitar is likened unto the eyelashes of the fair.

324:† The gulf of Persia so called.

324:‡ See note at page 287.

KHWĀJAH MUḤAMMAD, BANGASH.

THE materials for a notice of this poet are extremely meagre. Little is known about him, except that he lived in the reign of the Mughal Emperor, Aurangzeb, and belonged to the Bangakhor Bangas'h tribe of Afghāns, who hold the valley of that name, and of which Kohātt is the chief town. The Bangas'htribe, in bygone days, made a great figure in India; and from a peasant of it, the Nawwābs of Farrukhābād, in that country, traced their descent. *

Khwājah Muḥammad lived the life of a Darwesh, in poverty and religious abstraction, and followed the tenets of the Chastī sect. He was a disciple of Æabd-ur-Raḥīm, who was a disciple of Mī'ān Panjū, a celebrated Ṣūfi teacher, who came originally from

Hindūstān, and dwelt for many years in Afghānistān. He is said to have traced his descent from the Arab devotee, Muæīn-ud-Dīn, the founder of the Chastī sect. *

Khwājah Muḥammad appears to have been a man of some learning; and passed most of his time with his teacher or spiritual guide, already mentioned. It is not known whether he left any descendants; for although I despatched a person, specially, into the Bangas'h country to make inquiry, I cannot now discover, with any certainty, either his place of birth, residence, or the branch of the tribe to which he belonged. He is known, however, to have performed the pilgrimage to Makka and Madīnah; and that, after his return thence, he gave up writing poetry. His Dīwān, or Collection of Odes, from which the following poems have been selected, is a very rare book; in fact, scarcely procurable; for, as far as I can discover, the copy to which I had access is the only one known.

His writings are deeply tinged with the mysticisms of the Ṣūfis; but occasionally he devotes a poem to the remembrance of lost friends, and laments his bereavement from them.

The place and time of his decease are uncertain; and the whereabouts of the grave in which he was buried is not now known.

Footnotes

326:* Little did I imagine, whilst stationed in the Panjāb a few years since, when I was penning the notes for this short notice of a poet of the tribe, that I should behold the last of the Nawwābs, escorted by a party of my own regiment, conducted, on foot, with fetters on his legs, through the streets of Nassick, in Western India (where I then was stationed in command of a detachment), on his way to undergo perpetual banishment at Makka, for the share he took in the massacre at Farrukhābād, during the late rebellion in India. He had been sentenced to death; but his punishment was commuted to perpetual exile, in any place he might select. He chose Makka in Arabia, where, I have since heard, he subsists on alms. I spoke a few words to the wretched man at Nassick; the first he had heard in kindness, he said, for many long days. He appeared to be any thing but what one might expect, from all that has been proved against him. He was rather fair, slightly made, and about thirty years of age. To me, he appeared very wretched and heart-broken. He was only an Afghān in name: the centuries of admixture of Indian blood, by intermarriage with the people of the country, had left little of the Afghān blood remaining.

327:* See note at page 1.

THE POEMS OF KHWĀJAH MUHAMMAD, BANGASH.

I.

EITHER the ḥinnā * hath been unto thy white hands applied,

Or they have been made red in the blood of thy lover.

I am unable, O dear one! to endure thy glance's fire;

For I am weak, and infirm, and powerless, altogether.

Those languid eyes of thine have many in misery plunged:

It would be well, my beloved! shouldst thou their tyranny restrain.

Thy stricken ones, without union with thee, revive not again,

Though Abū-Sinā † himself to prescribe for them should come.

Those sable locks of thine are like unto spring's lowering clouds;

And from them shineth out thy countenance, like the sun.

Thy fascinated ones are entangled in the noose of thy ringlets;

But the wise bird upon the net can no confidence place.

The equal to thy beauty is not in the wide world to be found;

Whilst my poor heart breaketh at the affluence thou enjoyest.

Thou art celebrated throughout the world for thy benevolence too;

Wherefore, then, givest thou not ear unto KHWĀJAH's complainings?

II.

Separation from thee, O my friend! hath made me so disconsolate,

That naught in me remaineth, but misery and woe!

The ensanguined tears chase each other down my cheeks

My heart is rent to atoms, and my breast is all consumed.

The clear colour of my face dependeth upon thy existence;

And now, without thee, it is colourless, and tinged with blood.

I was unacquainted with the world's profits and losses—benefits and ills:

By the sight of thyself, without wine thou didst inebriate me.

Though I yearn and long for it, I cannot procure it in the world:

The rapturous sight of thee is become unattainable to me.

I become immersed therein: at times I sink; at times I rise again;

But out of the vortex of the ocean of thy love I cannot emerge.

The whole country unto me hath dark become without thee;

O thou, the bright sun among all saints and holy men!

Thou art a mighty river, in waves and billows rolling;

But no one drinketh one mouthful from the mighty stream.

My mind will not become comforted by any other person,

Than by thee only; O thou, of all poles now the pole * unto me!

I was wont to say, that in life we always together should be;

For I was utterly ignorant regarding the dread torrent of death.

The extent of thy goodness, my beloved! was beyond computation;

For thou didst not, from the veil, thy countenance to any one show.

Thou wert the altar of the aspirations and exigencies of all!

For at the threshold of the Highest, acceptable were thy prayers.

III.

I would relate unto thee the wondrous works of the ravishers of the heart,

But I know naught concerning it—they abstract it from my breast.

I will bear whatever cruelty the beloved may heap upon me:
God forbid that any one recreant unto love should be found!
I obtain no relief, even though in her service my life I lay down;
For my heart still reproacheth me, that I have not done enough.
There is no such cool water, whereby my thirst shall be quenched;
And I shall thus wander, with breast on fire, till time shall end.
I shed floods of tears, but she showeth no sympathy towards me:
Let not any one, O God! a mistress have, so cruel and unkind!
This also, both high and low, great and small, will understand—
When doth any one, without being ailing, unto the physician go?
The afflictions of the sick they increase: there is no cure for them;
For there are no skilful physicians remaining: they have all left the land!
Happy are the whole and the healthy, that need not medicine;
For those, with this malady afflicted, obtain no ease to their pain.
"I have meted unto every one his destiny," so the Ḳur'ān saith:
Who then shall change the lot HE unto KHWĀJAH MUḤAMMADassigned?

IV.

Shouldst thou become the possessor of the world's throne and sceptre,
Be not arrogant! for in the end thou wilt be plundered and despoiled.
All will be equally on a par, one with the other, after death,
Whether it be the beggar, the wealthy man, or the prince.
Since thy place, at last, is the dark earth beneath,

Manifest neither gladness nor predilection for the world's affairs.
It will become shattered to atoms by the stones of death,
To whatever degree thou mayest the body's glass vessel guard.
If thou considerest it thy duty, the necessities of the poor to relieve,
The Almighty will never let thee be under necessity unto any one.
When a friend presenteth himself, show thy bounty to the utmost;
Since there are merely these five days of existence for thee.
Adorn thy piety by good actions and praiseworthy deeds;
For a bride without adornment and jewels 'tis unusual to see.
The whole of this darkness shall be expelled from thine heart,
If thou lightest up within it, the lamp of love divine.
When are such things brought about by armies or by legions,
As are accomplished by the fervid enthusiasm of love?
If the lover be small in stature, but be great in heart,
Then of what use is Æāj's gigantic stature unto him? *
Love hath brought dishonour, both in this world and the next,
Upon one Majnūn; † upon another Manṣūr, Ḥillāj's son. ‡
What would the sportsman in the forest know concerning it,
If the partridge did not acquaint him by so loudly calling?
The fame of Kasrā's § justice hath unto all time remained,
But tyranny's scar remaineth branded Ḥujāj's forehead upon. §§
The unfinished and incomplete woof of the world's warp behold!

The weaver by no means soever can it to perfection bring!

If thou art a lover, of slander and aspersion have no fear!

But become thou the target of every one's arrow of reproach.

What are the sins of KHWĀJAH MUḤAMMAD in the eye of God,

When the ocean of His mercy in waves of beneficence rolleth?

V.

How much longer, O base one! for the world's love wilt thou wander?

Quaff of the inebriating cup of love divine, that both sugar and honey is!

O thou, its seeker! about the, world to come, that is eternal, be concerned!

Place not thy affections on the transient world, tho' all its dust were gold!

But the counsel of monitors taketh no effect whatever upon thee;

For like unto a breast-work round thine heart, is the love of the world!

Happy the inspired, who are filled with the remembrance of the beloved!

The general world are unacquainted with the raptures and bliss thereof!

The Perfect One's praise is the embellisher of the mouth, if thou art wise:

Come, polish the mirror of thine heart from the tarnishing dust thereon!

O, what rapture have those lovers that drink of the wine of love!

With the beloved, solely occupied, they are free from all griefs and woes!

Cast away, O KHWĀJAH MUḤAMMAD! both life and goods for it;

But for a tittle of the perfect saint's pain and affliction pray!

VI.

Entertain not, O brother! great friendship towards the world:

Dost thou not, the raids of separation, on all sides perceive?

'Tis to depart and pass away: the world is not thy tarrying place:

Whether king or beggar, all will certainly to the grave go down!

Whether the prelate, or the priest, or the accomplished in learning,

Not one, by any contrivance, shall from death's debt escape!

They who are by sanctity inspired, pursue not mundane love;

With that of the Beloved One, there is no love to be compared!

Since thou showest such yearning after the world's greatness,

What is it after all? reflect well, and of thy dear friends think!

I was calmly reposing in my abode, along with my beloved,

When the horsemen of separation carried me hand-bound away!

All my loved ones, from time to time, have been taken from me:

The tablets of my heart have been blotted all over by grief!

I, KHWĀJAH MUḤAMMAD, in bereavement's flame, consume;

Hence sighs and lamentations, irrepressibly, issue from my mouth!

VII.

Since He created thee for well-doing and virtuous actions,

It behoveth not, O man! that thou shouldst evil commit.

Unto the Creator, day and night, render due meed of praise:

Let it not be that thou for a moment fail in doing so!

Upon the throne of contentment sit, and a sovereign become;

And under what obligation wilt thou then, to lord or chieftain be?

The world's duration is but short: it will soon pass away!

If thou art anxious as to thy award hereafter, now is thy time!

Be prudent, and do not the world's transient pleasures pursue!

Let it not be that the prosperous be ruined by the adverse. *

The torrent of death hath carried whole peoples away;

Then what stay canst thou make upon the face of the flood?

Thou wilt be awakened, at last, by the herald's summons,

Notwithstanding thou mayest upon the softest couch repose!

In no way shalt thou be able the toils of death to escape,

Even shouldst thou with seventy thousand screens thyself surround!

Since sweet existence is ever melting like unto snow away,

How much longer, with harp and rebeck, wilt thou revel and rejoice?

Sometimes the green corn is cut down; sometimes the ripe:

What dependence canst thou place, then, upon youthfulness or age?

Fear, O KHWĀJAH MUḤAMMAD! fear, fear for thyself!

There, what answer wilt thou make, if the Almighty question thee?

The hopes of KHWĀJAH MUḤAMMAD are upon THY mercy placed:

If THOU rebukest him he hath not the power to reply!

VIII.

If thou takest into consideration the many favours of the Almighty,

When wilt thou be able, for even one of them, fitting thanks to return?

One of the favours HE hath bestowed upon thee is Islām's true faith:

The other, that HE hath placed thee the great Ḥumā's shadow *beneath.

Let it not happen, that in the end, thou shouldst lament about that,

For which, like the nightingale, thou constantly sacrificest thyself.

The world shall embrace thy feet and thy hands with affection,

If thou make thyself the dust of the feet of holy men.

Thou shalt, at that time, attain unto the object of thy wishes,

When thou shalt make thy life and goods an oblation unto them.

It behoveth thee to consider each respiration as the last;

For death many people hath homeless and desolate made.

Mankind come into the world, and soon from it depart:

How canst thou then place any hope upon this transient abode?

But I will eschew even the sovereignty of the world itself,

If THOU make KHWĀJAH MUḤAMMAD a beggar, at his loved one's door.

IX.

If thou possessest the love and regard of the Almighty,

Thou wilt tear thyself away both from brother and from friend.

Like unto Majnūn, thou wilt begin in wilds to wander:

Thou wilt never take account of the thorns and brambles by the way.

Until thou castest not off entirely all thy superfluous flesh,

O contender in the race! thou wilt never reach the goal.

Day and night thou pursuest this transient world,

And hast, O foolish one! turned from the immortal away.

At last, He will take away from thee, by force, for ever,

This borrowed garment, * that is so very precious unto thee.

The beasts of the field, when grazing, eat not up every herb,

But thou turnest not away thy face from any one thing.

Until it shall be melted the saint-like teacher's crucible within,

Thou wilt not be able to separate this silver from its tin alloy.

Notwithstanding, before him, thou mayest the beloved praise;

Still, thou canst not manhood from the impotent hope.

I, KHWĀJAH MUḤAMMAD, am immersed in the ocean of grief,

If thou, my master! wilt save me from this raging flood.

X.

Give ear, O brother! unto the request I make unto thee:—

Be not, by the contemptible deception of the world, led astray!

By its deceit, it maketh people despiteful unto each other:

It passeth around a golden cup with deadliest poison filled.

The millstones of fate, round the heads of mankind revolve;

And some time or other, the turn for thy head shall come.

By the severe bridle of fasting, curb the lusts of the flesh;

For with a halter thou wilt be unable, this steed to restrain.

The object of food is to keep body and soul together, and no more,

Although thou mayest have in thy possession all sorts of things.

To clothe the body is necessary, and it behoveth us so to do,

Though but two or three yards of blanket or of canvas it be.
Thy every breath is a pearl and coral of inestimable price:
Be careful, therefore, and guard every respiration well!
Let the whole of thy words be conformable with thy deeds;
And in no wise in vain and foolish conversation indulge!
Tell me what extent of torment thou wilt be able to bear;
And commit no more sin than may be equivalent thereunto.
By the rain of spring will become all saturated at last,
The paper dress in which thou mayest have clothed thyself.
Unto the money-changer, its exterior and interior will be known;
Notwithstanding thou shouldst, with gold, brass ever so enwrap.
The bead of this arrow will not come out from thy bones,
Until thy flesh shall have been by the sharp diamond incised. *
It was because he made use of words of arrogance and pride,
That Satan himself was wholly from God's mercy debarred.
Without doubt, all good and all misfortune are from the Almighty:
Wherefore then unto doubt, givest thou a place in thine heart?
In thy ways indeed, thou art still more silly than children,
Even now that thy years are beyond forty and fifty passed.
Shouldst thou drink one mouthful from the cup of love,
Like unto Khizr † and Mihtar Iliyās, ‡ thou wilt never die!
I am filled with terror and dismay, beyond all bounds;

For the Tempter waylayeth me before and on every side!

I, KHWĀJAH MUḤAMMAD, am prostrate at thy threshold,

If thou, O my master! wilt but take me by the hand!

XI.

The love of the world hath made thee so insensate,

That thou hast wholly forgotten the duties of religion.

Like unto the cat, thou art ever upon the watch:

Thou art of no use soever to any one, save the rat.

Outwardly, thou hast clothed thyself in sanctity's dress,

O deceiver! thou vender of barley, but shower of wheat!

When the opportunity hath passed away, then wilt thou grieve;

And when the cup of death shall be given thee to quaff.

Thou hearest with thine ears the cries of the outcast;

And the cries at thy decease too, shall reach others' ears.

Mankind HE hath created to walk in righteousness' ways:

Thou art not a beast; then not sinfully, but worthily act!

When thou leavest the body's house, take viaticum with thee;

For there, O beloved! are no means for obtaining it.

Thou art a pilgrim, and wilt depart: anxious therefore be:

Bind up thine effects, and reflect upon the long journey before!

The path in front the Tempter haunteth: go not alone!

Arise! search about thee! and thy companions select!

If one, even with every effort, cannot the goal attain;

No man can reach it without striving so to do.

Every morning and evening raise thy voice unto God!

Tears of blood shed in the depth of thy heart's emotion!

All other love, save one, is naught but deadly poison:

From the cupbearer's goblet, then, joyfully take one draught!

Groan and lament, but so that no one may hear thee!

Remember thy beloved in thine heart, but with silent lips!

The world is black, and maketh man's face so too at last;

But drink thou the wine of love, and red-faced become!

Without anxiety, O Khwājah Muḥammad! sleep not;

Since thou hast been by death's repeated warnings apprised!

I, KHWĀJAH MUḤAMMAD, am of sins and offences full;

But, O hider of faults! I place my trust in Thee!

XII.

From all ills, shield Thou me, O God, my Protector!

For save Thee, there is none other, my Protector!

Unto Thee I have intrusted the affairs of both worlds:

Of all things, both of faith and country, Thou art the Protector!

The flesh and the devil, alas! waylay me everywhere:

I have no means of escape, save through Thee, O Protector!

Of the world's calamities and woes, I shall have no dread;

Since, everywhere, Thou art my shield from ill, O Protector!

When I draw near unto Thee, go Thou before, O my guide!

For on this road I have no other friend but Thee, O Protector!

Every morn I cry unto Thee: with Thee I for union yearn;

Then, one morn, accept the prayer of my heart, O Protector!

Upon sinful KHWĀJAH MUḤAMMAD Thy love bestow,

That he may ever praise and call upon thy name, O Protector!

XIII.

Wherefore dost thou not follow righteousness, O my stony heart!

When thy beloved friends, one after the other, continually disappear?

O Thou! who hast bound so many loads upon thy back, and set out—

How wilt thou pass along the path in front, so narrow and confined?

Burn thyself and become ashes, if thou truly lovest the beloved:

Draw near, O suitor! learn thou from the moth true love!

Give up this world! leave it to the negligent and the remiss!

From heedlessness' dark film, make thou the mirror bright!

The garment's hem of my patron saint, I have, with both hands seized:

In the conflict with the flesh and the devil I shall conquer perhaps.

As the breath of the charmer to the afflicted, such is a sight of thee:

I will become thy sacrifice, thou anchorite at the loved-one's door!

Let both my life and goods be an oblation, O mediator! unto thee;

But the face of the beloved, so beautiful, show thou unto me!

Rivers have overflowed, and distant lands have become flooded;

But, alas! of thirst I die, at the brink of a mighty stream!

Give not away, wholly, to sorrow, O KHWĀJAH MUḤAMMAD!

For the Perfect One will confer honour upon the servants at His gate!

XIV.

Unto the whole and healthy, I am unable of my heart's state to speak;

And should I not tell it, I am unable its pain to endure.

To this degree I am become a reproach all people amongst,

That I am altogether unable out of my own house of sorrow to go.

From grief, on account of slander, I am fallen, with eyes closed;

For through shame, I am unable to look any one in the face.

My throat hath become so embittered by the cup of separation,

That I cannot taste aught of the sweetness of this world.

I cannot make my beloved acquainted with my condition;

For through fear of the kill-joy, I am unable my case to state.

I would leave the beloved, and depart to a far distant land;

But I am unable in any way the bonds of affection to break.

The tears of separation flow so continually down my cheeks,

That I cannot upon my eyeballs retain the image of my beloved.

Like the tulip, * the blood of my own vitals I am ever consuming;

For I, KHWĀJAH MUḤAMMAD, am unable, openly, to speak.

But I am altogether a recreant and a speaker of falsehood;

Since, to the love of the beloved, I cannot my life devote.

XV.

I am a complainant against absence: a complainant am I!

For it separated me, weeping and wailing, my loved-one from!

My love is the immortal soul, and I the form containing it;

And from its soul, the separation of the body is bitter indeed!

My very vitals have become entirely consumed in the flames:

Alas! alas! O separation! what dost thou require of me?

I am not criminal, that I grieve and complain so much:

'Tis that my heart is broken, and my breast with fire consumed!

If prosperity attend me in all other things, what shall I do with them?

For without thee, the whole world hath become desolate to me!

The anguish of my heart, on thy account, every moment increaseth

Henceforth of remedy or cure I shall quite hopeless become!

The physicians neglected to make her acquainted with my case;

And, at the Last Day, I will seize them by the collars therefore!

O KHWĀJAH MUḤAMMAD! make thou resignation thy daily task:

Entertain no hope that, from this world, thou shalt constancy find!

Since according to my desire thou never tamest unto me,

Say, say, O relentless fate! in what I have offended thee!

XVI.

Show thou no yearnings for the greatness of this world;

For many tribes, at death's wail, have desolate become!
Those dear friends, who were like spring's flowers unto,
In the sultry heats of autumn, grew withered, and decayed.
They are all now prostrate fallen, the dank earth upon,
Who, with turbans placed so jauntily, rode their fiery steeds.
And they who were wont upon the couches of the fair to lie—
Of their deaths, many anniversaries have come and passed away.
Those youths and fair maidens are now buried in the dust,
Whose hands were still more soft than even velvet itself.
The excellent of their time have passed from the world away,
Around whom their disciples gathered their discourses to hear.
Upon what wound of mine will the physicians salve apply?
For, with the diamonds * of separation I am all covered with wounds.
When I call to mind the pleasant meetings of friends so dear,
I, KHWĀJAH MUḤAMMAD weep, but not for any crime.

XVII.

The whole of my grief is love for thee, love, love for thee!
My heart is to atoms broken: it hath become blood, all blood!
My very vitals are become gorged with red, red blood,
Though clothed in garments outwardly white, all white!
Thou inflictest fresh wounds upon me, again and again,
Altho' of my former ones unhealed are many, very many!

Thou hast not shown aught of kindness in life towards me:
Of what use shouldst thou do so, when I die, when I die!
Thou hast expelled me entirely from the garden, my love!
And the black crows, within it consume the ripe, ripe fruit!
Thy dark tresses have the whole land with fragrance filled:
Thy curls are as the musk-pods of Chin, all perfume, all perfume!
Those sleepy eyes of thine are lions, both fierce and ravenous;
For they bear away KHWĀJAH MUḤAMMAD unto death, cruel death!

XVIII.

Since thou art the sovereign over the whole of the fair,
Inquire after the condition of the wretched and distressed!
Break not hearts! for they are rubies of Badakhshān
It is difficult to repair such broken things again!
My heart and soul are entirely bound up in love for thee;
Look then, these thine own heart-bound ones upon!
The flowers of the parterre have all revived thereby;
For the zephyr hath come from the nosegay of thy face.
When they beheld, with their eyes, thy stature and figure,
The waists of all the adorned ones crooked became.
They have deprived me altogether of sense and understanding—
Those gentle, tender words of thine, so pleasant and so sweet.
My head than the seventh heaven shall be higher exalted,

If thou makest me one of the sitters in thy court.

Like unto thee, there is none other of disposition so noble;

Didst thou, indeed, from the angels this nature acquire?

The heart of Khwājah that thus speaketh, hath been carried away

By the wiles and persuasion of those closed-mouthed ones.

Life and goods, as an oblation to them, will I give;

For I, KHWĀJAH MUḤAMMAD, am the disciple of the fair!

XIX.

They, who were enamoured of the red roses of the parterre,

Have now the nightingales of grief and sorrow become.

With cries and lamentations thou grievest for them;

Since the roses have all been scattered by autumn's dread blast.

They, who were then intoxicated with the flowers' perfume,

Have now become requited by separation's dread pangs.

Their pastimes and their laughter were apart from the world:

The world's pleasures and joys became deadly poison to them.

As yet, they had not tasted of union's sweet fruit,

When loving friends became severed in sorrow and grief.

For a few short days, the bliss of conjunction they enjoyed;

But now years of separation have their portion become.

Should they now flee from destiny, they cannot escape;

Since grief is the portion of lovers from the beginning of time.

The physicians of the age, if they are cognizant of much,

How are they thus so ignorant of KHWĀJAH MUḤAMMAD'S pangs?

With sighs and with groans, I will lament unceasingly;

For I ever long that the hour of my union were come!

XX.

Many youths and maidens have the dark dust's captives become,

The fair faces of whom are the source of the grief of our hearts!

Place not your hopes upon this transient world, for 'tis no permanent abode!

The whole of us, each in his own good time, shall follow after them!

They who were the great men of the land, and possessed the wealth thereof;

From the world have wholly disappeared, both name and trace of them.

They, before whom the poor were wont in humility to stand,

In the tomb, on their backs fallen, have now mouldered away.

For munificence and for justice their names still remain,

Though Hāṭim Tā-yī *, and Nosherwān † have long from the world departed.

Neither by power, nor by entreaty is there any escape from death:

Happy the sanctified, who are occupied with eternal things!

My heart hath become rent to atoms by the diamond * of separation;

For, one after the other, all my dear friends have been severed from me.

All must hence depart: for what can KHWĀJAH MUḤAMMADhope,

When holy and venerated prophets have unto the dust gone down?

XXI.

Fruitlessly in the world thy lifetime thou hast passed,

Whether it extended unto sixty, or unto eighty years!

The fortunate have carried away advantage from it;

But thou, save evil, hast no other result acquired!

The friends of thy acquaintance have all gone from thee;

And still thou perceivest it not, O man, with open eyes asleep!

When grief and sorrow man afflict, he sleepeth not:

Art thou a beast, or a man of human parents born?

Thy fathers and grandfathers all hath death cut off;

And thou, above all others, wilt not alone escape!

Alive in the world not one will remain behind:

No one can have taken on himself thy obligations to fulfil!

Thy beard from age is white, and thy back is bent:

How much longer then canst thou expect erect to remain?

Thy sixty years have passed, and thou art old become;

Yet thou accountest thyself of the age of fourteen still!

If thou art wise, turn devotee, and the world forsake;

For they who this life choose, are in both worlds free!

The veil of scepticism from thy face draw aside;

And unto the Master's will let thy assent be given!

Become thou the servant at the wine-sellers' door,

That wine from the cup of love be given unto thee!

Thou One and Only God! unto righteousness direct me,

That, the straight path upon, I may come unto Thee!

If I have evil committed, a rude slave consider me;

And pardon me, according to Thine own peculiar way!

When man giveth aught to another, again he taketh it;

But Thou art God, and takest not back thy gifts again!

O Thou all-possessing Deity! the sinner Khwājah Muḥammad free!

For the rich always grant liberty their aged slaves unto!

Thou art the hider of thy servant's sins, O Lord!

In mercy, of KHWĀJAH MUḤAMMAD'S rend not Thou the veil!

THE END.

Footnotes

328:* See second note at page 195.

328:† The name of a celebrated Arabian physician, erroneously called Avicenna in the West.

329:* Among the three hundred and fifty-six persons who, among the Ṣūfis, are accounted holy men, nine only are deemed qualified to invest others with authority as teachers: these nine consist of the pole of poles, three poles, and five props, and these nine alone can be deemed perfect teachers or spiritual guides. It is to his spiritual guide, the pole of whom he was a disciple, that the poet addresses the lines above.

332:* Og, king of Bashan.

332:† See note at page 29.

332:‡ The name of a Ṣūfi teacher, who is said to have attained the highest stage of Ṣūfi-ism, and who proclaimed, "I am the truth;" or, in other words, "I am God." The constant repetition of this impious phrase alarmed the orthodox priesthood, and he was therefore seized and impaled.

332:§ The name of a Persian king, Cyrus.

332:§§ See note at page 201.

334:* The prosperous here signifies " immortal joys," and the adverse, "worldly pleasures."

335:* Muḥammad the Prophet is probably meant here; but see note at page 137.

336:* The body, the borrowed garment of the soul.

338:* It is believed that the wound which a diamond touches will never heal.

338:† See note at page 48.

338:‡ Elias, said to have been a grandson of Shem, son of Noah.

339:* To become face-blackened, is to become disgraced; and red-faced, to be honoured and exalted.

342:* The tulip of a blood-red colour.

343:* See note at page 338.

346:* See third note at page 207.

346:† See second note at page 201.

347:* See note at page 338.

Printed in Great Britain
by Amazon

36837650R00206